W9-BXG-067

African American Eras

Segregation to Civil Rights Times

African American Eras

Segregation to Civil Rights Times

Volume 1:
Activism and Reform
The Arts
Business and Industry

U·X·L
A part of Gale, Cengage Learning

GALE
CENGAGE Learning™

Detroit • New York • San Francisco • New Haven, Conn • Waterville, Maine • London

GALE
CENGAGE Learning™

African American Eras:
Segregation to Civil Rights Times

Product Managers: Meggin Condino
   and Julia Furtaw

Project Editor: Rebecca Parks

Rights Acquisition and Management:
   Leitha Etheridge-Sims, Kelly Quin

Composition: Evi Abou-El-Seoud

Manufacturing: Rita Wimberley

Imaging: John Watkins

Product Design: Pamela Galbreath

© 2011 Gale, Cengage Learning

For product information and technology assistance, contact us at **Gale Customer Support, 1-800-877-4253.**
For permission to use material from this text or product, submit all requests online at **cengage.com/permissions.**
Further permissions questions can be emailed to **permissionrequest@cengage.com.**

Cover photographs reproduced by permission of Getty Images (photos of March on Washington and Josephine Baker) and the Library of Congress (photo of Martin Luther King Jr.).

While every effort has been made to ensure the reliability of the information presented in this publication, Gale, a part of Cengage Learning, does not guarantee the accuracy of the data contained herein. Gale accepts no payment for listing; and inclusion in the publication of any organization, agency, institution, publication, service, or individual does not imply endorsement of the editors or publisher. Errors brought to the attention of the publisher and verified to the satisfaction of the publisher will be corrected in future editions.

Library of Congress Cataloging-in-Publication Data

African American eras. Segregation to civil rights times.
   p. cm.
Includes bibliographical references and index.
   ISBN 978-1-4144-3596-1 (set) -- ISBN 978-1-4144-3597-8 (v. 1) --
ISBN 978-1-4144-3598-5 (v. 2) -- ISBN 978-1-4144-3599-2 (v. 3) --
ISBN 978-1-4144-3600-5 (v. 4) 1. African Americans--History--1863-1877--Juvenile literature. 2. African Americans--History--1877-1964--Juvenile literature. 3. African Americans--Segregation--History--Juvenile literature. 4. Segregation--United States--History--Juvenile literature. 5. African Americans--Civil rights--History--19th century--Juvenile literature. 6. African Americans--Civil rights--History--19th century--Juvenile literature. 7. African Americans--Biography--Juvenile literature. 8. United States--Race relations--Juvenile literature.
I. Title: Segregation to civil rights times.
E185.6.A254 2010
973'.0496073--dc22
                                                                    2010012405

Gale
27500 Drake
Farmington Hills, MI 48331-3535

ISBN-13: 978-1-4144-3596-1 (set)   ISBN-10: 1-4144-3596-7 (set)
ISBN-13: 978-1-4144-3597-8 (Vol. 1)   ISBN-10: 1-4144-3597-5 (Vol. 1)
ISBN-13: 978-1-4144-3598-5 (Vol. 2)   ISBN-10: 1-4144-3598-3 (Vol. 2)
ISBN-13: 978-1-4144-3599-2 (Vol. 3)   ISBN-10: 1-4144-3599-1 (Vol. 3)
ISBN-13: 978-1-4144-3600-5 (Vol. 4)   ISBN-10: 1-4144-3600-9 (Vol. 4)

This title is also available as an e-book.
ISBN-13: 978-1-4144-3705-7 ISBN-10: 1-4144-3705-6
Contact your Gale, a part of Cengage Learning sales representative for ordering information.

Printed in Mexico
1 2 3 4 5 6 7 14 13 12 11 10

Table of Contents

VOLUME 2

chapter nine *Law and Justice* 551

chapter twelve **Religion** . . . . *757* chapter thirteen

Science and Technology 817

Reader's Guide

U•X•L *African American Eras: Segregation to Civil Rights Times* provides a broad overview of African American history and culture from the end of the Civil War in 1865 through the civil rights movement up to 1965. The four-volume set is broken into thirteen chapters. Each chapter covers a major subject area as it relates to the African American community. Readers have the opportunity to engage with history in multiple ways within the chapter, beginning with a chronology of major events related to that subject area and a chapter-specific overview of developments in African American history. They are next introduced to the men and women who shaped that history through biographies of prominent African Americans, as well as topical entries on major events related to the chapter's subject area. Primary sources provide a firsthand perspective of the people and events discussed in the chapter, and readers have the opportunity to engage with the content further in a research and activity ideas section.

The complete list of chapters is as follows:

- Activism and Reform

- The Arts

- Business and Industry

- Communications and Media

- Demographics

- Education

- Government and Politics
- Health and Medicine
- Law and Justice
- Military
- Popular Culture
- Religion
- Science and Technology

These chapters are then divided into seven sections:

Chronology: A timeline of significant events in the African American community within the scope of the chapter's subject matter.

Overview: A summary of major developments and trends in the African American community as they relate to the subject matter of the chapter.

Headline Makers: Biographies of key African Americans and their achievements within the scope of the chapter's subject matter.

Topics in the News: A series of topical essays describing significant events and developments important to the African American community within the scope of the chapter's subject matter.

Primary Sources: Historical documents that provide a firsthand perspective on African American history as it relates to the content of the chapter.

Research and Activity Ideas: Brief suggestions for activities and research opportunities that will further engage the reader with the subject matter.

For More Information: A section that lists books, periodicals, and Web sites directing the reader to further information about the events and people covered in the chapter.

OTHER FEATURES

The content of U•X•L *African American Eras: Segregation to Civil Rights Times* is illustrated with 240 black-and-white images that bring the events and people discussed to life. Sidebar boxes also expand on items of high interest to readers. Concluding each volume is a general bibliography of books and Web sites, and a thorough subject index that allows readers to easily locate the events, people, and places discussed throughout the set.

COMMENTS AND SUGGESTIONS

We welcome your comments on U•X•L *African American Eras: Segregation to Civil Rights Times* and suggestions for other history topics to consider. Please write: Editor, U•X•L *African American Eras: Segregation to Civil Rights Times*, 27500 Drake Rd., Farmington Hills, MI 48331-3535; call toll-free: 1-800-877-4253; or send e-mail via http://www.galegroup.com.

Chronology

1862 Congress passes the Homestead Act, which provides people with 160 acres of free land in the American West. The act, which applies to African Americans, sets the stage for the so-called "Colored Exodus" of the late 1870s and early 1880s.

1862 Freedmen's Hospital is founded in Washington, D.C., by the U.S. secretary of war. Its purpose is to meet the medical needs of African Americans, including newly freed slaves.

1865 **March 3** Congress passes the Freedmen's Bureau Act, creating the Bureau of Refugees, Freedmen, and Abandoned Lands for the purposes of helping former slaves obtain property, employment, and an education.

1865 **December 2** The Thirteenth Amendment to the United States Constitution, which formally outlaws slavery in the United States, is ratified.

1866 United States Congress commissions six all-black U.S. Army units. The units, which become known as the Buffalo Soldiers, serve the United States in the Indian wars and in the Spanish-American War, among others.

1868 Howard University College of Medicine is founded in Washington, D.C., as one of the few medical schools open to African Americans.

1868 **July 9** The Fourteenth Amendment is added to the Constitution. Its most important provisions declare that African Americans who are born in the United States are citizens, that all persons are entitled to due process of law, and that no person shall be denied the equal protection of the laws.

1869 **May 1** Ebenezer Bassett becomes the first African American to serve the United States as a diplomat when President Ulysses S. Grant appoints him to be minister resident (the nineteenth-century equivalent of an ambassador) to Haiti.

1870 **February 3** The Fifteenth Amendment to the United States Constitution, which outlaws discrimination against voters based on race, is ratified.

1870 **February 23** Hiram Revels of Mississippi becomes the first African American to serve as a United States senator.

1875 **March 1** The Civil Rights Act of 1875, which forbids discrimination based on race for all public accommodations, is signed into law.

1877 **March** Under the Compromise of 1877, which enabled Republican candidate Rutherford B. Hayes to be elected president, the Republican Party agrees to withdraw the U.S. military from the South and end Reconstruction.

1883 **October 15** The Civil Rights Act of 1875 is declared unconstitutional by the Supreme Court, opening the way for Southern states to enact Jim Crow laws and institute policies of segregation.

1892 Journalist Ida B. Wells publishes *Southern Horrors: Lynch Law in All Its Phases,* the first comprehensive study of lynchings in the United States.

1895 **September 18** Booker T. Washington delivers a speech popularly known as the "Atlanta Compromise," in which he encourages African Americans to have patience and prove themselves worthy of equality to whites.

1896 **May 18** In the court case *Plessy v. Ferguson,* the United States Supreme Court rules that segregation is legal as long as blacks are provided "separate but equal" accommodations and facilities.

1899 **September 18** Scott Joplin publishes his first successful ragtime composition, "Maple Leaf Rag," which becomes the first instrumental sheet music to sell over one million copies.

1903 Author and activist W. E. B. Du Bois publishes *The Souls of Black Folk,* his landmark collection of essays about race relations in the United States.

1905 Madame C. J. Walker, a former employee of Annie Malone's Poro Systems, goes into business for herself, selling hair straighteners, creams, and other styling products designed specifically for African American women.

1906 **April** William Joseph Seymour begins the Azusa Street Revival, which is often credited as a key development in the growth of the Pentecostal faith. The Azusa Street Revival becomes the longest-running continuous revival in United States history.

1908 **December 26** Boxer Jack Johnson defeats Canadian heavyweight Tommy Burns in Australia to become the first African American world heavyweight champion.

1909 **February 12** Civil rights activists gather to form the organization that becomes known as the National Association for the Advancement of Colored People.

1910 Sickle-cell anemia is scientifically described for the first time. James Herrick, a Chicago physician, publishes a report describing the disease in Walter Clement Noel, a young black student from Grenada in the West Indies.

1919 **March** Oscar Micheaux's *The Homesteader,* the first feature-length film written and directed by an African American, premieres.

1920 Marcus Garvey, as part of his Back to Africa project, moves the headquarters of the Black Star shipping line to Liberia, a country in western Africa.

1925 Dancer and singer Josephine Baker arrives in Paris and quickly becomes the most popular American performer in Europe.

1927 **January 7** The first officially recorded game featuring the Harlem Globetrotters is played in Illinois.

1931 **November 7** The tragic death of Juliette Derricotte in a car accident in Dalton, Georgia, sparks a national outrage over segregated hospitals. Derricotte does not receive adequate medical care because the local hospital does not admit African Americans.

1936 **November 3** Seventy-six percent of African Americans who vote in the presidential election cast their vote for Franklin D. Roosevelt, a Democrat. The election marks the beginning of a major shift of African American voters away from the Republican Party.

1937 **April 25** The Brotherhood of Sleeping Car Porters becomes the first all-black union in American history to negotiate a labor agreement with a major corporation when it enters into a collective bargaining agreement with the Pullman Company.

1940 **February 29** Actress Hattie McDaniel becomes the first African American to win an Academy Award for her portrayal of Mammy in the film *Gone with the Wind* (1939).

1941 **June 25** President Franklin D. Roosevelt signs Executive Order 8802, making it illegal for government agencies and private companies that do business with the government to refuse to hire African Americans.

1945 **November** John Harold Johnson launches the lifestyle magazine *Ebony,* which quickly becomes the most popular African American magazine in the nation.

1945 **November 1** Brooklyn Dodgers owner Branch Rickey signs Negro League baseball player Jackie Robinson to play in the major leagues, the first African American in modern major league baseball.

1952 After completing a jail sentence for burglary, Malcolm Little adopts the new name Malcolm X and becomes the leading spokesperson for the Nation of Islam.

1954 **May 17** The Supreme Court unanimously rules in *Brown v. Board of Education* that segregated schools are unconstitutional. The Court's ruling overturns its previous decision in *Plessy v. Ferguson* (1896) and marks the beginning of the end of legalized racial segregation.

1954 **October 30** The last racially segregated unit in the United States military is disbanded, completing the military's transition from completely segregated to completely integrated in just over five years.

1955 **August 28** Emmett Till, a fourteen-year-old African American boy from Chicago, Illinois, is taken from his uncle's house in Money, Mississippi, and murdered for allegedly whistling at a white woman.

1955 **December 1** Rosa Parks is arrested after refusing to give up her seat to a white passenger on a Montgomery, Alabama, city bus; the arrest leads to a year-long bus boycott and the eventual desegregation of Montgomery city buses.

1957 Martin Luther King Jr. and Ralph Abernathy co-found the Southern Christian Leadership Conference (SCLC), a group that teaches the use of nonviolent direct action to protest injustice and promote civil rights for African Americans.

1957 **August 13** A postal worker alerts the suburb of Levittown, Pennsylvania, that a black family has moved into the neighborhood. This incident sparks a wave of violence and terrorism against the family as white residents attempt to force them to leave the neighborhood.

1957 **September 24** President Dwight D. Eisenhower deploys a U.S. Army division to Little Rock, Arkansas, and federalizes the Arkansas National Guard in order to protect nine African American students and enforce integration at Little Rock Central High School. The students become known as the "Little Rock Nine."

1958 Dancer Alvin Ailey forms the Alvin Ailey American Dance Theater in New York City, one of the most influential modern dance companies in the country.

1959 **March 11** The play *A Raisin in the Sun* by Lorraine Hansberry premieres, becoming the first Broadway play written by an African American woman.

1960 **February 1** Four college students stage a sit-in at a Woolworth's lunch counter in Greensboro, North Carolina, launching a massive campaign that results in the desegregation of lunch counters throughout the city.

1960 **April 14** Berry Gordy Jr. founds the recording label Motown Records in Detroit, Michigan.

1962 **October 1** James Meredith is admitted to the University of Mississippi as its first African American student; the event leads to riots among white supremacists.

1963 **January 14** Newly elected Alabama governor George C. Wallace famously declares in his inauguration day address that he will support "segregation now, segregation tomorrow, segregation forever."

1963 **August 28** At least two hundred thousand demonstrators participate in the March on Washington for Jobs and Freedom; millions of viewers around the world are moved by the event and by Martin Luther King's "I Have a Dream" speech.

1964 **March** Malcolm X leaves the Nation of Islam and founds his own religious organization, the Organization of Afro-American Unity, built on a belief in world brotherhood.

1964 **May 25** The Supreme Court rules in *Griffin v. County School Board of Prince Edward County* that state governments in the South cannot close their public schools as a strategy for avoiding the racial integration mandated by the Court's decision in *Brown v. Board of Education.*

1964   **July 2**   The Civil Rights Act of 1964, which outlaws segregation based on race in virtually all instances, becomes law.

1964   **December 10**   Martin Luther King Jr. is awarded the Nobel Peace Prize for his campaigns of nonviolent resistance.

1965   The federal programs Medicare and Medicaid are created, finally bringing an end to the long practice of segregated hospitals and medical discrimination.

1965   **February 21**   Malcolm X, while attending a meeting in Harlem, is shot dead by three members of the Nation of Islam.

1965   **August 6**   President Lyndon B. Johnson signs into law the Voting Rights Act of 1965, which prohibits all forms of racial discrimination in voting and the administration of elections. The Voting Rights Act and the Civil Rights Act of 1964 are widely regarded as the most important pieces of legislation enacted in the country in the twentieth century.

Era Overview

The American Civil War ended in 1865 with a victory for the North and freedom for African American slaves. The federal government quickly enacted several constitutional amendments aimed at establishing and protecting the rights of African Americans. The federal government was able to protect these rights during the period of time immediately following the Civil War known as Reconstruction. The presence of federal troops in the South during Reconstruction allowed African Americans to make impressive advances in a variety of fields. Numerous African Americans were elected to local and state offices as blacks exercised their right to vote. Schools were built throughout the South to help educate and train freed slaves for new careers in mainstream American society.

Federal troops remained in the South for more than a decade to enforce Reconstruction policies. Reconstruction ended in 1877 after the Northern Republicans agreed to withdraw federal troops from the South in exchange for Southern Democratic support of the Republican presidential candidate Rutherford B. Hayes (1822–93). The withdrawal of federal protection was devastating to the Southern black population. Many African Americans found themselves in circumstances as bad or worse than before the war. Southern blacks once again worked the plantation fields owned by whites— now as sharecroppers, trapped by debt just as they had once been bound by slavery.

To make matters worse, state governments throughout the South began to institute "black codes," which were laws aimed at restricting the rights of African Americans. These laws supported strict segregation throughout the

South. Separate public facilities—everything from schools to hospitals to water fountains—were created for blacks. These facilities were almost never equal in quality to those offered for white citizens. The constitutionality of this kind of segregation was tested in the United States Supreme Court case *Plessy v. Ferguson* in 1896. The Court ruled that "separate but equal" facilities for blacks did not violate the Fourteenth Amendment, which gave African Americans full citizenship. The "separate but equal" concept was used to justify segregation for many decades.

The South in particular saw increasing violence against blacks at the end of the nineteenth century, mainly in the form of lynching. Lynchings are executions held outside the bounds of the law, usually by large groups, and often without much proof that the victim had committed a crime. African American journalist and editor Ida B. Wells (1862–1931) exposed the racist motivations for lynchings in her pamphlets *Southern Horrors* (1892) and *A Red Record* (1895). She campaigned vigorously for stronger anti-lynching laws.

Even in the midst of segregation and lynchings, many African Americans in the South were furthering their educations thanks to schools such as the Tuskegee Institute in Alabama. Booker T. Washington (1856–1915), born into slavery, was the leader of the Tuskegee Institute and a persuasive voice in the struggle for African American acceptance by white society. Washington's philosophy was to provide African Americans with basic trade skills so they could prove their worth to whites as productive members of society. He felt that protests and demands for increased liberty would prove disastrous for blacks, and that the key component in defusing racial tension was time. Many African American intellectuals in the North, such as W. E. B. Du Bois (1868–1963), felt that blacks should not have to wait for whites to give them the rights they deserved. Du Bois was a driving force behind the creation of the National Association for the Advancement of Colored People (NAACP) in 1909. He utilized the organization's official publication, *The Crisis*, to rally African American readers in the struggle for civil rights.

In the first decades of the twentieth century, many African Americans began moving to growing cities in the North and Midwest in search of greater economic opportunities and freedoms. This became known as the Great Migration. By 1930, millions of African Americans had migrated to urban centers such as New York City, Detroit, and Chicago. One of the largest concentrations of African Americans in the North was found in Harlem, a neighborhood in New York City. The relative economic prosperity enjoyed by African Americans in the North, combined with the influx of cultural influences from the South, were key factors in the Harlem

Renaissance. The Harlem Renaissance was a flourishing of African American art and culture that began in the 1920s and continued into the 1930s.

Equally notable was the growing acceptance of African Americans by mainstream American society. While many white Americans reacted negatively to African American boxer Jack Johnson (1878–1946) when he won the heavyweight boxing title in 1908, Joe Louis (1914–81) was praised as an American hero when he secured the title in 1937. When Jackie Robinson (1919–72) debuted as the first African American baseball player in the major leagues in 1947, uncertainty among white fans quickly gave way to respect for his unquestionable talents.

African Americans made great strides in other fields as well. In 1939, Charles Drew (1904–50) invented a blood storage method that allowed for the creation of blood banks, thereby helping to save the lives of millions. Singer Marian Anderson (1897–1993) earned worldwide acclaim for her performances of both opera and traditional songs. And in 1940, Benjamin O. Davis Sr. (1877–1970) became the first African American to achieve the rank of general in the United States Army. In each case, however, these pioneers struggled against the widespread racism that still divided American culture. Drew resigned from the Red Cross in 1941 when the United States Army ordered that blood from black donors must be separated from blood donated by whites. In 1939, Anderson was barred from performing at Constitution Hall in Washington, D.C., because she was black. And while Davis served as a general in the U.S. Army during World War II (1939–45), the soldiers themselves were still divided on the battlefield according to their race.

One important factor in changing American perceptions about blacks was popular media. Even as the roles for African Americans in Hollywood films remained largely stereotypical, performers like Bill "Bojangles" Robinson (1878–1949) won over audiences with their talent and charm. Hattie McDaniel (1895–1952) became the first African American to win an Academy Award for her supporting performance as a servant in the 1939 film *Gone with the Wind*. Still, it would be fifteen years before another African American woman, Dorothy Dandridge (1922–65), would be nominated in the Best Actress category, and twenty-four years before Sidney Poitier (1927–) would become the first African American man to win an Oscar for Best Actor.

Even more significantly, the media played a key role in shaping American views on the growing struggle for civil rights for African Americans. The South was still as segregated in the 1950s as it had been in the 1800s, even as black Americans made important contributions to the worlds of art, science, and business. One of the most important challenges to segregation occurred in 1954. That year the United States Supreme Court ruled in the case *Brown v. Board of Education of Topeka* that separate schools for blacks and whites are, by definition, unequal, and therefore against federal law. Soon after, segregation was challenged on other fronts as well; for example, Alabama resident Rosa Parks (1913–2005) earned fame when she refused to give up her seat to a white bus passenger in 1955. Her arrest sparked the Montgomery bus boycott, one of the first major protest campaigns of the modern civil rights era. In 1957, nine African American students in Little Rock, Arkansas, defied the state's governor and National Guard troops to attend a high school that had previously admitted only white students.

The leading voice of the civil rights struggle in the South was Martin Luther King Jr. (1929–68), a clergyman and advocate of nonviolence in the struggle for civil rights. King's influence resulted in peaceful demonstrations such as sit-ins and boycotts of businesses that supported segregation, and earned him the Nobel Peace Prize in 1964. However, the peaceful efforts of King and other activists were often met with violence by whites. Activists such as Medgar Evers (1925–63) and James Chaney (1943–64) were brutally murdered because of their efforts to help African Americans secure their constitutional right to vote. Across the South, African American churches were bombed, and peaceful demonstrators were beaten—often by police and at the direction of state and local government officials.

In 1963, more than two hundred thousand demonstrators participated in the March on Washington for Jobs and Freedom, aimed at securing basic civil rights for African Americans nationwide. Massive media coverage of the event helped sway millions of white Americans to support civil rights reform. The following year, the Civil Rights Act of 1964 was passed by the United States Congress. This legislation formally ended segregation and guaranteed civil rights for all Americans regardless of race. More than a century after Abraham Lincoln issued the Emancipation Proclamation to free African American slaves, the federal government finally followed through on guaranteeing their basic rights as Americans.

chapter one *Activism and Reform*

1865 December 6 The Thirteenth Amendment to the United States Constitution, which formally outlaws slavery in the United States, is ratified.

1868 July 9 The Fourteenth Amendment to the United States Constitution, which formally grants citizenship and due process rights to former slaves and their descendants, is ratified.

1870 February 3 The Fifteenth Amendment to the United States Constitution, which outlaws discrimination against voters based on race, is ratified.

1871 April 20 The Civil Rights Act of 1871, also known as the Ku Klux Klan Act, is signed into law as a protection for blacks against racially motivated attacks.

1875 March 1 The Civil Rights Act of 1875, which forbids discrimination based on race for all public accommodations, is signed into law.

1877 The Compromise of 1877, which results in federal troops being withdrawn from Southern states, effectively ends Reconstruction in the South.

1883 October 15 The Civil Rights Act of 1875 is declared unconstitutional by the Supreme Court, opening the way for Southern states to enact Jim Crow laws and institute policies of segregation.

1892 October 26 Ida B. Wells publishes *Southern Horrors: Lynch Law in All Its Phases,* which brings attention to the growing trend of mob executions that occur primarily against African American men.

1895 September 18 Booker T. Washington delivers a speech popularly known as the "Atlanta Compromise," in which he encourages African Americans to have patience and prove themselves worthy of equality to whites.

1896 The National Association of Colored Women's Clubs is created through the efforts of Josephine St. Pierre Ruffin and Mary Church Terrell.

1896 May 18 The United States Supreme Court rules that segregation is legal as long as blacks are provided "separate but equal" accommodations and facilities in the court case *Plessy v. Ferguson.*

1905 July 11 W. E. B. Du Bois organizes a conference of African American professionals that results in the formation of the Niagara Movement.

1909 February 12 Civil rights activists gather to form the organization that becomes known as the National Association for the Advancement of Colored People (NAACP).

1910 November The first issue of the magazine *The Crisis,* published by the NAACP and edited by W. E. B. Du Bois, is released.

1930 July Wallace D. Fard founds the Nation of Islam (NOI) in Detroit, Michigan.

1937 The Southern Negro Youth Congress is founded.

1940 The NAACP Legal Defense and Educational Fund, led by Thurgood Marshall, is created to challenge unfair civil rights laws.

1942 The Congress on Racial Equality, one of the key activist groups during the civil rights era, is formed in Chicago.

1947 April 9 The Congress on Racial Equality challenges segregation by sending sixteen riders, eight white and eight black, together on public interstate bus trips across the South. The trips are known collectively as the Journey of Reconciliation.

1952 Malcolm Little adopts the new name Malcolm X and becomes the leading spokesperson for the Nation of Islam.

1954 May 17 The Supreme Court rules in *Brown v. Board of Education* that segregated schools are not equal and are therefore unconstitutional, paving the way for desegregation.

1955 November 7 The Supreme Court bans segregation on interstate bus travel, reinforcing earlier rulings.

1955 December 1 Rosa Parks is arrested after refusing to give up her seat for a white passenger on a Montgomery, Alabama, city bus; the arrest leads to a year-long bus boycott and the eventual desegregation of Montgomery city buses.

1957 February 14 The Southern Christian Leadership Conference is created, and Martin Luther King Jr. is selected as president.

1957 September President Dwight Eisenhower sends National Guard and U.S. Army troops to escort nine black students into the newly desegregated Little Rock Central High School in Arkansas over protests from the state's governor.

1960 February 1 Four college students stage a sit-in at a Woolworth's lunch counter in Greensboro, North Carolina, launching a massive campaign that results in the desegregation of lunch counters throughout the city.

1960 April 15 The Student Nonviolent Coordinating Committee is formed in Raleigh, North Carolina.

1961 May 4 Freedom Riders begin a journey across the South to test state segregation laws on interstate buses.

1961 November 1 The Interstate Commerce Commission begins to enforce existing rulings outlawing segregation on buses and in bus terminals.

1962 October 1 James Meredith is admitted to the University of Mississippi as its first African American student; the event leads to riots among white supremacists.

1963 April Activists launch a wide-scale campaign to desegregate the city of Birmingham, Alabama; the campaign leads to the arrest of Martin Luther King Jr. and his writing of the famous "Letter from Birmingham Jail."

1963 June 11 Civil rights activist Medgar Evers is murdered by a white supremacist in Jackson, Mississippi.

1963 August 28 At least two hundred thousand demonstrators participate in the March on Washington for Jobs and Freedom; millions of viewers around the world are moved by the event and by Martin Luther King's "I Have a Dream" speech.

1963 September 15 White supremacists bomb the Sixteenth Street Baptist Church in Birmingham, Alabama, killing four African American girls.

1964 June 21 Three civil rights workers, two white and one black, are murdered by a group of Mississippi white supremacists that includes at least one police officer.

1964 June 28 Malcolm X founds the Organization of Afro-American Unity to bring together all people of African descent after leaving the Nation of Islam.

1964 July 2 The Civil Rights Act of 1964, which outlaws segregation based on race in virtually all instances, becomes law.

1964 December 10 Martin Luther King Jr. is awarded the Nobel Peace Prize for his campaigns of nonviolent resistance.

1965 February 21 Malcolm X is assassinated by three Black Muslims at the Audubon Ballroom in Manhattan.

1965 March 7 Demonstrators participating in a peaceful march from Selma to Montgomery, Alabama, are attacked and beaten by police under direction from Governor George Wallace.

1965 August 6 The Voting Rights Act of 1965, which outlaws discrimination against voters based on race and largely mirrors the Fifteenth Amendment, is signed into law.

After the Civil War ended in 1865, the United States government passed several laws meant to protect the rights of African Americans. However, exercising these rights proved to be far more difficult than Northern lawmakers could have imagined. It would take the efforts of countless activists, reformers, and supporters, and a century of struggle to finally fulfill the dream of freedom that seemed within reach of African Americans after the end of slavery.

Congress passed the first of several amendments to the Constitution that guaranteed the rights of African Americans in 1865. These amendments ended slavery permanently, recognized African Americans as full citizens, and outlawed discrimination against eligible voters based on race. The government even sent federal troops into the South during the period of time known as Reconstruction to ensure that African Americans could enjoy these rights. Federal courts and lawmakers had little power to enforce these rules once Reconstruction ended in 1877. Throughout the South, the laws were skirted around or ignored outright, and the sheer size and power of the Southern voting bloc was hard for rights activists to overcome. Eventually, many of the reform laws were ruled unconstitutional or were interpreted so narrowly that they proved useless. Southern states also passed new laws that added all sorts of restrictions and rules to keep blacks from voting and exercising other basic rights.

One important tactic used by Southern lawmakers was segregation. The Supreme Court ruled in 1896 that blacks could be given accommodations and facilities that were "separate but equal" to what whites received. Throughout the South, businesses and public services were divided in ways that were indeed separate, but seldom equal. For example, schools for African American children received only a fraction of the funding that schools for white students received. Black passengers were granted areas of seating on buses and trains, but were required to give up their seats if those seats were needed for white passengers.

At the same time, whites in the South began to terrorize the black population through the practice of lynching, a punishment (usually an execution by hanging, and sometimes by burning) carried out by a mob without the involvement of the legal system. Lynchings were vicious, violent attacks against African Americans who had been accused of committing offenses against whites. They were often led or organized by members of white supremacist groups such as the Ku Klux Klan, who believed that blacks were inferior to whites. These offenses were almost never proven, and in many cases were later disproven. Ida B. Wells (1862–1931), an

African American journalist and activist, was instrumental in bringing these horrific crimes to the attention of readers in the Northern states and in Europe.

In this highly charged environment, African American leaders like Booker T. Washington (1856–1915) promoted positive behavior and self-reliance among blacks as a way to avoid worsening race relations. Washington argued that if blacks learned valuable trade skills and held their tongues regarding the harsh treatment they were receiving, whites would eventually realize their value as members of American society. Washington summed up these arguments in an 1895 speech now known as the "Atlanta Compromise" because many African Americans felt that Washington had asked them to compromise their belief in fairness and justice in order to secure the goodwill of whites.

This led to a new school of activism among blacks, characterized best by the work of W. E. B. Du Bois (1868–1963). Du Bois believed that blacks should demand basic rights such as the right to vote. In 1905 he started a civil rights organization called the Niagara Movement, which was the precursor to the National Association for the Advancement of Colored People (NAACP). As an officer of the NAACP, Du Bois edited the magazine *The Crisis,* which featured news and commentary related to the civil rights struggle as well as some of the finest examples of African American literature being produced at the time. For several decades, the NAACP remained the only major organization actively fighting to reinstate the legal rights that had already been granted to African Americans after the Civil War.

In that regard, the NAACP was often successful. Thanks to the legal expertise of Thurgood Marshall (1908–93) and others during the 1930s and 1940s, the organization won several Supreme Court rulings that stated segregation was illegal in schools and aboard interstate transportation. However, the federal government still had difficulty enforcing these rulings in the South. Activists struck upon the idea of actively challenging Southern laws that violated these federal rulings. Rosa Parks, for example, refused to give up her seat aboard a city bus in Montgomery, Alabama, and was arrested. One year later, after a lawsuit and very successful boycott of the city bus system, a federal ruling was issued that required the city to end its segregation policies aboard its buses.

Even as African Americans increasingly took up the struggle for their rights in the South, most followed the philosophy of Martin Luther King Jr. (1929–68). He believed that nonviolence and civil disobedience were the answer to achieving their goals. For this reason, the major campaigns of the civil rights struggle were marked by events like sit-ins, in which activists simply occupied stores and businesses in an effort to persuade them to serve blacks. Even though those demonstrating for civil rights avoided violence as a means to achieve equality, their opponents often resorted to violent and unprovoked physical and verbal attacks. Numerous civil rights workers were killed by white supremacists, including Mississippi voting rights activist Medgar Evers (1925–63) and King himself.

Some activists like Malcolm X (1925–65), a longtime spokesperson for the Nation of Islam (NOI), believed that violence was appropriate and even necessary for blacks who had to defend themselves against whites. Malcolm X also represented a growing number of African Americans who felt that whites would never fully accept blacks, and therefore blacks should form their own independent communities or even a separate nation for their own well-being.

Still, an increasing number of black and white Americans took up the cause of civil rights, resulting in the massive March on Washington for Jobs and Freedom in 1963. The event was a victory in its shifting of mainstream public opinion toward support of the civil rights cause. Many historians believe that the event cemented congressional support for the Civil Rights Act of 1964 and the Voting Rights Act of 1965. These new laws finally granted African Americans the basic rights—to vote and to live free of discrimination—that they had struggled for a century to achieve.

Headline Makers

★ W. E. B. DU BOIS
(1868–1963)

W. E. B. Du Bois was one of the most influential African American activists during the first half of the twentieth century. As an author, he wrote landmark historical works such as *The Negro* (1915) and *Black Reconstruction in America* (1935). He also wrote *The Souls of Black Folk* (1903), a critically important text arguing in favor of civil rights for African Americans. As an editor, Du Bois headed *The Crisis,* a magazine aimed at an African American audience that published works by many of the most significant figures of the Harlem Renaissance (a flowering of African American arts that occurred in the 1920s). And as an activist, Du Bois was a founding member of the National Association for the Advancement of Colored People (NAACP). In fact, Du Bois was the only African American granted an executive position in the NAACP at the time it was founded.

W. E. B. Du Bois. *The Library of Congress*

A Comfortable Upbringing and Impressive Education

Du Bois was born in Great Barrington, Massachusetts, to Mary Silvina Burghardt, a woman from a notable local family, and Alfred Du Bois, a Haitian-born man who vanished from his son's life at an early age. Du Bois grew up in a family accustomed to freedom and land ownership, rights rarely enjoyed by African Americans in the years before his birth. He attended school almost exclusively with white students, but they seldom made an issue of his racial heritage, and Du Bois proved to be an exceptional academic. On one occasion, however, a female student new to his school refused to accept his calling-card. "Then it dawned upon me with a certain suddenness," he wrote in *The Souls of Black Folk*, "that I was different from the others; or like, mayhap, in heart and life and longing, but shut out from their world by a vast veil."

Du Bois graduated from Great Barrington High School in 1884, the same year his mother died. Even before he finished school, Du Bois had already found success as a journalist, publishing columns in the *Springfield Republican* and the *New York Globe*. In 1885, Du Bois traveled south to Nashville, Tennessee, to attend college at Fisk University. Fisk University was a learning institution established in 1866 to meet the educational needs of recently freed slaves. Du Bois graduated in 1888 and was admitted to Harvard University in the fall of the same year. He earned a bachelor's degree with honors in 1890, and he immediately began graduate studies at Harvard, focusing on history and economics. During this time, he was awarded a fellowship that allowed him to study in Europe. He traveled to Germany to attend the University of Berlin in 1892. Two years later, he returned to the United States and continued his studies at Harvard. He became the first African American to receive a Ph.D. from the university in 1895.

Sociological Studies of African American Communities

While still finishing his doctoral dissertation for Harvard, Du Bois accepted a teaching position at Wilberforce University, a private college run by the African Methodist Episcopal Church. He taught several language classes, including Latin, Greek, and German. His true interest, however, was in the field of sociology, which he was not able to teach at Wilberforce. When Du Bois had an opportunity to teach sociology at the University of Pennsylvania in 1896, he took it. That same year, Du Bois married a former student of his named Nina Gomer; the two would remain together for over fifty years. Du Bois arrived in Philadelphia with his new wife and began a sociological study of the African American community in the city. This research led to the book *The Philadelphia Negro: A Social Study* (1899). Du Bois was one of the first to examine social issues like crime and pregnancy from an African American perspective, which had been all but ignored by others in the field.

Du Bois accepted a teaching position at Atlanta University in Georgia after two years of teaching and gathering data in Philadelphia. There, he continued his research into the everyday challenges faced by African Americans. Du Bois also began taking on a more activist role, collaborating with Booker T. Washington (1856–1915) to organize an exhibition highlighting the achievements of African Americans for the 1900 World's Fair in Paris. He became involved in the First Pan-African Congress, held in London in 1900. The purpose of the meeting was to recognize the commonalities in all those of African descent, regardless of where they lived. Pan-Africanism promoted the idea of maintaining an African cultural heritage for blacks worldwide and securing civil rights for those who were not treated as equals due to their race.

Du Bois wrote *The Souls of Black Folk* (1903) during his tenure at Atlanta University. The collection of essays and sketches built upon the idea that African Americans must take an active and positive role in achieving equality with whites. This was somewhat contrary to the philosophy offered by Booker T. Washington, another influential activist of the era. Washington believed that African Americans should focus on demonstrating their skills in trades so that whites would realize their value from a practical standpoint; this would, in turn, help whites to view African Americans as equals. Du Bois objected to this strategy for two reasons. First, it relied upon a "wait and see" attitude with regard to receiving equal treatment. Second, it emphasized trade skills but downplayed the importance of classical studies and the arts, which Du Bois felt were critically important for the development of African American culture.

A Key Leader of the NAACP

In 1905, Du Bois became one of the founding members of the Niagara Movement, an organization dedicated to ending racial segregation and taking an active role in the furthering of African American rights. This group was the forerunner of the National Association for the Advancement of Colored People (NAACP), founded in 1909. Du Bois was selected to be the director of publicity and research. His position with the NAACP led to his duties as the editor of the group's magazine, *The Crisis,* which debuted in 1910. *The Crisis* provided Du Bois with a forum for commenting on current events in the world of racial relations and the struggle for equality. "The object of this publication," he wrote in his editorial for the first issue, "is to set forth those facts and arguments which show the danger of race prejudice, particularly as manifested today toward colored people."

Du Bois also made the magazine into a respected periodical of the arts, publishing works by writers such as Countee Cullen (1903–46) and Zora Neale Hurston (1891–1960). Most notably, however, *The Crisis* published "The Negro Speaks of Rivers" (1921), the first poem by Langston Hughes (1902–67)—a key figure in the Harlem Renaissance. The magazine proved to be a success, growing from a circulation of one thousand in 1910 to one hundred thousand in 1918. Even though it was the official magazine of the NAACP, it regularly sold more copies than there were members of the organization, and even served to draw in new members.

Du Bois relocated from Atlanta to New York City during his years with the NAACP and *The Crisis.* He continued writing books and participating in public demonstrations, and his activism became increasingly focused on political issues. He believed that the race issue in the United States was much like the traditional division between social classes, and saw communism and socialism—which emphasize equality among all people—as potential solutions for the problem. Du Bois continued to move farther away from

W. E. B. Du Bois (third from the left) stands with other speakers from a 1949 rally sponsored by the Cultural and Scientific Conference for World Peace, an organization branded by the State Department as a vehicle for Communist propaganda. © *Bettmann/ Corbis*

the passive strategy supported by Booker T. Washington and toward a more active role that led some to view him as an agitator or troublemaker. The Federal Bureau of Investigation (FBI), fearful of the spread of Communist and socialist ideas in the United States, kept a file on Du Bois that ultimately contained over nine hundred pages of witness statements, published comments, and surveillance records.

In 1934, Du Bois resigned from the NAACP and from his job as editor of *The Crisis.* The departure came after Du Bois wrote editorials that praised the benefits of some blacks-only institutions such as colleges. He did not simply accept the stated NAACP mission of an end to all segregation, which could possibly mean the closing of African American colleges like Fisk and the Tuskegee Institute. He saw the issue as being more complex and saw institutions exclusive to African Americans as a way for them to gain strength to enact change. Some Southern politicians, however, pointed to Du Bois's editorials as being supportive of the unequal forms of segregation already found across the country.

Retirement in Ghana

Du Bois returned to Atlanta University as the head of its department of sociology after leaving the NAACP. He also published *Black Reconstruction in America,* a collection of essays that attempted to explain how and why

African Americans had fared so poorly in the South in the years following the Civil War. Du Bois also worked on a project that was never far from his mind: an "Encyclopedia Africana," covering the history of African people and their descendants around the world. Du Bois encountered problems funding the project, but he continued writing other books and remaining politically active well into his senior years. He returned to the NAACP as director of special research in 1944, devoting much of his effort to opposing colonialism in Africa. At the time, much of Africa was still controlled by the governments of European countries. In 1950, Du Bois ran for a seat in the United States Senate at the age of eighty-two, representing New York as a candidate for the American Labor Party. Although he did not win, he received over two hundred thousand votes. That same year, his wife Nina died.

Du Bois remarried in 1952, to author and activist Shirley Graham. Throughout the 1950s, Du Bois traveled around the world, particularly concerned with countries that enacted socialist or Communist policies such as the Soviet Union and China. The Soviet Union even awarded him the International Lenin Peace Prize in 1959. These visits proved controversial in the United States, where anti-Communist sentiment was at an all-time high. In 1961, he was invited by President Kwame Nkrumah to visit the newly independent nation of Ghana, a former British colony on Africa's western coast. Nkrumah offered to fund Du Bois's "Encyclopedia Africana" through the Ghanaian government. Du Bois accepted, and he and Shirley relocated to Ghana. His health declined soon after, and he was unable to complete the project. Both he and his wife became citizens of Ghana in 1963, after they were denied new passports by the United States government. On August 27, 1963, Du Bois passed away in Accra, Ghana, at the age of ninety-five.

★ MEDGAR EVERS
(1925–1963)

Medgar Evers was a civil rights activist in Mississippi who worked for the voting rights of African Americans and organized boycotts against segregated businesses. His murder by a white supremacist in 1963 attracted new attention to the injustices suffered by African Americans in the South. The subsequent trials of his accused murderer brought to light the racism still prevalent in American—and particularly Southern—society.

Evers was born in Decatur, Mississippi, to James and Jessie Evers. He was the third of four children. He grew up on a small farm in an area where white locals had a history of committing violent acts against African Americans. One significant childhood memory was of a family friend beaten to death for allegedly showing disrespect to a white woman. The killers were never arrested or prosecuted, and the dead man's bloody clothes were left on a

Medgar Evers. *The Library of Congress*

fence post as a warning to other African Americans in the area. Even under such difficult conditions, Evers performed well in school. He walked more than ten miles each way to the high school in Newton, south of Decatur, to continue his education.

Veteran of World War II

World War II (1939–45) put Evers's education on hold. Evers enlisted in the U.S. Army in 1943 and served in an all–African American unit. He spent much of his time in France, and he was stunned at the acceptance he received from white citizens there. He even dated a white woman for a time, something that was all but impossible back in his hometown. Evers served three years in the U.S. Army before being honorably discharged and returning to Decatur in 1946. While he was away, the United States Supreme Court outlawed some of the restrictions that had been enacted to prevent blacks from voting in the South. In addition, the state government of Mississippi voted to allow returning soldiers the right to vote without paying a "poll tax," which was generally enforced only to keep poor blacks from casting their vote.

Evers was determined to vote in the state's Democratic primary in 1946, which took place on his twenty-first birthday. He planned to vote against an incumbent, Theodore Bilbo, who was actively racist and opposed any sort of advancement of African American rights. Evers and his brother, along with four other African American war veterans, walked through town to the courthouse, which served as the polling place. They were denied entrance by twenty white men armed with shotguns and rifles. Rather than risk their lives to vote, the veterans gave up and went home. However, Evers's passion for achieving equality was far from extinguished.

Evers completed high school and enrolled in Alcorn College along with his brother Charles. Evers excelled in several areas in college; he studied business, participated in sports, and served as editor for the school newspaper. He met and married Myrlie Beasley, another student, shortly before graduating. After receiving his degree, he began working as an insurance salesman for Magnolia Mutual in Mound Bayou, Mississippi. His territory as a salesman was a rural one, and his customers were the poorest of African Americans whose living conditions and treatment by local whites strengthened his resolve to improve the civil rights of blacks. In 1954, while visiting his dying father in the hospital, he witnessed a mob attempting to kill an African American man who had fought with a white man and had been brought to the hospital for treatment.

NAACP Field Secretary for Mississippi

Evers decided to join the National Association for the Advancement of Colored People (NAACP) as an organizer, and he also applied for law school at the University of Mississippi in 1954. The Supreme Court had recently ruled that segregation in public schools was illegal, and Evers had hoped the ruling would allow him to attend one of the state's traditionally "whites only" schools. However, his application was denied. Officials from the NAACP took note of Evers's drive and determination, and he was selected as the group's first field secretary for the state of Mississippi. He and his family relocated to Jackson, the state capital, and set up the field office for which he was responsible.

Evers worked to organize the local African American community, registering eligible voters and organizing boycotts of businesses that discriminated against blacks. In 1958, he was arrested for riding in a seat reserved for whites as a way of protesting segregation on local bus lines. Although Evers was himself denied entrance to the college, he was a key figure in the admission of James Meredith as the first African American to attend the University of Mississippi in 1962.

The response of some local whites to Evers's efforts was fierce; it began with death threats, and then escalated to acts of destruction and violence. Evers was one of the most famous civil rights activists in the state, which made him a prime target for racists. His name was included on a "death list" circulated among white supremacists in the South. In May 1963, his family's home was firebombed; his wife, fearful that gunmen were waiting outside to shoot when she fled the house, stayed inside. The house did not sustain major damage. On June 11, Evers attended an NAACP rally in Jackson that lasted until after midnight. That same day, President John F. Kennedy (1917–63) had given a speech in which he proposed to make segregation illegal. When Evers arrived home and got out of his car, he was shot in the back by a sniper. He died soon after at a local hospital on June 12, 1963, at the age of thirty-seven. He was buried in Arlington National Cemetery, in Washington, D.C.

A Long Wait for Justice

The murder shocked the African American community and resulted in near riots. President Kennedy issued a statement condemning the killing, and the FBI took control of the search to find Evers's murderer. Within two weeks, a fertilizer salesman named Byron de la Beckwith (1920–2001) was arrested for the crime. The evidence against Beckwith seemed overwhelming: the rifle scope from the alleged murder weapon had one of his fingerprints, his car was seen in the area near Evers's home at the time of the killing, and he had asked two cab drivers for directions to Evers's home just days before the murder. In addition, Beckwith was a member of the White Citizens Council, a white supremacist organization. However, Beckwith produced witnesses—including two police officers—who testified that he was far away from Evers's home at the time of the murder.

Beckwith's murder trial began in 1964. In court, he was confident and friendly with court officials and even with members of the jury, who were all white males from the area. The governor of Mississippi visited Beckwith during the trial, and some accounts state that the jury witnessed the governor hugging the defendant

in the courtroom. For the African Americans in attendance, however, Beckwith showed only contempt. Despite the evidence against him, he appeared certain that his white male peers on the jury would find him not guilty. Both the prosecution and defense were surprised when the jury came back after over thirty hours of deliberation and told the judge that they could not agree on a verdict. They were split nearly down the middle with no hope of reaching an agreement—a situation known as a hung jury.

Because the trial could not be completed, prosecutors were free to file murder charges against Beckwith a second time, which they did. This led to a new trial in 1965, which also ended in a hung jury. Rather than risk acquittal with a third trial, prosecutors chose not to file charges until more convincing evidence arose or until conditions improved enough for African Americans that they could be sure to receive an impartial jury. Unlike other crimes, cases involving murder do not have to be taken to trial within a certain period of time, known as a statute of limitations. Prosecutors could wait as long as necessary to guarantee a fair trial. It finally took place more than thirty years after Evers's murder.

Unlike the juries in the first two trials, the jury for the new trial was at last representative of the population in Jackson: it contained eight African Americans and several women. New evidence included witness testimony that Beckwith had bragged about committing the murder. In 1994, at the age of seventy-three, Beckwith was at last found guilty of murdering Evers; he was sentenced to life in prison without the possibility of parole. He died in prison in 2001.

In 1996, director Rob Reiner (1947–) released the film *Ghosts of Mississippi,* which details the murder of Evers and the long road to justice. In the film, Whoopi Goldberg (1955–) portrays Evers's widow Myrlie, who continued to push for a third trial even after decades had passed. Evers's two adult sons appear as themselves in the film, and his daughter plays the role of a juror. After the successful trial of Beckwith, Myrlie Evers-Williams (c. 1933–) was selected as chairman of the NAACP. She served as chairman from 1995 until 1998, continuing the activist work of her former husband.

★ MARTIN LUTHER KING JR.
(1929–1968)

Martin Luther King Jr. is perhaps the first person most Americans think of when considering the most significant figures of the civil rights movement. He was a minister, an activist, an orator, and an author whose strategy of nonviolent resistance earned him both praise and ridicule. His accomplishments were many, despite the fact that he was assassinated at the age of thirty-nine.

Martin Luther King Jr. was born Michael King Jr. on January 15, 1939. He belonged to the fourth generation in a family of Baptist ministers. The family lived in a middle-class neighborhood of Atlanta, Georgia. His father, Michael King Sr., adopted the name Martin Luther for both himself and his son in honor of the sixteenth-century German religious leader. His father was also involved in the National Association for the Advancement of Colored People (NAACP), an organization dedicated to securing equal rights for African Americans. His father's accomplishments, both as a religious leader and a community activist, provided a positive model for King's own future.

Martin Luther King Jr.
The Library of Congress

The Montgomery Bus Boycott

In 1944, at the age of fifteen, King began attending Morehouse College, a highly prestigious, private college for men. He studied sociology and was also ordained as a minister for the National Baptist Church. After receiving his degree from Morehouse, King traveled to Pennsylvania to study at the Crozer Theological Seminary. He received a degree in the study of religion in 1951, and served as both the president and the valedictorian for his class. King continued his religious studies at Boston University. While in Boston, he also met a music student named Coretta Scott (1927–2006). The two fell in love and married on June 18, 1953, in Alabama, Scott's home state. King completed his religious studies in 1955, earning a doctorate.

King accepted a position as the leader of the Dexter Avenue Baptist Church in Montgomery, Alabama, in 1954. Not long after he had moved to the city, Montgomery became ground zero for the civil rights struggle in the South. Rosa Parks (1913–2005), a secretary for the NAACP, refused to change seats aboard a Montgomery city bus when ordered by the driver to make room for boarding white passengers. She was arrested, and African American community leaders organized a one-day boycott of city buses as a sign of protest. The boycott was effective, and the leaders created a new organization to spearhead additional boycotts. That organization was called

Martin Luther King Jr. is fingerprinted after being arrested for his leadership of the Montgomery bus boycott in 1956.
Don Cravens/Time & Life Images/Time & Life Pictures/ Getty Images

the Montgomery Improvement Association (MIA), and King was selected to oversee the group and serve as its spokesman. He was twenty-six years old.

The bus boycott was extended, with the MIA asking all African Americans in Montgomery to avoid taking the bus until a policy of equal treatment was instituted. The boycott lasted for more than a year. King was instrumental in rallying the community behind the boycott and orchestrating alternate transportation options for black supporters. Meanwhile, a discrimination lawsuit filed in support of other black bus passengers reached the United States District Court, where it was ruled that segregating black passengers from white passengers on Montgomery city buses was illegal. This victory for the MIA thrust King further into the national spotlight. He was selected as the president of a newly formed organization called the Southern Christian Leadership Conference (SCLC) in the first months of 1957. An office for the new organization was established on Auburn Avenue in Atlanta, Georgia—the very street where King grew up.

The Potential of Nonviolent Protest

In 1958, King wrote *Stride Toward Freedom: The Montgomery Story*, a detailed account of the bus boycott and King's growing interest in nonviolent resistance as a means of achieving equality. King visited Harlem, New York, for a book-signing event on September 20, 1958. At the event, he was approached by a mentally disturbed African American woman named Izola Ware Curry who believed King was conspiring with Communist leaders. She stabbed him in the chest with a steel letter opener. Though King survived the attack, he underwent major surgery to remove the letter opener and was forced to spend several months recovering from the injury. Curry was diagnosed with schizophrenia, and was committed to a psychiatric facility instead of prison.

After he recovered, King traveled to India with his wife. He spoke with Prime Minister Jawaharlal Nehru (1889–1964), and learned more about Indian resistance leader Mohandas Gandhi (1869–1948). Gandhi's methods of nonviolent protest had been instrumental in achieving India's independence from Great Britain in 1947. King strengthened his resolve to use only nonviolent means in his civil rights demonstrations.

In 1960, King moved to Atlanta with his family and became the co-pastor of the Ebenezer Baptist Church along with his father, who had served as pastor there for thirty years. After King's success in Montgomery, other protest movements formed throughout the South. One of these was the Albany Movement, a group of student protesters in Albany, Georgia, who sought broad reforms throughout their city. The protests were not focused on a specific goal, like the Montgomery bus boycott, but instead were aimed at many businesses. King went to Albany to assist protestors, but found the movement's lack of focus to be a problem. Ultimately, over seven hundred protestors were arrested there, including King. King struck a bargain with government officials: He agreed to leave the city if they would be willing to release the rest of the protestors on bail. Although King upheld his end of the agreement, the city did not.

More successful was King's participation in a campaign in Birmingham, Alabama, in April 1963. The goal of the campaign was to boycott and peacefully disrupt businesses during the normally busy Easter shopping season. Government officials ordered the protestors to stop, but King and other leaders decided that the order was unjust, and continued protesting. King was arrested along with hundreds of others, and was placed in solitary confinement. During this time, he wrote a document known as the "Letter from Birmingham Jail" (1963), in which he explains his reasons for ignoring what he felt was an unjust law. He was released after eight days.

As police stepped up arrests of protestors, campaign leaders encouraged children to join in the nonviolent demonstrations. This did not reduce police brutality against the protestors, and televised footage of police beating children increased support for the protestors. King took charge of negotiations with city officials, and on May 10, the two sides agreed to a truce. The city ended segregation of public utilities like drinking fountains and rest rooms, and also agreed to end segregation at some dining locations. Local white supremacists responded violently to the agreement, and on September 15, 1963, an African American church was bombed by members of the Ku Klux Klan, killing four girls. King returned to Birmingham to speak at their funeral.

Marches in Washington and Selma

Between these two trips to Birmingham, King was involved in organizing one of the greatest demonstrations of the civil rights era. In August, over two hundred thousand people participated in the March on Washington for Jobs and Freedom. This event brought the issues of the troubled South to the doorstep of the United States government. At the time, it was the largest gathering ever seen in Washington, D.C. Standing before the crowd, King delivered what would become his most famous speech, commonly referred to as "I Have a Dream." Although President John F. Kennedy had already proposed the creation of civil rights legislation, the March on Washington increased support from the American public and other politicians for what would become the Civil Rights Act of 1964. King himself was selected by *Time* magazine as "Man of the Year" for 1963—the first African American to be so honored. In 1964, he received the Nobel Peace Prize for his emphasis on nonviolence in his campaigns for civil rights.

Though King did not endorse violence, his opponents were often all too ready to use it against him and his fellow demonstrators. In 1965, King helped organize voter registration in Selma, Alabama, where African Americans had been subject to arrests and beatings by police when trying to secure their right to vote. Civil rights leader James Bevel (1936–2008) planned a peaceful march from Selma to Montgomery, Alabama, a distance of about fifty miles, on March 7, 1965. The purpose was to ask the governor, George Wallace (1919–98), to support their right to vote, and to protest the killing of a peaceful demonstrator by police the prior month. Approximately six hundred people showed up for the march, but as they attempted to leave Selma, they were attacked with clubs and tear gas by police who were reportedly acting on Governor Wallace's orders. The event came to be known as "Bloody Sunday," and over a dozen demonstrators were badly injured. King quickly organized another march, but he was asked by President Lyndon B. Johnson (1908–73) to postpone it until he could ensure the safety of the participants. King complied, and within one week President Johnson introduced the Voting Rights Act to Congress. The bill guaranteed that no eligible American voter could be denied the right to vote based on his or her race.

King's techniques had proven effective, but many African Americans were growing tired of peaceful responses to violent attacks by white supremacists and even government-controlled police. Some turned toward the black power movement, which advocated violence as a means to achieve equality. Some African Americans believed that staying separate from whites would benefit their own culture and preserve their racial identity. King dismissed these ideas, and the civil rights movement became fragmented rather than united.

King began to focus his activism on other areas after 1966. One issue of great concern to him was the Vietnam War (1954–75). King considered the war to be damaging to the poor in South Vietnam, where American troops fought, as well as to the poor and working-class young Americans who were being sent to fight there. In addition, he felt that the massive amount of money spent to fund the war would be better spent improving the lives of Americans and protecting the rights of blacks. At the time, few spoke out in support of King's statements. However, public opinion about the war would change dramatically over the next five years.

Memphis Strike and a Tragic End

In December 1967, King launched a campaign meant to address the issue of poverty in the United States for people of all races and ethnicities. This was known as the Poor People's Campaign. King participated in a sanitation workers' strike in Memphis, Tennessee, at the end of March 1968. He returned to Memphis on April 3, with the intention of marching again the following week. He gave a speech that night addressing the death threats he had recently received, including a bomb threat that had delayed his flight to Memphis. Just after 6 PM on Thursday, April 4, while standing outside his room at the Lorraine Motel, King was struck in the face by a single bullet. He was rushed to a local hospital, but was pronounced dead an hour later.

News of King's murder resulted in riots and demonstrations across the country, with over forty deaths linked to the unrest. President Johnson proclaimed April 7 a national day of mourning for King. On April 9, a funeral service was held for King in Atlanta, with over one hundred thousand people accompanying his body as it traveled through the streets of the city. Meanwhile FBI agents began the most extensive investigation they had ever undertaken in a search for King's killer. They found the murder weapon and linked it to James Earl Ray (1928–98), an escaped convict who had rented a room in a boardinghouse with a clear view of King's motel room. Although Ray had disappeared, he was captured in England two months later and sent back to the United States to await trial. Ray chose to plead guilty to the murder in exchange for a plea bargain: he would not be executed, but would instead spend the rest of his life in jail. Still, some doubt remained in the minds of those connected with the King family and those who were present at the shooting. In 1999, the King family won a wrongful death suit against a man named Loyd Jowers (1927–2000), who owned a restaurant near the Lorraine Motel at the time of the shooting. Jowers had admitted to being involved in a plot to kill King, and he claimed that a Memphis police officer named Earl Clark was actually the shooter.

Following King's murder, Coretta Scott King created the Martin Luther King Jr. Center for Nonviolent Social Change in Atlanta. In 1983, lawmakers recognized the importance of King's legacy by passing a bill to create a federal holiday in his honor. Martin Luther King Jr. Day is celebrated on the third Monday of January each year, in recognition of his January 15 birth date.

Malcolm X. *Robert Parent/ Time & Life Pictures/ Getty Images*

★ MALCOLM X
(1925–1965)

Malcolm X was a civil rights activist known best for his scathing criticisms of white American culture and for his support of both Islamic religion and black separatism. Black separatism is the belief that African Americans would be better off forming their own nation separate from whites, or returning to their ancestral lands in Africa. In his final years, Malcolm X reevaluated his anger toward whites and began to offer a message of unity among people of all races. Malcolm X was murdered in 1965 by militant Black Muslims (as the African American members of the Nation of Islam were popularly called) who felt he was turning his back on their extremist ideals.

A Childhood Marked by Violence and Tragedy

Malcolm X was born Malcolm Little in Omaha, Nebraska, to a Baptist minister named Earl Little and his homemaker wife Louise, who was originally from Grenada. Malcolm was one of eight children. His father was active in the struggle for civil rights at a time when it was still especially dangerous for an African American to stand up for equality. Earl Little supported Marcus Garvey (1887–1940), a black activist who led a movement to establish a homeland in Africa for Americans of African descent. The Black Legion, a white supremacist organization linked to the Ku Klux Klan and active in the Midwest, threatened and harassed Earl Little enough to cause him to move his family from Nebraska to Wisconsin, and then again to Lansing, Michigan.

The Little family home in Lansing was burned to the ground in 1929, though luckily no one was injured. Earl believed the fire to be the work of the Black Legion, but could not prove it. In 1931, when Malcolm was just six years old, Earl was run over by a streetcar and died soon after. Though police contended that he simply fell from a streetcar, there was some evidence that he had been struck on the head. Many believed that the Black Legion had finally followed through on their death threats.

Louise's mental state deteriorated after the death of her husband, and in 1938 she was committed to a state institution. Malcolm and the other Little children were placed in foster care. Despite the loss of his only parent, Malcolm remained an exceptional student, and he dreamed of becoming a lawyer. He was discouraged from pursuing this dream by a teacher who told him that such a career was not realistic for an African American. He turned his back on educational pursuits and dropped out of school. In 1941, at the age of fifteen, he left Michigan and went to live in Boston with one of his half-sisters. Malcolm drifted from job to job and relocated several times, once back to Michigan and once to Harlem, in New York City. He became a low-level criminal, and in 1946, he was caught and convicted of burglary. He was given a sentence of ten years, and he served around seven before earning parole.

A Prison Conversion and the Nation of Islam

While in prison, Malcolm spent his time educating himself. He reportedly read through the dictionary as a way of improving his vocabulary. Most significantly, however, he became part of a religious movement introduced to him by one of his brothers: the Nation of Islam. The Nation of Islam was a Muslim organization that sought to unite all people of African descent. At least some followers also supported the formation of a separate nation for African Americans, much like Marcus Garvey and Malcolm's own father. The Nation of Islam differed from traditional Muslim beliefs in many ways, most notably in the idea that blacks were the original and highest form of humankind. From prison, Malcolm began corresponding with the Nation of Islam's leader, Elijah Muhammad. He became a devoted member of the Nation of Islam and replaced his last name with the letter "X." He felt that Little was a name forced upon his ancestors by the system of slavery that had brought them to America and taken away their true African identity.

Malcolm became a minister for the Nation of Islam after being released from prison in 1952, working at temples in Detroit, Boston, Philadelphia, and Harlem. His success brought him into the national spotlight. The message he offered was very different from that of other civil rights leaders such as Martin Luther King Jr. Whereas King promoted nonviolence and active participation in American society, Malcolm encouraged African Americans to withdraw from interaction with whites, whom he felt had proven themselves untrustworthy and unable to accept blacks as equals. He also felt that nonviolence was unsatisfactory as a response to violence from whites: "Concerning nonviolence," he stated in a speech, "it is criminal to teach a man not to defend himself when he is the constant victim of brutal attacks."

He became recognized as the national spokesman for the Nation of Islam, and in 1958, he married a fellow member named Betty. They would eventually have six children, all daughters. The organization grew significantly with Malcolm as the face and voice of the Nation of Islam, reaching thirty thousand members by 1963. His outspoken nature attracted the attention of the Federal Bureau of Investigation (FBI), which kept a close watch on his activities. By all appearances, he had become the most important person in the organization even though Elijah Muhammad was still the group's recognized leader and prophet. In 1957, Malcolm founded the official newspaper of the Nation of Islam, called *Muhammad Speaks.*

Wider Interests and a Break with Elijah Muhammad

In 1959 and 1960, Malcolm traveled to other countries, including some in Africa. He met with world leaders, including Fidel Castro (1926–), the leader of Cuba. His growing interest in political activism intensified a rift between him and the Nation of Islam, which was more concerned with religious activism. In addition, he discovered that Elijah Muhammad had engaged in extramarital affairs with several women in his organization, and had even fathered children with them. This behavior was strictly forbidden by the teachings of the Nation of Islam, and Malcolm took it as a personal betrayal that his mentor did not follow the basic teachings of the faith.

Tension between Muhammad and Malcolm came to a head after the assassination of President John F. Kennedy, when Malcolm was officially reprimanded for comments he made about the killing. He had suggested that the violence found in white society had finally come back to haunt whites instead of just African Americans, who were usually the victims of such crimes. He was forbidden from speaking in public for three months by the Nation of Islam. After his period of silence was complete, he announced that he would be leaving the Nation of Islam permanently and would instead form his own Muslim organization.

Malcolm followed through on this promise by creating Muslim Mosque, Inc., on March 12, 1964. He also reached out to civil rights activists whom he had previously criticized, hoping to forge a united front despite their differing methods of activism. Three weeks later, he gave one of his most well-known speeches in a church in Ohio. In the speech called "The Bullet or the Ballot," Malcolm encourages African Americans to become politically active when it is to their advantage to do so. However, he also warns that African Americans may resort to violent means if the government fails to address their needs. At the time of his speech, the Civil Rights Act first introduced by President Kennedy had yet to be passed by the United States Senate. Southern Democrats were fighting bitterly to prevent the passage of the bill, which specifically outlawed any discrimination based on race or ethnic heritage. While Malcolm had earlier in his life dismissed the possibility of working with whites to improve the rights of African Americans, his speech reveals his willingness to cooperate with those committed to making change happen.

Malcolm X (right) stands next to Martin Luther King Jr. in the Capitol building following debates over a civil rights bill in 1964. After Malcolm X broke away from the Nation of Islam, he was more willing to partner with the civil rights leaders he had previously criticized. *AP Images*

Travels in the Middle East and a Philosophical Transformation

Soon after, he made a pilgrimage to Mecca, the most sacred location in Islam, located in Saudi Arabia. He learned the differences between Islam as it was taught in the Nation of Islam and more traditional Islamic beliefs. He was also surprised by the diversity of those gathered under the banner of Islam: People of all races interacted with peace, love, and respect for each other. Throughout the year, he spent time speaking with African and Middle Eastern activists and leaders, which gave him a broader understanding of the issue of race relations around the world. In May 1964, he founded the Organization of Afro-American Unity, a nonreligious organization aimed at strengthening relations between African Americans and others of African descent.

Malcolm's experiences in the Middle East and Africa transformed his view of the world. He adopted a new name that reflected his acceptance of traditional Islam, El-Hajj Malik El-Shabazz. In a conversation with photographer and author Gordon Parks (1912–2006) on February 19, 1965—just two days before he was killed—he expressed regret over some of his past remarks about white people, stating that he made "a fool of himself" by blindly following the Nation of Islam. He also affirmed his dedication to establishing brotherhood between people of all races and religions.

Meanwhile, leaders of the Nation of Islam had not taken his departure well. He was criticized heavily in *Muhammad Speaks,* the newspaper he had founded, and some within the organization offered veiled threats that were widely reported in the media. On February 14, 1965, his family's home in East Elmhurst, New York, was firebombed and burned to the ground. No one was injured. However, one week later, on February 21, 1965, Malcolm was gunned down while speaking at a meeting for the Organization of Afro-American Unity. The three gunmen emerged from the crowd of approximately four hundred attendees and shot him at least fifteen times. Although he was rushed to Columbia Presbyterian Hospital, Malcolm was pronounced dead upon arrival.

The three suspects, all of whom were members of the Nation of Islam, were arrested, tried, and convicted for their part in the murder. Beginning in 1964, Malcolm had been working with author Alex Haley on a book about his life. The book was released as *The Autobiography of Malcolm X* in 1965, and was put together from interviews Malcolm had given to Haley. It is mainly through this book and through transcriptions of his speeches that Malcolm was later known. Unlike other activists such as Martin Luther King Jr. or W. E. B. Du Bois, Malcolm did not author any books or essays to express his beliefs. Despite this, he remains one of the best-known and most significant activists of the civil rights era.

★ THURGOOD MARSHALL
(1908–1993)

Thurgood Marshall was one of the most significant figures in civil rights law. He was a lawyer with the National Association for the Advancement of Colored People (NAACP), and argued some of the most significant civil rights cases of the twentieth century. His most notable victory was as the lead lawyer in the landmark Supreme Court case *Brown v. Board of Education*, which struck down legalized segregation in public schools in 1954. He went on to become the first African American judge to serve as a Supreme Court justice.

Thurgood Marshall. *Hank Walker/Time & Life Pictures/ Getty Images*

A Civil Rights Activist from an Early Age

Marshall was born in Baltimore, Maryland, the second child of Norma Arica Williams and William Canfield Marshall. His mother was an elementary school teacher, and his father held various positions, including railroad porter and steward at an exclusive boat club that only allowed white members. Marshall was a mischievous youth and often got into trouble at school. On occasion, the principal punished him by forcing him to memorize a passage from the United States Constitution, which thoroughly cemented his relationship with constitutional law. His father was also interested in the law, and often recounted details of trials he had watched in the local courtroom. Marshall's father also taught him never to tolerate racial insults. When he was fifteen, Marshall was arrested after he got into a fight with a white man who pulled him off a trolley and uttered a racial slur. The charges were dropped, but from then on Marshall would never stop fighting against bigotry and prejudice.

Marshall graduated from high school and enrolled in Lincoln University with an eye toward studying law. He completed his degree in 1930, and expressed an interest in attending law school at the University of Maryland in Baltimore. The school, however, did not accept African Americans. Instead, Marshall attended law school at Howard University, a prestigious institution originally established for black students. He graduated at the top of his class in 1933, and he opened a private law practice in Baltimore.

One of Marshall's former deans at Howard, Charles H. Houston (1895–1950), became involved with the National Association for the Advancement of Colored People (NAACP). He encouraged Marshall to lend his talents to the organization, and Marshall agreed. In 1935, he assisted Houston in arguing *Murray v. Pearson,* a case in which an African American student named Donald Gaines Murray was denied admission to the University of Maryland School of Law—the same school Marshall had wanted to attend. Marshall argued the case, contending that the school's "separate but equal" policy meant that they should provide Murray admission to another school of equal quality. Since no other public law school was available in the state of Maryland, the judge ruled that Murray must be allowed to attend.

Marshall's success at arguing civil rights cases led to his being hired as legal counsel for the NAACP in 1936. Two years later, he became the main counsel for the organization. He argued his first case before the United States Supreme Court in 1940. The case was *Chambers v. Florida,* in which he represented three African American defendants found guilty of murder and sentenced to death. Marshall argued that police had exerted undue pressure on the men to make them confess. The Supreme Court agreed and overturned their convictions.

In 1940, Marshall also became director of the new NAACP Legal Defense and Educational Fund, intended to increase funding for the legal casework they were handling. He was also chosen as a board member for both the American Civil Liberties Union and the National Lawyers Guild. He argued more cases before the Supreme Court, including *Smith v. Allwright* in 1944. In this case, he convinced the Court that "whites-only" voting primaries in Texas violated existing laws, and the practice was ended. In 1948, Marshall returned to the Supreme Court to argue the case of *Shelley v. Kraemer.* In this case, an African American family in St. Louis was forbidden from taking possession of a home they purchased because the deed had prior restrictions barring blacks from owning the property. The court ruled in favor of Marshall and the family.

Brown v. Board of Education

Marshall was perhaps best known for his work in ending segregation in schools. His career had started with just such a case, and in 1950 he argued two more cases before the Supreme Court. Both cases involved students who were supplied "separate" educational experiences at universities that the students and the NAACP felt were not equal to what was offered to white students. Marshall won both cases, helping to chip away at segregation within the educational system. His most famous case also involved segregation and education. In 1951, a group of parents in Topeka, Kansas, filed a lawsuit to end segregation in their local elementary schools. At the time, the country was divided on the issue of school segregation; every state in the South required it by law, but just as many states throughout the rest of the country had already outlawed the practice. It was 1954 by the time the case, called *Brown v. Board of Education,* reached the Supreme Court, where Marshall argued that separate schools, even if similar in facilities and appearance, are inherently unequal. The justices of the Supreme Court agreed unanimously and declared that segregation in schools was unconstitutional.

The fight to end segregation in schools did not end there, however. Even after the Supreme Court had ruled to outlaw segregation, Southern states fought the integration of black and white students at every step. Some states even passed laws that directly contradicted the ruling of the Supreme Court. In the case of *Cooper v. Aaron* in 1958, school board members in Little Rock, Arkansas, sued to end the process of desegregation, arguing that the law in their state still required segregation in schools. Marshall argued the opposing view when the case was elevated to the Supreme Court, stating that the ruling of the federal court was more important than state law. As with *Brown v. Board of Education,* the justices agreed unanimously with Marshall. Of the thirty-two cases he argued as a lawyer before the Supreme Court, Marshall won twenty-nine of them.

In 1961, President John F. Kennedy recommended Marshall for a position as a judge for the United States Court of Appeals. He served in that position for four years, issuing ninety-eight majority decisions. None of these decisions was ever reversed by the Supreme Court. In 1965, President Lyndon B. Johnson appointed Marshall as solicitor general, in which he argued cases on behalf of the United States government. His success in this position led President Johnson to appoint Marshall to the Supreme Court on June 13, 1967, where he continued to serve for twenty-four years.

⭐ ROSA PARKS
(1913–2005)

Rosa Parks is best remembered for a single significant event: She refused to give up her seat to a white passenger on a Montgomery, Alabama, bus in 1955. This simple act of defiance led to her arrest and a subsequent boycott of the Montgomery bus system by the city's African American residents. This, in turn, led to one of the most important early victories of the civil rights movement, the ending of segregation on Montgomery public buses.

Involvement with the NAACP

Parks was born Rosa Louise McCauley in Tuskegee, Alabama, the oldest child of James and Leona Edwards McCauley. At a young age, she and her brother Sylvester moved to Pine Level, Alabama, with their mother. There, she attended an all-black school for girls that consisted of a single room. The school only taught up to grade six, so her mother sent her to a private school in Montgomery, Alabama. Unfortunately, the illnesses of both her grandmother and later her mother required her to remain home and care for them. School was put on hold.

Rosa Parks. *Don Cravens/ Time & Life Pictures/ Getty Images*

In 1932, she married a Montgomery barber named Raymond Parks. Raymond was a self-educated civil rights activist and a member of the National Association for the Advancement of Colored People (NAACP). He encouraged his wife to return to high school and complete her education, which she did in 1934. She also joined her husband in his activism, becoming one of the few women involved in the Montgomery chapter of the NAACP. In 1943, she became the secretary of the chapter, and she worked to improve the level of voter registration among local African Americans. She also worked as a seamstress and performed various odd jobs.

In that same year, Parks had her first conflict with a city bus driver. A process had been established for those using Montgomery's segregated buses, which had two sets of entrance doors—one at the front of the bus and one at the rear. Black riders were required to enter through the front entrance to pay the fare, and then exit through the front and re-enter the bus through the back entrance. The back section of the bus was designated as the "colored" section. One day, Parks entered the front of a Montgomery bus, paid her fare, and walked straight to the back of the bus without first exiting and reentering. Even though she was already in the back section of the bus, the driver demanded that she exit the front and board again through the rear. She refused to do it, and he threw her off the bus. After the incident, Parks made it a point to avoid taking any bus driven by that same driver, a man named James F. Blake.

Parks Keeps Her Seat, Sparks a Boycott

By 1955, Parks had worked as a youth advisor for the NAACP and had been given an opportunity to attend a nonsegregated workshop with both black and white students. In August, she met Dr. Martin Luther King Jr., a minister and civil rights activist who had just arrived in town to lead one of its Baptist churches. On December 1, 1955, Parks boarded a bus and paid the fare before realizing that the driver was Blake, the very same one who had thrown her off twelve years earlier. This time, she exited the front of the bus and boarded in back, as she was required to do. However, there was another rule the blacks aboard the bus were expected to follow. If the white section of the bus became full, all the black passengers in the front row of the black section would be required to move back, even if there were no seats available in the back. The front section of the bus filled up, and one white passenger still required a seat. Blake instructed all the black passengers in the first row of their section to move back. Three of the four passengers moved back. The fourth was Rosa Parks.

Blake again warned Parks that she had to move, but she refused. He called the police to the scene, and Parks was arrested for failing to comply with orders issued by the driver. The president of the Montgomery NAACP chapter, Edgar Daniel Nixon (1899–1987), posted bail and arranged for a lawyer to represent her. Parks's actions were not part of an arranged plan, but the organization had been looking for a case that would publicize the unfairness of the Montgomery bus system. Activists and ministers quickly formed a group called the Montgomery Improvement Association, and under that banner they called for a boycott of the Montgomery bus system. The group selected new minister Martin Luther King Jr. as its leader and spokesman.

Most people expected the boycott to be a short-term protest designed to send a message to local government officials. It wound up lasting 381 days and significantly hurt city revenues generated by the bus system. The boycott began on Monday, December 5—the same day as Parks's trial, in which she was found guilty and ordered to pay a ten-dollar fine. Contrary to popular belief, it was not Parks's court case that resulted in the end of segregation on Montgomery city buses. A civil court case was filed that named four other plaintiffs—all African American women who were treated badly by Montgomery bus drivers. Still, it was Parks's arrest that ignited the fire of protest among the black population of Montgomery and resulted in the successful boycott.

The boycott ended on December 21, 1956, after the court ruled that the buses could no longer be segregated. Parks and others still suffered from discrimination at the hands of whites in the community, and she and her husband both had difficulty staying employed. In 1957, the family relocated, settling in Detroit, Michigan. She worked in a friend's sewing factory beginning in 1961. She continued in the struggle for civil rights by attending both the March on Washington in 1963 and the Selma to Montgomery March in 1965. Also in 1965, newly elected congressman John Conyers Jr. (1929–) of Detroit invited Parks to work as a secretary in his office. She remained there until 1988, when she retired at the age of seventy-five. In 1992, she completed a short autobiography with Jim Haskins titled *Rosa Parks: My Story*. In her later life, she received numerous awards for her significant contribution to the civil rights movement, including the Spingarn Medal from the NAACP and the Presidential Medal of Freedom from President Bill Clinton (1946–). When she died in 2005, her body was approved to lie in state in the Rotunda of the United States Capitol building. She was the first woman and the second African American to receive this honor.

❖ JIM CROW LAWS STRIP BLACKS OF CONSTITUTIONAL RIGHTS

The end of the Civil War in 1865 began a series of legislative acts to guarantee the freedom of former slaves and integrate them as full citizens of the United States. The Thirteenth Amendment was officially adopted as a part of the United States Constitution on December 6, 1865. This amendment guaranteed a permanent end to slavery throughout the United States. The Fourteenth Amendment, passed in 1868, guaranteed all African Americans status as full citizens. The Fifteenth Amendment, approved in 1870, stated that a person could not be denied the right to vote based on race. These amendments ultimately failed to prevent decades of racism and unfair treatment. One of the most glaring examples of this was legalized segregation, in which separate facilities and services were provided for blacks and whites. The system of state and local laws that formed legal segregation were referred to collectively as "Jim Crow" laws. Based on a song in a minstrel show, the term Jim Crow became a racial slur.

Blacks Banished from White Society

U.S. Army forces remained active in the former Confederate states of the South in the years following the Civil War. They ensured that federal laws outlawing slavery and ensuring African American men the right to vote were enforced. This period of rebuilding and adjusting to life without slavery in the South is known as Reconstruction. The Civil Rights Act of 1875 made it unlawful for public services and accommodations to provide unequal treatment based on race. This was the final major protection offered to blacks during the Reconstruction era. Reconstruction ended in 1877, when federal troops withdrew from the South and allowed these states full control of their own governments.

The rights that African Americans had enjoyed during the time of Reconstruction were swiftly stripped away by Southern state governments after the federal troops left. New laws denied blacks access to businesses and services. Blacks also faced discrimination in the northern and western parts of the country. Several African Americans sued on behalf of their rights, and the United States Supreme Court considered these cases together in 1883. All involved African Americans being excluded from public places: a hotel dining room in Kansas, an opera house in New York City, a theater in San Francisco. The Supreme Court ruled that the Civil Rights Act of 1875 was unconstitutional, because the Thirteenth and Fourteenth Amendments were meant to protect African Americans from racial discrimination by the government, but their protection did not extend to private businesses. This meant that private businesses were free

African American Frustration Boils Over

There were no widespread protests against the U.S. Supreme Court decisions of 1883 and 1896 regarding legal segregation. The modern student of history may wonder why African Americans did not organize and rise up sooner against those who oppressed them. Quite simply, many blacks were too afraid to protest. Those who did were often beaten or even killed. During the 1890s alone, about one thousand African Americans, almost all men, were lynched—killed by mobs with no legal authority. The threat of such extreme violence was an effective deterrent to organized public protest.

Sometimes, however, anger and resentment within the black community erupted into deadly riots. In Chicago in 1919, the African American community was enraged by the drowning of a black teenager who accidentally went into a "whites only" beach area. Several days of fighting left dozens dead and hundreds injured. In Tulsa, Oklahoma, in 1921, a black man was accused of touching a white woman in an elevator. The black community rallied to protect him from lynching, and intense fighting broke out. Dozens of people were killed, and many homes were destroyed.

Other riots in American cities involved white citizens launching attacks on blacks or black neighborhoods. These race riots of the early twentieth century inspired the beginning of an organized civil rights movement. The National Association for the Advancement of Colored People (NAACP) was founded in 1909 in response to a riot in Springfield, Illinois, and quickly became a major force in the fight against lynching, Jim Crow laws, and disenfranchisement (taking away a person's right to vote).

to refuse service to blacks. Southern states were free to pass laws requiring racial segregation.

Segregation extended beyond private businesses. During the 1880s and 1890s, many states in the South passed laws requiring African Americans to use separate public facilities, such as hospitals, parks, and schools. The 1896 U.S. Supreme Court case *Plessy v. Ferguson* challenged the constitutionality of these laws. Homer Adolph Plessy was an African American businessman from Louisiana who deliberately broke a Louisiana law requiring segregation on trains in order to challenge the state's Jim Crow laws in general. Plessy was arrested after refusing to sit in the segregated part of a train. He was convicted and fined, and his appeal found its way eventually to the U.S. Supreme Court.

Again, arguments before the Supreme Court centered on the Thirteenth and Fourteenth Amendments and the limits of the protection they offered. The justices ruled that as long as public facilities available to blacks were "equal" to those offered to whites, that separation of black and white facilities was legal. In reality, public facilities for blacks were almost always inferior to those for whites. However, the "separate but equal" guideline kept the United States firmly and legally divided along color lines for almost sixty years.

African Americans Denied Access to Polls, Political Power

African American men had been guaranteed the right to vote in 1870, but whites in the South set up rules that kept blacks from the polls. By 1908, most Southern states had enacted laws that almost completely disenfranchised blacks. Some states required literacy tests for those who wished to vote; this kept older blacks who had never been able to attend school from voting. Many states also required a poll tax, meaning that each voter would have to pay money in order to vote. Blacks were generally much poorer than whites, and therefore could not afford to pay the tax. These rules were often applied selectively, meaning that only blacks were required to pay a tax or take a test. If these methods failed, groups of armed white men stood guard in small towns across the South to threaten and discourage any blacks who came to the polls.

African Americans issued several legal challenges to these laws. Those filing suit found an ally in Booker T. Washington (1856–1915). The renowned educator and founder of the Tuskegee Institute had been scoffed at by some civil rights activists because he publicly supported an "accomodationist" approach to bettering the lives of African Americans. He said blacks should seek integration into white society gradually, not aggressively. Washington secretly paid for several legal challenges to laws disenfranchising blacks. One by one, however, the U.S. Supreme Court rejected these challenges. In *Williams v. Mississippi* (1903), the Court upheld Mississippi's use of literacy tests and poll taxes because, technically, they applied to all citizens. *Giles v. Harris* (1903) and *Giles v. Teasley* (1904) were challenges to an Alabama law designed to make it difficult for African Americans to register to vote. The Supreme Court upheld a lower court dismissal of *Giles v. Harris* and claimed it had no jurisdiction to overturn the decision of the Alabama Supreme Court in *Giles v. Teasley*. Later legal challenges were sometimes successful, but states responded by coming up with new ways to limit African American voting. It was not until the passage of the Voting Rights Act of 1965 that African Americans were once again able to exercise their constitutional right to vote.

❖ IDA B. WELLS WAGES CAMPAIGN AGAINST LYNCHING

Racial tensions throughout the United States resulted in the deaths of many African Americans under the guise of justice in the 1890s. These victims were never tried or convicted of crimes, and in some cases were later proven innocent of any wrongdoing. These killings often escaped the attention of the media and the public because they occurred outside the bounds of the law. After learning of these atrocities, an African American woman named Ida B. Wells made sure that they would never again go unnoticed.

A Journalist Speaks Out Against the Horrors of Lynching

The term "lynching" has its origins during the American Revolutionary War (1776–83). It came from the name of Charles Lynch (1742–1820), a judge in Virginia who ordered various punishments for suspected supporters of the British during the war. These punishments were not based on existing laws. Since then, lynching has come to mean a severe punishment—usually murder—carried out by a group against one or more people without following a legal court process. In other words, those killed in a lynching are never formally convicted of committing a crime.

Ida B. Wells's pamphlet, Southern Horrors: Lynch Law in All Its Phases, *exposed the shame of lynching in the South.* Photographs and Prints Division, Schomburg Center for Research in Black Culture, The New York Public Library, Astor, Lenox and Tilden Foundations

SOUTHERN HORRORS.

LYNCH LAW

IN ALL

ITS PHASES

Miss IDA B. WELLS,

Price, · · · Fifteen Cents.

THE NEW YORK AGE PRINT.
1892.

Wells, a well-known activist and journalist living in Memphis, Tennessee, first became interested in the subject of lynching in 1892. In March of that year, three African American business owners in Memphis were attacked at their grocery store by resentful whites, and three of the white men were injured when the black men defended themselves. The black men were put in jail, but an angry white mob removed them and shot them dead. Several months later, another black man accused of attacking a white woman was pulled from jail, viciously attacked, and hanged from a telephone pole. Afterward, his body was cut down and burned in the middle of the street, then dragged to the courthouse and hung on display there. During the entire incident, local police looked on and made little effort to subdue the mob. Afterward, they made no effort to arrest those who had participated.

Photographs Reveal the Horror of Lynching

"Without Sanctuary: Lynching Photography in America" is a collection of more than 150 photographs of lynchings from multiple U.S. states dating from the late nineteenth to the early twentieth centuries. Collector James Allen gathered the photographs over the course of twenty-five years of research. The exhibit photographs, which have been shown in galleries and museums across the United States and continue to be displayed regularly, are also available in book form (published in 2000 as *Without Sanctuary: Lynching Photography in America*) and online at www .withoutsanctuary.org. The photographs themselves are extremely shocking. They often show large crowds of white men, women, and even children seeming to celebrate in a party-like atmosphere around the hanged, burned, and mutilated corpses of black men. Some of the photographs were even reproduced as postcards and sold as souvenirs. These graphic images help modern viewers understand the true horror of lynching.

Wells's article about the first lynching caused such a stir that angry whites destroyed the offices of the newspaper Wells owned. She moved to New York, where she published an article on lynching in the *New York Age* in June 1892. The article, later published as the pamphlet *Southern Horrors: Lynch Law in All Its Phases,* noted that the primary justification given for lynchings was to punish black men for raping white women. Wells pointed out that only one-third of those lynched in the United States were actually accused of rape. She listed several cases in which white women willingly had relationships with black men, but lied because they feared disgrace from other whites when the relationship became public. In these cases, the innocent black men were either killed or imprisoned. Wells argued that lynchings were not carried out as acts of justice, but as acts of terror to keep other African Americans in line.

Wells Goes Abroad on Antilynching Crusade

Wells moved to Chicago in 1893, and in 1894 she took a job writing a column for a mainstream daily newspaper. She began a campaign to end lynchings in the United States, and made trips to Europe to publicize the horrors that were taking place. She encountered many people who had difficulty believing that such horrible acts were taking place. She kept documents, records, and photographs as evidence of the crimes. Wells wrote detailed reports of various lynchings and published them in 1895 as *The Red Record: Tabulated Statistics and Alleged Causes of Lynching in the United States.* The book points out that blacks had recently been lynched for such alleged crimes as stealing hogs (which may have actually just been lost), an argument over incorrect change being given, and displaying a "saucy" attitude toward whites.

Statistics kept by the Tuskegee Institute (now Tuskegee University) reveal that lynchings peaked immediately after the Civil War. However, the decade of the 1890s saw a dramatic increase in lynchings, especially throughout the South. Over one thousand African Americans were killed during this ten-year period. After Wells launched her campaign to educate and rally sentiment against lynching, the number of lynchings steadily dropped, finally reaching fewer than ten per year during the 1940s. President Theodore Roosevelt (1858–1919) supported the antilynching cause during his time in office, as did Indiana governor Winfield T. Durbin, who enforced antilynching laws and dispatched a militia to prevent a mob from lynching a murder suspect in 1903.

❖ BOOKER T. WASHINGTON MAKES "ATLANTA COMPROMISE" SPEECH

Booker T. Washington was the most influential civil rights activist and African American educator at the close of the nineteenth century. His strategy for improving conditions for African Americans relied heavily upon education in trade skills such as farming. By proving their skills, Washington argued, African Americans would eventually be accepted by whites as equals. However, activists like W. E. B. Du Bois (1868–1963) felt that Washington's strategy relied too heavily upon a "wait and see" attitude for securing African American rights.

Washington was himself a slave on a Virginia plantation until the age of nine. He began his working life laboring at difficult jobs like coal mining, but was able to further his education at the Hampton Institute. He ultimately became a teacher there. When a new African American trade school was being formed in Alabama, Washington was recommended for the job of principal. At twenty-five, he took charge of the Tuskegee Institute and shaped it into one of the premier African American educational facilities in the United States. Education at Tuskegee stressed the importance of self-reliance. Washington believed that African Americans, so long viewed as inferior by many whites, had to prove their worth by demonstrating their practical value to American society. To this end, he encouraged the mastery of trade skills such as bricklaying and metalworking. This was also a way for African Americans to provide for themselves while they waited for whites to accept them into mainstream society.

The "Atlanta Compromise" Speech

Washington's strategy and philosophy is most famously demonstrated by a speech he gave in 1895 at the Atlanta Cotton States and International Exposition. The speech is commonly known as the "Atlanta Compromise." In the speech, he emphasized cooperation and brotherhood between whites and blacks, and dismissed suggestions that blacks should separate themselves or return to Africa for their own benefit. He acknowledged the difficult struggle African Americans faced, but advised: "It is at the bottom of life we must begin, and not at the top. Nor should we permit our grievances to overshadow our opportunities."

In the speech, Washington went on to criticize civil rights activists who wanted to pursue a more aggressive strategy in working toward equality. The only effective tactic, he argued, would be for African Americans to prove themselves economically useful: "No race that has anything to contribute to the markets of the world is long in any degree ostracized." He also suggested that economic freedom was of greater importance than civil freedom.

Booker T. Washington makes a speech before a large crowd. *The Library of Congress*

"The Talented Tenth"

In 1903, W. E. B. Du Bois laid out a viewpoint on African American education that stood in direct contrast to Washington's proposal that blacks focus on learning trades in order to make immediate economic gains and avoid disturbing white people. His article "The Talented Tenth" appeared in a collection of articles by various African Americans called *The Negro Problem*. Du Bois argued that about ten percent of the black population was capable of benefitting from a classical liberal education in a college or university and becoming public intellectuals and world leaders— what he called an "aristocracy of talent and character." He believed that the great efforts and achievements of these gifted individuals could quickly elevate the African American community in general, both by serving as role models to other African Americans and by showing whites the capabilities of educated blacks. He called on his readers (whom he assumed to be white liberals) to identify these talented young African Americans and give them the best educational opportunities. "If you do not lift them up," he warned, "they will drag you down."

Du Bois and Others Criticize the Compromise

The fact that the speech is best known as the "Atlanta Compromise" is an indication of how later African Americans came to feel about Washington's ideas. They felt that his approach required them to compromise their beliefs in their fight for equality. Washington suggested that by not actively fighting for rights such as the right to vote or the end of segregation, African Americans would earn acceptance among whites slowly and without great opposition.

Early in his career, Du Bois supported some of Washington's goals, and even collaborated with him on an exhibition of African American achievements for the 1900 World's Fair in Paris. Du Bois offered much praise for Washington's accomplishments in his 1903 book *The Souls of Black Folk*. However, he also noted that "there is among educated and thoughtful colored men in all parts of the land a feeling of deep regret, sorrow, and apprehension at the wide currency and ascendancy which some of Mr. Washington's theories have gained." According to Du Bois, Washington's strategy required African Americans to give up political power, their quest for basic civil rights, and higher education that was not focused on learning a trade skill. Du Bois believed these were unacceptable compromises. Du Bois was quick to point out that he and others who disagreed with Washington did not expect equal rights to come quickly or easily.

Washington remained the dominant spokesperson for African Americans throughout the first decade of the twentieth century, and his autobiography *Up from Slavery* (1901) proved successful among both black and white readers. However, the ideas of Du Bois and others began to gain acceptance. Du Bois's viewpoint in particular was attractive to African American men who had already achieved some level of educational or economic success. In 1905, he helped to form a movement more or less in opposition to Washington's own, which called specifically for voting rights and the end of segregation. This led to the formation of the National Association for the Advancement of Colored People (NAACP) in 1909. After Washington's death in 1915, many African Americans began to drift away from his humble, patient approach to achieving equality and instead embraced activism as the best path toward securing their civil rights.

❖ NATIONAL ASSOCIATION OF COLORED WOMEN'S CLUBS IS FORMED

The National Association of Colored Women's Clubs (NACWC) is one of the oldest African American women's organizations in the United States, established in 1896. It served as a uniting force for smaller women's organizations and clubs in over thirty states. The two main forces behind the creation of the NACWC were Josephine St. Pierre Ruffin (1842–1924) and Mary Church Terrell (1863–1954).

Ruffin was an early supporter of women's suffrage, or the right to vote. She launched the first American newspaper published by an African American woman in 1884. Ten years later, she organized the Women's Era Club, one of the earliest clubs specifically for African American women. She created the National Federation of Afro-American Women in 1895 in an attempt to bring together the best-educated and most-successful African American women in the country. Ruffin was one of two African American women asked to participate in the founding of the National Association for the Advancement of Colored People (NAACP) in 1909.

Terrell was one of the first African American women to earn a college degree, in 1884. Terrell became a teacher and later a member of the Washington, D.C., Board of Education. She also became a leader in the National American Woman Suffrage Association, the most prominent women's suffrage organization in the 1890s.

Ruffin's National Federation of Afro-American Women combined with the Colored Women's League of Washington, D.C., in 1896. The resulting

Members of the National
Association of Colored
Women's Clubs picket the
White House in protest of
a quadruple lynching in
Georgia, July 30, 1946.
© *Bettmann/Corbis*

group was named the National Association for Colored Women's Clubs. Terrell was elected as the group's first president, and Ruffin served as its vice president. They decided the group's motto would be "Lifting as We Climb." The NACWC was actually an umbrella organization made up of many other clubs across the country. Its founders published a periodical called the *National Association Notes* to share news among the various clubs.

One of the main goals of the NACWC was to counteract stereotypes of African Americans. Throughout the South, Jim Crow laws had been instituted to keep blacks separate from whites. The civil rights successes that occurred after the Civil War were quickly being reversed or ignored. Many Americans still believed stereotypes about blacks being uneducated, dishonest, and lewd. The women of the NACWC fulfilled a duty to present a positive image of the African American community, and worked hard to help less advantaged blacks achieve similar success.

The NACWC involved itself in several key causes throughout the first half of the twentieth century. The group was instrumental in publicizing Ida B. Wells's antilynching campaign, and its members also fought for desegregation of all-white women's clubs around the country. The NACWC raised over five million dollars in bonds to support the war effort when the United States entered World War I (1914–18). In 1920, they preserved the historic home of Frederick Douglass (1818–95) in Washington, D.C., which was later classified as a national historic site. In the 1930s, the organization created the National Association of Colored Girls and donated to the defense of the Scottsboro boys, nine African Americans accused of raping two white women in Alabama. In the 1950s, they donated money to help the first black students who integrated an all-white high school in Little Rock, Arkansas. During the 1960s, they networked with civil rights groups throughout the South to support the struggle for desegregation and voting rights, and participated in the March on Washington in 1963. The group continued to be active even after African Americans received their full rights in the 1960s, supporting education and community projects in the thirty-two states in which it was active in 2010.

❖ THE NIAGARA MOVEMENT GIVES RISE TO THE NAACP

The Niagara Movement arose from the desire of a handful of African American activists to end racial segregation and take an active role in the furthering of African American rights. The movement was named for the place of its first meeting, near Niagara Falls. Among the leaders of the group were W. E. B. Du Bois and William Monroe Trotter (1872–1934). The organization formed the basis for what would later become the National Association for the Advancement of Colored People (NAACP).

The founding members of the Niagara Movement, including W. E. B. Du Bois (second from right, center row) pose in front of Niagara Falls, 1905. *Photographs and Prints Division, Schomburg Center for Research in Black Culture, The New York Public Library, Astor, Lenox and Tilden Foundations*

A Small Group of Activists Meets at Niagara Falls

Civil rights activist Du Bois and a number of prominent African Americans organized a meeting in 1905 to discuss the state of black rights in the United States. The members included lawyers, publishers, and other well-educated and successful men. Du Bois was named the general secretary of the group. The meeting occurred in July in Fort Erie, on the Canadian side of the Niagara River. The aim of the meeting was to establish an organization dedicated to ending segregation and other unfair practices against African Americans. Another stated goal was to secure for African American men the right to vote. At that time, women were not allowed to vote in the United States, and were not initially a part of the Niagara Movement. Women did become part of the group in the years that followed.

The group created a declaration of principles. The declaration called for voting rights for black men, and economic and educational opportunities for all Americans in equal measure. The document specifically called for improvements in the areas of education, justice, health, and employment, among others. To achieve these goals, the members vowed to "complain loudly and insistently" when encountering unfair conditions. "To ignore, overlook, or apologize for these wrongs is to prove ourselves unworthy of freedom," the declaration read. "Persistent manly agitation is the way to liberty, and toward this goal the Niagara Movement has started and asks the cooperation of all men of all races."

The declaration contained criticism of the current state of affairs far stronger than many activists of the time were willing to make. According to the members, the African American population "needs sympathy and receives criticism, needs help and is given hindrance, needs protection and is given mob-violence, needs justice and is given charity, needs leadership and is given cowardice and apology, needs bread and is given a stone." The document ended with a list of responsibilities that all African Americans should fulfill; these included showing respect for others, educating one's children, and obeying the law.

The first meeting in 1905 had around 30 participants. By the close of that year, membership had increased to 170, with chapters launched in 21 states. The group continued for several years, but never achieved the success Du Bois and the other founders had envisioned.

Black and White Activists Work Together to Form NAACP

Though the Niagara Movement was seen as an organization for educated African American men, several white activists shared similar aims. One of these activists was Mary White Ovington (1865–1951), a New Yorker involved in labor and women's rights issues in addition to fighting for racial equality. In 1908, Ovington read an article written by William English Walling (1877–1936) concerning a race riot that occurred in Springfield, Illinois, Abraham Lincoln's hometown. The riot started when two African American men were independently accused of committing violent crimes against white residents. A mob formed, demanding that the sheriff release the men so that they could be dealt with outside the confines of the law. In the end, dozens of homes were destroyed and seven people were killed, including one innocent African American who was hanged.

After reading the story, Ovington contacted Walling. They put out a call for activists to organize for a conference on civil rights. The call was issued on February 12, 1909—the one hundredth anniversary of Abraham Lincoln's birth. It is this date that is generally acknowledged as the start of what would become the NAACP. The first conference was held on May 30, 1909, in New York City. It was not until the following year, however, that the organization chose its permanent name and its executive officers. The goals of the organization meshed well with the earlier Niagara Movement, and several key members of that group—most notably Du Bois—joined the NAACP. Du Bois was chosen as one of the group's first officers, and was in fact the only African American officer initially chosen for the organization.

The group began publishing its own magazine, edited by Du Bois. The magazine, called *The Crisis*, helped to spread the message of the organization across the country. By 1917, the NAACP consisted of around nine thousand members. Just two years later, membership had reached ninety thousand. The group provided legal support for those fighting against unfair or discriminatory laws, and also worked to reduce occurrences of lynching in the United States.

Major Achievements of the NAACP

Protests and legal pressure by NAACP members were behind many civil rights advances in the twentieth century. One of its first major court cases occurred in 1917 when the NAACP fought and won a battle to force the U.S. military to allow African Americans to be commissioned as officers in World War I. About six hundred African Americans were commissioned as officers during the war. Future U.S. Supreme Court justice Thurgood Marshall (1908–93), one of the NAACP's attorneys, teamed with Charles Hamilton Houston (1895–1950) in 1935 to win a legal battle to get a black student admitted to the University of Maryland. When renowned African American opera singer Marian Anderson (1902–93) was barred from performing at Constitution Hall by the women's organization Daughters of the American Revolution in 1939, it was the NAACP (with the help of First Lady Eleanor Roosevelt) that arranged for her concert to be moved to the Lincoln Memorial, where she performed for an audience of 75,000.

During the 1940s, the NAACP kept steady pressure on the federal government to make racial discrimination illegal. President Franklin Roosevelt (1882–1945) signed orders banning racial discrimination in federal employment and in industries related to World War II efforts. His successor, President Harry Truman (1884–1972), issued executive orders banning segregation in the armed forces, racial discrimination in hiring for civil service positions, and racial discrimination by contractors for the armed forces.

The NAACP's most famous legal achievement came in 1954, when a team of lawyers led by Thurgood Marshall triumphed in the U.S. Supreme Court case *Brown v. Board of Education.* The Supreme Court ruled in *Brown* that segregated public school facilities are unconstitutional, overturning the precedent (accepted legal rule) set by the 1896 Supreme Court case *Plessy v. Ferguson.* The case marked the beginning of the end of segregation in all areas of society, not just in education.

NAACP member Rosa Parks refused to give up her seat on a Montgomery, Alabama, bus to a white passenger in 1955. Her arrest sparked the Montgomery bus boycott, and ushered in a decade of intense involvement by the NAACP in civil rights protests. Throughout the late 1950s and 1960s, the NAACP would coordinate with other civil rights groups, including the Southern Christian Leadership Conference and the Student Nonviolent Coordinating Committee, to lead voter registration drives throughout the South.

The NAACP continued to fight against discrimination and to support positive advances in race relations into the twenty-first century. The organization numbered three hundred thousand members in 2009. That same year, the organization celebrated its one hundredth anniversary.

❖ VIOLENCE MEETS VOTER REGISTRATION EFFORTS

African American men in the South technically had the right to vote since 1870. African American women were able to vote with the rest of American women after the passage of the Nineteenth Amendment in 1920. Yet African Americans in the South were denied the right to exercise their right to vote by unfair laws that required them to take a literacy test or pay a poll tax before they could vote. Their lack of education and poverty made these barriers difficult to overcome for most African Americans. Those blacks who did attempt to vote were physically intimidated by whites. In many parts of the South, five percent or less of the African American population was even registered to vote.

Attempts to challenge laws that disenfranchised (took voting rights away from) blacks met with failure in lawsuits filed during the late nineteenth and early twentieth centuries. The first case to successfully challenge the unfair voting laws occurred in 1915. In *Guinn v. United States*, the United States Supreme Court ruled that "grandfather clauses" were illegal. Grandfather clauses made voting eligibility dependent on whether a person was descended from someone who had voting rights. Most African Americans descended from slaves, who could not vote. Therefore, the grandfather clauses clearly discriminated against African Americans.

In 1944, the Supreme Court ruled in *Smith v. Allwright* that "white primaries" in Texas were unconstitutional. A white primary was a primary election in which African Americans were barred from voting, either explicitly or by rules of the political party holding the primary. Some states tried to come up with new ways to keep African Americans from voting, but these were struck down in federal courts during the 1940s and 1950s. Unfortunately, this case-by-case approach to protecting African Americans' voting rights did not result in widespread enfranchisement of African Americans.

NAACP and SNCC Lead the Way in Voter Registration

The National Association for the Advancement of Colored People (NAACP) and the Student Nonviolent Coordinating Committee (SNCC) organized major voter registration drives in the South. Amzie Moore (1911–82), Aaron Henry (1922–97), and Medgar Evers (1925–63) coordinated voter registration efforts in Mississippi, where their attempts met with particularly violent responses. Evers had been field secretary for the NAACP in Mississippi since 1954. He had been active in helping to integrate the University of Mississippi and in investigating the lynching of Emmett Till (1941–55), a black teenager accused of whistling at a white woman in Money, Mississippi. His activities drew the anger of white supremacists in Mississippi, and Evers was threatened repeatedly. Evers was shot dead in his driveway in 1963. His murderer, Byron de la Beckwith, escaped justice for decades after all-white juries deadlocked twice during his trials. He was eventually convicted based on new evidence in 1994 and died in prison in 2001.

Evers's death was not the end of the violence surrounding voter registration efforts in the South. Three activists helping with voter registration disappeared in Mississippi on June 21, 1964. They were James Chaney, a twenty-one-year-old black Mississippi native; Andrew Goodman, a twenty-year-old white New York native; and Michael Schwerner, a twenty-four-year-old white organizer for the Congress of Racial Equality (CORE). The national uproar that followed their disappearance prompted President Lyndon B. Johnson (1908–73) to order the director of the Federal Bureau of Investigations (FBI), J. Edgar Hoover (1895–1972), to investigate the case. The bodies of the missing activists were found in an earthen dam several weeks after their disappearance. Seven members of the Ku Klux Klan were eventually charged with and convicted of the murders in 1967. In 2005, one more person, Edgar Ray Killen, who had been a local minister, was convicted for his role in the killings. He was said to be the person who planned and oversaw the murders.

Other volunteers risked their lives during the summer of 1964—dubbed Freedom Summer—to register voters across Mississippi and establish community support systems for African Americans. More than one thousand activists were arrested and more than three dozen black churches were burned or bombed. The violence did not stop the campaign from being successful.

March in Selma Gives Momentum to Voting Rights Act

A similar voting rights campaign began in Selma, Alabama, in the late 1950s. At that time, only .01 percent of the African American population of Dallas County, where Selma is located, were registered to vote. Beginning in 1963, the Dallas County Voters League (DCLV) attempted to register black voters, but they met with violent resistance from the White Citizens Council and the Ku Klux Klan. The DCLV called in assistance from the SNCC in 1963. They were aided in their cause by the passage of the Civil Rights Act the following year. The Civil Rights Act was a sweeping law that, among other things, made it illegal to apply voting registration requirements unequally. That summer, SNCC chairman John Lewis (1940–) led a march of fifty African Americans to the courthouse to register to vote. They were arrested.

The DCLV called in the assistance of Martin Luther King Jr. (1929–68) and the Southern Christian Leadership Conference (SCLC) in 1964. The SCLC and SNCC expanded voter registration efforts in Dallas County and the surrounding areas beginning in January 1965. The SCLC planned a nonviolent march to Montgomery, Alabama, for Sunday, March 7, to confront Alabama governor George Wallace (1919–98). The six hundred demonstrators who planned to march from Selma to Montgomery were never allowed to leave Selma. They were brutally attacked by police acting under orders from Governor Wallace in an incident later dubbed "Bloody Sunday." King held a demonstration on March 9 in which he led 2,500 protestors across the Edmund Pettus Bridge in Selma, held a prayer service, and turned back. He did not march on Montgomery in order to comply with a restraining order against the march. King also hoped to gain the support of sympathetic judges in Alabama who might issue a court order preventing police from stopping a future march. Three white ministers who had traveled to Selma to support King were beaten outside a Selma restaurant that night. One, a Unitarian Universalist minister from Boston named James Reeb, died of his injuries two days later.

Alabama judge Frank Minis Johnson ruled that the Selma to Montgomery march was protected by the First Amendment on March 18. Three days later, 8,000 activists began a peaceful march to Montgomery. Most returned to Selma after the first day to comply with Judge Johnson's court order, but 300 continued. They were joined by thousands more as they approached Montgomery, and 25,000 people joined the marchers on the final stretch of their long walk to the capitol in Montgomery. The demonstrations in Selma shifted public opinion in favor of the civil rights activists and gave President Johnson the momentum he needed to pass the Voting Rights Act, which outlawed discrimination against eligible voters in 1965. Although demonstrations continued after the Voting Rights Act became law, this act finally enforced the rights that activists had spent a decade struggling to earn.

❖ MALCOLM X BECOMES NEW FACE OF BLACK NATIONALISM

Black nationalism is the idea that African Americans should establish independence from white society and take pride in their own cultural heritage. Some black nationalists believe that blacks and whites should be completely segregated, or kept apart. This self-imposed segregation would prevent whites from exploiting or abusing blacks. Some call for a separate nation of blacks to be formed, either from part of the United States or from territory in Africa. The black nationalist position stood in stark contrast to that of many civil rights leaders who pressed for increased integration during the civil rights era. In the 1950s, a charismatic leader named Malcolm X (1925–65) helped bring new prominence and wider acceptance to the black nationalist agenda.

The Roots of Black Nationalism Run Deep

At least some aspects of black nationalism can be traced back to the early nineteenth century. A group called the American Colonization Society, founded by whites who supported the end of slavery, came up with a plan to help freed slaves establish a colony in Liberia, a U.S.–held territory on the western coast of Africa. Many of the members felt that African Americans would never be fully accepted into American society, and should therefore be allowed to start a new society back in Africa. Thousands of freed blacks relocated to Liberia during the 1820s and 1830s. The movement did receive criticism from those who felt that the real purpose of moving free blacks to Africa was to keep them from becoming a burden to mainstream American society.

Although the justifications were different, Marcus Garvey's Back to Africa movement in the 1920s was similar in its goals. Garvey (1887–1940), the Jamaican-born founder of the Universal Negro Improvement Association (UNIA), sought to unite all people of African descent into a single, powerful force. He tried to accomplish that goal by helping interested African Americans to settle in Liberia. Garvey also created business groups like the Negro Factories Corporation, which would allow African Americans to operate self-sufficiently and independent of whites within

American society. Garvey's desire to keep black and white societies separate put him in the odd position of sharing goals with members of the Ku Klux Klan, a white supremacist group that he met with and regarded somewhat favorably. He believed that Klan members were honest about their racism, while other whites were simply being deceptive. His association with the Klan and his segregationist philosophy drew sharp criticism from many African American activists, including W. E. B. Du Bois. Garvey was convicted of mail fraud in 1923 and deported to Jamaica in 1927. The UNIA continued to operate, but it lost much of its momentum without Garvey.

A New Generation of Black Nationalists Appears

A new group took up the cause of black nationalism less than a decade later. The Nation of Islam (NOI) is a religious organization that has played an important part in race relations in the United States. Founded in Detroit in the 1930s, the NOI offered a message of esteem and strength for African Americans. The NOI also strongly endorsed a separation between black and white societies.

Malcolm X, one of the most famous NOI leaders, subscribed to Garvey's views on race relations. His father had been a member of the UNIA, was often threatened by white supremacists, and died under suspicious circumstances when Malcolm was six years old. Malcolm joined the NOI while in prison for burglary. He became active in the organization after he was released from prison in 1952. His outspoken criticism of other black activists brought him attention. Malcolm often stated that the peaceful protests of Martin Luther King Jr. and other activists were pointless, and that they were just playing into the hands of whites. He also argued that nonviolence was an unacceptable strategy when whites committed brutal acts of violence against blacks on a daily basis. These controversial statements resulted in greater exposure and popularity for the NOI. The group built new temples and expanded existing ones as membership increased. The number of members grew from around five hundred to twenty-five thousand between 1952 and 1963, reflecting the growing popularity of both Malcolm and the NOI's philosophy of separatism.

The publicity that brought the group to national mainstream attention was a documentary called *The Hate that Hate Produced* that aired in 1959. The documentary featured interviews with key members of the Nation of Islam, including the group's leader Elijah Muhammad (1897–1975) and Malcolm X. This increased exposure for the group as a whole, but Malcolm X clearly emerged as the face and voice of the organization. His speeches and appearances began to receive greater attention, particularly because his message was so strikingly different from that of Martin Luther King Jr.

Malcolm X's views on African American self-reliance and pride were influential, especially among young African American men discouraged by their lack of opportunity for economic and educational advancement. They were also at odds with many civil rights activists who were trying to help African Americans become accepted members of mainstream society. These activists saw black nationalism as being too negative and working against the goals of the civil rights movement. Martin Luther King Jr., in his famous "Letter from Birmingham Jail" in 1963, referred to black nationalism as a force "of bitterness and hatred," and described it as a movement "made up of people who have lost faith in America."

Malcolm X Changes His Mind

Malcolm X announced that he was leaving the NOI to form his own Muslim organization in early 1964. That year, Malcolm traveled to the Islamic holy city of Mecca, and the journey transformed his way of thinking. After seeing people of all races united in peace and love under the banner of Islam, Malcolm rejected his earlier support of black separatism. He emphasized a message of brotherhood and human rights, rather than just focusing on civil rights for African Americans. On February 21, 1965, three members of the NOI gunned down Malcolm X during a speech in New York City. The negative publicity surrounding this tragic occurrence left a cloud over the NOI for years. Although calls for a separate African American society did not disappear entirely, the relative success of the Civil Rights Act of 1964 and the Voting Rights Act of 1965 caused black nationalism to have dwindling appeal for African Americans from the mid-1970s onward.

❖ KING PROMOTES NONVIOLENT CIVIL DISOBEDIENCE

Martin Luther King Jr. is considered by many to be the most significant leader of the struggle for civil rights in the United States. The son and grandson of Baptist ministers, he was raised with an understanding of the importance of community as a tool for positive change. His dedication to nonviolence shaped the civil rights movement throughout the South and led to his receiving a Nobel Peace Prize in 1964.

Nonviolence Brings an End to Segregated Buses in Montgomery

King arrived in Montgomery, Alabama, in 1954 to start his career as a pastor. He had accepted a position as pastor of the Dexter Avenue Baptist Church. His training involved many years of studying Christianity and other world religions. One religious figure and activist made a particular impression on him: Mohandas Gandhi (1869–1948), Hindu leader of a movement to secure India's independence from Great Britain. Gandhi was known for his use of nonviolence and civil disobedience to accomplish his goals. Civil disobedience could mean simply ignoring an unjust law. Often protestors using civil disobedience deliberately break a law that they consider unjust. If they are not arrested, the law quickly becomes unenforceable as more people break it. If they are arrested, others join in the disobedience, forcing police to either arrest them all or ignore the law. These techniques avoid violence and emphasize camaraderie, or friendship among people sharing a common experience. Another nonviolent tactic used by Gandhi and others is the boycott. During a boycott, participants avoid buying a product or using a service as a way of protesting that business or company.

King and other organizers in Montgomery used these techniques to great effect when protesting segregation on Montgomery city buses. The rule on these buses was that black passengers must give up their seats if there were no seats available for white passengers. Activists in Montgomery felt that the law was unjust, because federal laws had already stated that segregation was illegal. Police in Montgomery and other places in the South got around this by claiming that passengers were required by law to obey the bus driver. Therefore, the driver could order anyone, black or white, to change seats or move. Several African American passengers had already exercised nonviolent civil disobedience regarding the rule, and all had been arrested.

Activists decided to launch a boycott against the city bus system in 1955. All African Americans were urged to avoid taking the bus. Since black passengers outnumbered white passengers by at least two to one, the revenues for the bus company fell dramatically. At the same time, the African American community in Montgomery grew stronger. Blacks worked together to coordinate transportation around the city, since the buses could no longer be used. These bonds remained even after city officials ended segregation on the buses in 1956.

Young Protestors Face Violence with Bravery in Birmingham

In April 1963, King led demonstrators in Birmingham, Alabama, in a campaign to change the city's segregation laws. Boycotts alone were not enough, so demonstrators used civil disobedience to call attention to their cause. Throughout the city, demonstrators staged "sit-ins," which involved remaining inside a business that refused to serve African Americans. Although the demonstrators were nonviolent and generally respectful to others, their presence disrupted the normal operations of the businesses. Most expected to be arrested, and many were. King himself was sent to jail, which attracted media attention and brought the cause to the attention of people around the world. People in other parts of the country began to

Student Sit-ins Inspired by King

King wrote *Stride Toward Freedom* after his success with the Montgomery bus boycott. The book fully explained and defended his practice of nonviolent civil disobedience. The book directly inspired a group of African American students in Greensboro, North Carolina. These students decided to take action. Several lunch counters in the city, which operated like small diners within larger stores, would only serve white customers. Black residents could not boycott these restaurants, because they were already excluded as customers. On February 1, 1960, four African American college students sat down at the F. W. Woolworth lunch counter and waited patiently to be served. This type of demonstration is known as a "sit-in." Sit-ins had already proved effective in Oklahoma City and Chicago, among other places. This was the first publicized example of a sit-in that took place in the highly segregated South. The four students stayed at the lunch counter until the store closed, and were never served. The next day they returned, along with a few more African American students. By the third day, the number of peaceful demonstrators had increased to sixty, and other lunch counters in the city experienced similar sit-ins. Less than six months later, the Woolworth chain agreed to serve African Americans at all its lunch counters throughout the South.

The publicized success of the Greensboro sit-ins inspired students in Nashville, Tennessee, to begin similar protests. Although the demonstrators were polite and nonviolent, several white agitators attacked some of the demonstrators. Instead of arresting the white attackers, police arrested at least seventy-five demonstrators. Soon after, the home of a lawyer representing the arrested demonstrators was bombed. Fortunately, no one was hurt, and the demonstrations grew to even greater size. On May 10, six businesses agreed to desegregate their lunch counters on a trial basis. The trial was successful, and Nashville became a leading city of the desegregation movement in the South.

African Americans take seats at a Woolworth's lunch counter in Atlanta, Georgia, on October 20, 1960, during a sit-in demonstration. *Ap Images*

boycott the business chains that allowed discrimination in their stores in Birmingham.

Campaign leaders also called upon children to take part in the demonstrations. This highlighted their nonviolent intentions and their desire to bring change for future generations. Over one thousand children and young adults showed up to demonstrate in the city on May 2, 1963. Several hundred of these children were arrested, and police ran out of space to keep all the protestors jailed. They could not continue to arrest protestors, so police began to use violence to disperse them. The demonstrators still followed King's philosophy of nonviolence, even as many were subdued with attack dogs and fire hoses. The protestors earned sympathy by not responding with violence. Many whites reconsidered their views on the segregation issue, and support for the campaigners continued to grow. Every time a group of protestors was arrested, they were replaced by new sympathetic supporters. Though the decision to recruit children as

Firemen turn the full force of their fire hoses on civil rights demonstrators in Birmingham, Alabama, on July 15, 1963. The city's use of force against peaceful protestors, particularly children, helped sway public opinion in favor of civil rights. *AP Images*

protestors was controversial, the Birmingham campaign was successful. By July 1963, Birmingham had overturned most of its segregation ordinances.

❖ MONTGOMERY BUS BOYCOTT FORCES DESEGREGATION

The year 1955 was a frustrating time for many people involved in the struggle for civil rights in the United States. The United States Supreme Court had already ruled the previous year that segregation in public schools was illegal. And a full nine years had already passed since the same court had ruled against segregation on interstate buses. However, change was slow to come in many areas of the country, particularly the South.

Montgomery Bus System an Example of Institutional Racism

Institutional racism occurs when an organization or governing body operates under a policy that discriminates between different people based on race or ethnicity. The public transportation system in Montgomery, Alabama, was a clear example of institutional racism. The back section of the bus was designated for African Americans, while the front was reserved for white passengers. Black passengers had to enter through the front doors, pay the fare, exit the front doors, and reenter through the rear doors. In addition, if the white section of the bus was full and another white passenger boarded, any black passengers in the first row of the "colored" section were required to move back one row to make room for the white passenger, regardless of whether or not seating was available for them.

Black passengers who failed to obey these unfair rules could be thrown off the bus or arrested. In the 1950s, as more and more African Americans recognized the unfairness of the rules, conflicts between black passengers and Montgomery bus drivers became increasingly common. On March 2, 1955, a fifteen-year-old high school student named Claudette Colvin refused to give up her seat for boarding white passengers. She was arrested and taken to jail. In April of the same year, a thirty-six-year-old housewife named Aurelia Browder was arrested under similar circumstances. On October 21, an eighteen-year-old named Mary Louise Smith was arrested for not giving up her seat to a white woman.

Rosa Parks Ignites the Spark of Protest

Tensions regarding the bus policy had been mounting for years, and on December 1, 1955, circumstances finally reached a tipping point. Rosa Parks (1913–2005), a forty-two-year-old seamstress and secretary for the local chapter of the NAACP, was arrested for refusing to give up her seat to a white man. Her situation was no different from that of other women arrested before, but the fact that she was older and a respected member of the activist community in Montgomery drew attention. The president of the local NAACP, Edgar Daniel Nixon (1899–1987), and a local lawyer posted Parks's bail. They and other community leaders immediately began organizing a response: a one-day boycott of Montgomery's public transit system that would take place on Monday, December 5, which was also the day of Parks's trial. Flyers were printed by the Women's Political Council, an organization that had already attempted to affect changes to the bus system and had previously threatened a boycott. The flyer read in part, "If we do not do something to stop these arrests, they will continue. The next time it may be you, or your daughter, or mother." The flyer continued, "This woman's case will come up on Monday. We are, therefore, asking every Negro to stay off the buses Monday in protest of the arrest and trial." Although Parks was found guilty at the trial, the bus boycott proved successful.

Community organizers met again that same day and decided to extend the boycott to send a message to the local government. A new organization called the Montgomery Improvement Association (MIA) was formed. Martin Luther King Jr., a minister new to the area but eager to participate in civil rights causes, became the leader and spokesman of the organization. The group issued demands to those who controlled the public transit

A nearly empty bus during the Montgomery bus boycott. *Time & Life Pictures/ Getty Images*

system, and stated the boycott would end when these demands were met. These demands included more courteous treatment for black passengers, as well as a promise to hire black drivers. They also asked that seating be offered on a first-come, first-served basis, though they did not push the issue of separate entrances for blacks and whites.

The boycott was wildly successful at reducing revenues for the bus system. Before the boycott, nearly three-fourths of all passengers on Montgomery city buses were black. During the boycott, an estimated ninety percent of African Americans in Montgomery avoided taking the bus. The MIA offered alternative transportation methods for those participating in the boycott. Over three hundred cars were used for carpooling, and discounted cab fares were offered for some participants.

The organization and its leaders faced opposition on many fronts as the boycott dragged on. The homes of both King and Nixon were bombed, and King was convicted of violating a law that forbade the disruption of lawful businesses. The Federal Bureau of Investigation (FBI) even assigned an agent to "uncover all the derogatory information he could" about King. Parks also endured hardship, being fired from her job at a local department store. However, the boycott continued throughout the year.

A Supreme Court Ruling Ends Bus Segregation

During the boycott, civil rights lawyers prepared a civil lawsuit to be filed on behalf of several women—including Claudette Colvin, Mary Louise Smith, and Aurelia Browder—who had been arrested on Montgomery city buses. The suit was filed on February 1, 1956, and the named defendant was the mayor of Montgomery. In June, a district court ruling found that the bus segregation was unconstitutional, but the matter escalated all the way to the Supreme Court. On November 15, 1956, the Supreme Court upheld the earlier ruling that public buses in Alabama could no longer segregate passengers according to race.

A Montgomery city ordinance was passed in December to change the previous law. The boycott ended after 381 days on December 20, 1956. Many historians view this campaign as the first major success in the civil rights movement.

❖ FREEDOM RIDERS RISK DEATH IN FIGHT FOR DESEGREGATION

In December 1960, the United States Supreme Court confirmed a ruling that passengers traveling from one state to another cannot be segregated, regardless of the laws in individual states. A group of thirteen civil rights activists from the Congress of Racial Equality (CORE) decided to test this ruling by organizing a "Freedom Ride" aboard buses traveling from Washington, D.C., to New Orleans, Louisiana. The journey required them to pass through several Southern states, including South Carolina, Georgia, Alabama, and Mississippi. They began on May 4, 1961. Three Freedom Riders were attacked in South Carolina, and some local police made efforts to disrupt their journey. Still, the Freedom Riders continued onward to Alabama.

In Anniston, Alabama, mobs led by members of the Ku Klux Klan attacked one bus and its riders, setting the bus on fire and attempting to trap the passengers on board. The other bus continued to Birmingham, but there the riders were viciously attacked by another mob. It was later revealed that Birmingham's sheriff Bull Connor (1897–1973) knew in advance of the planned attack and decided not to send police to protect the riders. Fearful bus drivers for Trailways and Greyhound refused to carry the Freedom Riders any farther, and they were forced to take an airplane for the final leg of their journey.

A group of students from Nashville decided to continue the journey in their place. The students were arrested in Birmingham and returned by police to Tennessee. The students refused to allow themselves to be intimidated and returned to Birmingham to try again. The Greyhound Bus Company, under pressure from U.S. Attorney General Robert Kennedy (1925–68), agreed to carry the new Freedom Riders. They left Birmingham on May 20 and had police protection along the way to Montgomery. In

Freedom Riders faced violence from angry white mobs as they travelled through the South, including the firebombing of their buses. *AP Images*

Prominent Freedom Riders

F amous Freedom Riders include Stokely Carmichael (1941–98), John Lewis (1940–), and Bob Filner (1942–). Stokely Carmichael was a leader of the Student Nonviolent Coordinating Committee (SNCC), and later a leader of the Black Panther Party, a radical black power group that achieved prominence in the late 1960s and early 1970s. John Lewis was chairman of the SNCC and went on to become a United States congressman for the state of Georgia in 1987, an office he continued to hold as of 2010. Bob Filner was a student at Cornell University when he decided to participate in the Freedom Rides. He spent two months in jail after being arrested in Mississippi. Filner, a white participant in the Freedom Rides, represented California's fifty-first district in the United States House of Representatives starting in 1992.

Montgomery, the group's promised police protection disappeared, and they were attacked. The mob of angry whites viciously beat the Freedom Riders, both white and black, along with anyone who came to their aid. Among those trying to stop the violence were Floyd Mann, head of Alabama's state highway patrol, and John Seigenthaler, a U.S. Justice Department aide sent by Robert Kennedy. Seigenthaler was beaten unconscious. Mann ordered in state troopers to stop the violence. After hearing of the attack, Kennedy sent federal marshals to Montgomery.

Martin Luther King Jr. flew to Montgomery and held a meeting at a local Baptist church, surrounded by federal marshals. The presence of the marshals did not stop a crowd of whites from hurling stones through the windows. The marshals, backed up by local police, dispersed the crowd. Kennedy called for a "cooling off" period in the hopes of calming the situation, but the Freedom Riders rejected the plan. They boarded a bus to Jackson, Mississippi, and traveled to Mississippi without incident. They were arrested in Jackson for defying segregation laws. This outrage inspired other Freedom Riders across the South to join the cause. Wave after wave of Freedom Riders converged on Jackson, Mississippi, intent on continuing the original journey. Over three hundred Freedom Riders were ultimately arrested in Jackson and sent to Parchman Penitentiary, where they were forced to endure whips and cattle prods, and sleep without mattresses.

A police officer places a segregation sign in front of a railroad station on January 9, 1956, in Jackson, Mississippi. The railroad company had removed segregation signs from waiting rooms in compliance with an Interstate Commerce Commission order, but Mississippi state law required segregated facilities at rail depots. *AP Images*

Most of these Freedom Riders spend the summer of 1961 in appalling conditions at Parchman. Many were scarred for life by the beatings and mistreatment they endured. Though they never reached New Orleans, they did succeed in forcing the federal government to take a clear stand on desegregation. Citing the experiences of the Freedom Riders, Robert Kennedy forced the Interstate Commerce Commission (ICC) to enforce its own existing rules outlawing segregation on interstate buses. In 1955, the ICC had ordered the desegregation of interstate bus travel, but it neglected to enforce the rule. Kennedy petitioned the ICC to adopt and enforce strict, clear regulations regarding bus desegregation. Beginning on November 1, 1961, bus stations across the South finally complied.

❖ THE 1963 MARCH ON WASHINGTON WINS SUPPORT FOR CIVIL RIGHTS

The March on Washington for Jobs and Freedom took place in August 1963. It was a large political rally organized by religious and labor leaders.

Somewhere between 200,000 and 300,000 people, mostly African Americans, began at the Washington Monument and walked to the Lincoln Memorial, where a program of musical performances and speakers took place. The march was planned to coincide with the one-hundredth anniversary of Abraham Lincoln's Emancipation Proclamation, which freed all slaves in the South during the Civil War. The event is generally recognized as the single most important demonstration of the civil rights movement in the United States.

Campaigns Across the South Unite for Common Goal

In the early 1960s, campaigns for civil rights took place all across the South. Several different organizations assisted campaigners, including the Southern Christian Leadership Conference (SCLC) led by Martin Luther King Jr., the National Association for the Advancement of Colored People (NAACP), the Congress of Racial Equality (CORE), the Student Nonviolent Coordinating Committee (SNCC), the National Urban League (NUL), and the Brotherhood of Sleeping Car Porters (BSCP). In 1963, leaders from all these organizations got together and agreed to combine forces. The result would be a demonstration in Washington, D.C., intended to persuade members of Congress to pass civil rights legislation and to provide greater economic opportunities for African Americans.

At the time of the march, President John F. Kennedy (1917–63) had already presented the civil rights bill to Congress, which would outlaw discrimination based on race or ethnic heritage. However, Congress had not yet voted on it, and many believed the bill would not pass. Civil rights leaders hoped that by orchestrating such a massive demonstration, whites across the country would take note of the injustices still occurring in the South, and pressure their representatives to support the bill. In addition to the passage of civil rights laws, organizers created a list of other demands. These included an end to segregation in all schools across the country, a higher minimum wage, and a new jobs program for unemployed workers of all races. March coordinators also demanded that the federal government withhold funding for states that failed to enforce civil rights laws. This was an ongoing problem in the South. For example, even though the Supreme Court had ruled that segregated schools were illegal in 1954, most schools in the South were still segregated almost ten years later.

Preparation for such a massive event required months of planning and organizing. Specially chartered buses and planes were arranged to help demonstrators reach the city in time. The original goal was to attract one hundred thousand people—an unheard-of number at the time, when mass demonstrations were rare. Members of Kennedy's administration feared that the turnout would overwhelm the city, and persuaded the organizers to hold the demonstration on a weekday so that many potential attendees would be forced to stay at work instead. The organizers chose Wednesday, August 28, 1963, as the day of the demonstration. They asked all participants to remain nonviolent, and discouraged civil disobedience for the event.

Demonstrators Stage the Largest Rally in Washington's History

As the date of the march approached, the federal government and local residents feared that the protestors would bring chaos and rioting to the city. March leaders arranged for one thousand off-duty African American police officers from around the country to serve as marshals for the event, and arranged for an additional one thousand specially trained activists to help maintain order. Still, over twenty thousand military and police troops were either put into action or placed on alert for the event.

In the end, these precautions were unnecessary. At least two hundred thousand—and possibly more than three hundred thousand—demonstrators participated in the March on Washington, making it the largest demonstration

Martin Luther King Jr. stands before the crowd at the 1963 March on Washington.
CNP/Getty Images

in the city's history up to that time. The crowd remained orderly, and even began the march from the Capitol to the Lincoln Memorial without the event organizers, who were delayed. Nearly three thousand members of the press from around the world covered the event. Millions of Americans were moved by televised highlights of the march. For many, the most memorable part of the event was King's speech, now commonly referred to as "I Have a Dream." He had given variations of the speech in previous years to crowds of activists around the country. Originally, the most well-known part of the speech was not meant to be included, and speakers were told to adhere to a strict seven-minute time limit. However, encouraged by the historic nature of the event, King brought the crowd to a roaring cheer with his uplifting sermon and final words: "Free at last! Free at last! Thank God Almighty, we are free at last!"

After the march, some organizers felt that it had not been successful. They believed that the press had portrayed the event as less than serious. They also felt that commentators had been more interested in the fact that so many African Americans could gather peacefully than in their actual message. However, the March on Washington succeeded in two important goals. First, it demonstrated to millions of white Americans the true character of the civil rights movement. Before then, many whites had feared the movement and its aims. Second, it inspired and strengthened the resolve of the many different groups and campaigns in the South. Activists from different cities and regions were finally able to see that they were not alone in their struggles. Many historians credit the March on Washington with directly influencing the passage of the Civil Rights Act of 1964 and the Voting Rights Act of 1965.

Primary Sources

◆ WELLS'S REMEDY FOR LYNCHING (1895)

Activist Ida B. Wells was famous for her articles about lynching in general and her scrupulous reporting on dozens of individual lynching incidents throughout the South. Lynching is the mob killing of an individual—usually an African American man—who is accused, but not yet convicted, of a crime. The number of lynchings was alarmingly high in the last decades of the nineteenth century, which is when Wells began a crusade to expose the injustice. Her brave reporting on this topic was a key factor in the decline of lynchings in the twentieth century.

Here, in an excerpt from *A Red Record. Tabulated Statistics and Alleged Causes of Lynching in the United States, 1892–1893–1894. Respectfully Submitted to the Nineteenth Century Civilization in "the Land of the Free and the Home of the Brave,"* published in 1895, Wells offers her "remedy" for the problems of lynching. She insists that she supports just punishment for all African Americans who commit crimes, but that accused criminals, black and white, must all be given due process of law. She calls upon readers of her book to take a vocal and public stand against lynching. Wells also appeals to economic self-interest: Large companies and industries are unlikely to build or invest in parts of the country where the rule of law is not respected.

• •

It is a well established principle of law that every wrong has a remedy. Herein rests our respect for law. The Negro does not claim that all of the one thousand black men, women and children, who have been hanged, shot and burned alive during the past ten years, were innocent of the charges made against them. We have associated too long with the white man not to have copied his vices as well as his virtues. But we do insist that the punishment is not the same for both classes of criminals. In lynching, opportunity is not given the Negro to defend himself against the unsupported accusations of white men and women. The word of the accuser is held to be true and the excited blood-thirsty mob demands that the rule of law be reversed and instead of proving the accused to be guilty, the victim of their hate and revenge must prove himself innocent. No evidence he can offer will satisfy the mob; he is bound hand and foot and swung into eternity. Then to excuse its infamy, the mob almost invariably reports the monstrous falsehood that its victim made a full confession before he was hanged.

With all military, legal and political power in their hands, only two of the lynching States have attempted a check by exercising the power which is theirs. Mayor Trout, of

Roanoke, Virginia, called out the militia in 1893, to protect a Negro prisoner, and in so doing nine men were killed and a number wounded. Then the mayor and militia withdrew, left the Negro to his fate and he was promptly lynched. The business men realized the blow to the town's financial interests, called the mayor home, the grand jury indicted and prosecuted the ringleaders of the mob. They were given light sentences, the highest being one of twelve months in State prison. The day he arrived at the penitentiary, he was pardoned by the governor of the State.

The only other real attempt made by the authorities to protect a prisoner of the law, and which was more successful, was that of Gov. McKinley, of Ohio, who sent the militia to Washington Courthouse, O., in October, 1894, and five men were killed and twenty wounded in maintaining the principle that the law must be upheld.

In South Carolina, in April, 1893, Gov. Tillman aided the mob by yielding up to be killed, a prisoner of the law, who had voluntarily placed himself under the Governor's protection. Public sentiment by its representatives has encouraged lynch law, and upon the revolution of this sentiment we must depend for its abolition.

Therefore, we demand a fair trial by law for those accused of crime, and punishment by law after honest conviction. No **maudlin** sympathy for criminals is solicited, but we do ask that the *law* shall punish all alike. We earnestly desire those that control the forces which make public sentiment to join with us in the demand. Surely the humanitarian spirit of this country which reaches out to denounce the treatment of the Russian Jews, the Armenian Christians, the laboring poor of Europe, the Siberian exiles and the native women of India—will no longer refuse to lift its voice on this subject. If it were known that the cannibals or the savage Indians had burned three human beings alive in the past two years, the whole of Christendom would be roused, to devise ways and means to put a stop to it. Can you remain silent and inactive when such things are done in our own community and country? Is your duty to humanity in the United States less binding?

Maudlin
Overly emotional or self-pitying

What can you do, reader, to prevent lynching, to thwart anarchy and promote law and order throughout our land?

1. You can help disseminate the facts contained in this book by bringing them to the knowledge of every one with whom you come in contact, to the end that public sentiment may be revolutionized. Let the facts speak for themselves, with you as a medium.

2. You can be instrumental in having churches, missionary societies, Y. M. C. A.s, W. C. T. U.s and all Christian and moral forces in connection with your religious and social life, pass resolutions of condemnation and protest every time a lynching takes place; and see that they are sent to the place where these outrages occur.

3. Bring to the intelligent consideration of Southern people the refusal of capital to invest where lawlessness and mob violence hold sway. Many labor organisations have declared by resolution that they would avoid lynch infested localities as they would the **pestilence** when seeking new homes. If the South wishes to build up its

Pestilence
Infectious disease

waste places quickly, there is no better way than to uphold the majesty of the law by enforcing obedience to the same, and meting out the same punishment to all classes of criminals, white as well as black. "Equality before the law," must become a fact as well as a theory before America is truly the "land of the free and the home of the brave."

4. Think and act on independent lines in this behalf, remembering that after all, it is the white man's civilization and the white man's government which are on trial. This crusade will determine whether that civilization can maintain itself by itself, or whether anarchy shall prevail; whether this Nation shall write itself down a success at self government, or in deepest humiliation admit its failure complete; whether the precepts and theories of Christianity are professed and practiced by American white people as Golden Rules of thought and action, or adopted as a system of morals to be preached to heathen until they attain to the intelligence which needs the system of Lynch Law.

The belief has been constantly expressed in England that in the United States which has produced Wm. Lloyd Garrison, Henry Ward Beecher, James Russell Lowell, John G. Whittier and Abraham Lincoln there must be those of their descendants who would take hold of the work of inaugurating an era of law and order. The colored people of this country who have been loyal to the flag believe the same, and strong in that belief have begun this crusade.

DU BOIS ON THE CONSERVATION OF RACES (1897)

W. E. B. Du Bois was one of the foremost thinkers on the subject of race relations at the dawn of the twentieth century. He believed that African Americans should be integrated with white society, in contrast to the beliefs of African American leaders like Marcus Garvey, who argued that blacks should set up societies apart from whites in order to achieve true equality. But Du Bois also saw the value in maintaining "black-only" institutions as a way to uplift the race. This philosophy was different from that of other integrationists, particularly those in the National Association for the Advancement of Colored People (NAACP) who saw such institutions as maintaining the harmful system of segregation. Du Bois explained his philosophy on race relations and, particularly on the value of African American institutions for the preservation of black cultural heritage, in the following excerpt from a 1897 paper written for the American Negro Academy.

....

Here, then, is the dilemma, and it is a puzzling one, I admit. No Negro who has given earnest thought to the situation of his people in America has failed, at some time in life, to find himself at these cross-roads; has failed to ask himself at some time: What, after all, am I? Am I an American or am I a Negro? Can I be both? Or is it my duty to cease to be a Negro as soon as possible and be an American? If I strive as a Negro, am I not **perpetuating** the very **cleft** that threatens and separates Black and White America? Is not my only possible practical aim the **subduction** of all that is Negro in me to the American? Does my black blood place upon me any more obligation to assert my nationality than German, or Irish or Italian blood would?

It is such **incessant** self-questioning and the hesitation that arises from it, that is making the present period a time of **vacillation** and **contradiction** for the American Negro; combined race action is **stifled**, race responsibility is **shirked**, race enterprises **languish**, and the best blood, the best talent, the best energy of the Negro people cannot be **marshalled** to do the bidding of the race. They stand back to make room for every rascal and **demagogue** who chooses to cloak his selfish deviltry under the veil of race pride.

Is this right? Is it rational? Is it good policy? Have we in America a distinct mission as a race—a distinct sphere of action and an opportunity for race development, or is **self-obliteration** the highest end to which Negro blood dare **aspire**?

If we carefully consider what race prejudice really is, we find it, historically, to be nothing but the friction between different groups of people; it is the difference in aim, in feeling, in ideals of two different races; if, now, this difference exists touching territory, laws, language, or even religion, it is **manifest** that these people cannot live in the same territory without fatal collision; but if, on the other hand, there is substantial agreement in laws, language and religion; if there is a satisfactory adjustment of economic life, then there is no reason why, in the same country and on the same street, two or three great national ideals might not thrive and develop, that men of different races might not strive together for their race ideals as well, perhaps even better, than in isolation. Here, it seems to me, is the reading of the riddle that puzzles so many of us. We are Americans, not only by birth and by citizenship, but by our political ideals, our language, our religion. Farther than that, our Americanism does not go. At that point, we are Negroes, members of a vast historic race that from the very dawn of creation has slept, but half awakening in the dark forests of its African fatherland. We are the first fruits of this new nation, the **harbinger** of that black to-morrow which is yet destined to soften the whiteness of the **Teutonic** to-day. We are that people whose subtle sense of song has given America its only American music, its only American fairy tales, its only touch of **pathos** and humor amid its mad money-getting **plutocracy**. As such, it is our duty to conserve our physical powers, our intellectual **endowments**, our spiritual ideals; as a race we must strive by race organization, by race **solidarity**, by race unity to the realization of that broader humanity which freely recognizes differences in men, but sternly **deprecates** inequality in their opportunities of development.

For the accomplishment of these ends we need race organizations: Negro colleges, Negro newspapers, Negro business organizations, a Negro school of literature

Manifest
Accepted as true or
obvious

Harbinger
An indication of
things to come

Teutonic
Of northern European
ethnic origin

Pathos
A quality that inspires
sympathy or pity in
others

Plutocracy
A system of
government in which
the wealthy hold all
power

Endowments
Talents or gifts

Solidarity
A state of unity and
cooperation

Deprecates
Disapproves of

Imperative
Critically necessary or
unavoidable

Iniquity
Wickedness

Implicit
Accepted without
question

Zealously
With energy and
devotion

Whoremongers
People lacking morals

and art, and an intellectual clearing house, for all these products of the Negro mind, which we may call a Negro Academy. Not only is all this necessary for positive advance, it is absolutely **imperative** for negative defense. Let us not deceive ourselves at our situation in this country. Weighted with a heritage of moral **iniquity** from our past history, hard pressed in the economic world by foreign immigrants and native prejudice, hated here, despised there and pitied everywhere; our one haven of refuge is ourselves, and but one means of advance, our own belief in our great destiny, our own **implicit** trust in our ability and worth. There is no power under God's high heaven that can stop the advance of eight thousand thousand honest, earnest, inspired and united people.

But—and here is the rub—they MUST be honest, fearlessly criticising their own faults, **zealously** correcting them; they must be EARNEST. No people that laughs at itself, and ridicules itself, and wishes to God it was anything but itself ever wrote its name in history; it MUST be inspired with the Divine faith of our black mothers, that out of the blood and dust of battle will march a victorious host, a mighty nation, a peculiar people, to speak to the nations of earth a Divine truth that shall make them free. And such a people must be united; not merely united for the organized theft of political spoils, not united to disgrace religion with **whoremongers** and ward-heelers; not united merely to protest and pass resolutions, but united to stop the ravages of consumption among the Negro people, united to keep black boys from loafing, gambling and crime; united to guard the purity of black women and to reduce the vast army of black prostitutes that is today marching to hell; and united in serious organizations, to determine by careful conference and thoughtful interchange of opinion the broad lines of policy and action for the American Negro.

◈ MARTIN LUTHER KING JR.'S NOBEL PEACE PRIZE ACCEPTANCE SPEECH (1964)

In 1964, Martin Luther King Jr. was awarded the Nobel Peace Prize for his efforts to improve African American civil rights through nonviolent means. King's commitment to nonviolence was not universally shared by the African American community. Other civil rights activists, such as Malcolm X of the Nation of Islam, believed that African Americans should respond to white violence with violent self-defense. They criticized King's approach as weak and ineffective. King, however, did not waver from his belief that it was the right way to obtain justice, and eloquently defended nonviolence in his Nobel Peace Prize acceptance speech, presented in Oslo, Norway, on December 10, 1964. An excerpt from that speech is reprinted below.

••••••••••••••••••••••••••

Martin Luther King Jr. accepts the Nobel Peace Prize in 1964. *National Archives and Records Administration (NARA)*

Your Majesty, Your Royal Highness, Mr. President, Excellencies, Ladies and Gentlemen:

I accept the Nobel Prize for Peace at a moment when 22 million Negroes of the United States of America are engaged in a creative battle to end the long night of racial injustice. I accept this award on behalf of a civil rights movement which is moving with determination and a majestic scorn for risk and danger to establish a reign of freedom and a rule of justice. I am mindful that only yesterday in Birmingham, Alabama, our children, crying out for brotherhood, were answered with fire hoses, snarling dogs and even death. I am mindful that only yesterday in Philadelphia, Mississippi, young people seeking to secure the right to vote were brutalized and murdered. And only yesterday more than 40 houses of worship in the State of Mississippi alone were bombed or burned because they offered a sanctuary to those who would not accept segregation. I am mindful that **debilitating** and grinding poverty afflicts my people and chains them to the lowest rung of the economic ladder.

Therefore, I must ask why this prize is awarded to a movement which is **beleaguered** and committed to unrelenting struggle; to a movement which has not won the very peace and brotherhood which is the essence of the Nobel Prize.

Debilitating
Containing the ability to weaken

Beleaguered
Surrounded by troubles

Contemplation
Carefully considered thought

Antithetical
Opposite in meaning or intent

Passivity
Inaction

Elegy
A song of mourning

Tortuous
Twisting or crooked

Flotsam and jetsam
Unimportant debris

Cynical
Distrustful or lacking optimism

Militaristic
Reliant upon war and military force

Thermonuclear
Relating to the fusion of atomic particles, as in certain types of atomic bombs

Mortar
A type of cannon, or the shells fired from such a cannon

Prostrate
Lying face down to show weakness or submission

Audacity
Boldness

After **contemplation**, I conclude that this award which I receive on behalf of that movement is a profound recognition that nonviolence is the answer to the crucial political and moral question of our time—the need for man to overcome oppression and violence without resorting to violence and oppression. Civilization and violence are **antithetical** concepts. Negroes of the United States, following the people of India, have demonstrated that nonviolence is not sterile **passivity**, but a powerful moral force which makes for social transformation. Sooner or later all the people of the world will have to discover a way to live together in peace, and thereby transform this pending cosmic **elegy** into a creative psalm of brotherhood. If this is to be achieved, man must evolve for all human conflict a method which rejects revenge, aggression and retaliation. The foundation of such a method is love.

The **tortuous** road which has led from Montgomery, Alabama to Oslo bears witness to this truth. This is a road over which millions of Negroes are travelling to find a new sense of dignity. This same road has opened for all Americans a new era of progress and hope. It has led to a new Civil Rights Bill, and it will, I am convinced, be widened and lengthened into a super highway of justice as Negro and white men in increasing numbers create alliances to overcome their common problems.

I accept this award today with an abiding faith in America and an audacious faith in the future of mankind. I refuse to accept despair as the final response to the ambiguities of history. I refuse to accept the idea that the "isness" of man's present nature makes him morally incapable of reaching up for the eternal "oughtness" that forever confronts him. I refuse to accept the idea that man is mere **flotsam and jetsam** in the river of life, unable to influence the unfolding events which surround him. I refuse to accept the view that mankind is so tragically bound to the starless midnight of racism and war that the bright daybreak of peace and brotherhood can never become a reality.

I refuse to accept the **cynical** notion that nation after nation must spiral down a **militaristic** stairway into the hell of **thermonuclear** destruction. I believe that unarmed truth and unconditional love will have the final word in reality. This is why right temporarily defeated is stronger than evil triumphant. I believe that even amid today's **mortar** bursts and whining bullets, there is still hope for a brighter tomorrow. I believe that wounded justice, lying **prostrate** on the blood-flowing streets of our nations, can be lifted from this dust of shame to reign supreme among the children of men. I have the **audacity** to believe that peoples everywhere can have three meals a day for their bodies, education and culture for their minds, and dignity, equality and freedom for their spirits. I believe that what self-centered men have torn down men other-centered can build up. I still believe that one day mankind will bow before the altars of God and be crowned triumphant over war and bloodshed, and nonviolent redemptive good will proclaim the rule of the land. "And the lion and the lamb shall lie down together and every man shall sit under his own vine and fig tree and none shall be afraid." I still believe that We Shall overcome!

This faith can give us courage to face the uncertainties of the future. It will give our tired feet new strength as we continue our forward stride toward the city of freedom. When our days become dreary with low-hovering clouds and our nights become darker than a thousand midnights, we will know that we are living in the creative turmoil of a genuine civilization struggling to be born.

Today I come to Oslo as a trustee, inspired and with renewed dedication to humanity. I accept this prize on behalf of all men who love peace and brotherhood. I say I come as a trustee, for in the depths of my heart I am aware that this prize is much more than an honor to me personally.

Every time I take a flight, I am always mindful of the many people who make a successful journey possible—the known pilots and the unknown ground crew.

So you honor the dedicated pilots of our struggle who have sat at the controls as the freedom movement soared into orbit. You honor, once again, Chief Lutuli of South Africa, whose struggles with and for his people are still met with the most brutal expression of man's inhumanity to man. You honor the ground crew without whose labor and sacrifices the jet flights to freedom could never have left the earth. Most of these people will never make the headline and their names will not appear in Who's Who. Yet when years have rolled past and when the blazing light of truth is focused on this marvelous age in which we live—men and women will know and children will be taught that we have a finer land, a better people, a more noble civilization—because these humble children of God were willing to suffer for righteousness' sake.

I think Alfred Nobel would know what I mean when I say that I accept this award in the spirit of a curator of some precious heirloom which he holds in trust for its true owners—all those to whom beauty is truth and truth beauty—and in whose eyes the beauty of genuine brotherhood and peace is more precious than diamonds or silver or gold.

Research and Activity Ideas
....

1. Ida B. Wells is best known for her detailed chronicles of lynchings that occurred in the early 1890s. Read her book *Red Record,* and make a list of the different offenses African Americans allegedly committed that resulted in lynching. Is there any pattern or consistency to the crimes that led to lynching? Do you think lynch mobs were mainly concerned with enforcing justice, or do you think they had other goals? Can you find any cases where members of a lynch mob were actually punished for their murderous actions?

2. The Freedom Riders planned to travel across the South to test federal rulings about segregation on interstate bus travel. Create a map that shows the route traveled by the Freedom Riders along with the dates when they reached each city along the way. Be sure to note the struggles the riders faced at each stop. Include pictures or news articles to help bring the events to life for modern audiences.

3. Thurgood Marshall was highly successful in arguing before the Supreme Court on civil rights issues. His most famous success was *Brown v. Board of Education,* which effectively ended legal school segregation. Create your own classroom version of the Supreme Court, with two students serving as lawyers for opposing viewpoints and at least three as Supreme Court justices. Debate this issue: are segregated schools inherently unequal even if students at both schools are given the exact same buildings, textbooks, supplies, etc.? Be sure to present examples and arguments to support your view. After the two sides are presented, allow the members of the "court" to vote on their ruling.

4. The idea of separatism, or keeping blacks and whites completely separated into two distinct societies, had supporters on both sides of the civil rights movement. Many white supremacists felt that blacks would degrade white society, and some favored sending them back to Africa. At the same time, black nationalists like Malcolm X felt that African Americans would never achieve equality as long as they shared a society with whites. In other words, these two groups largely supported the same goal but for totally different reasons. Write a short paper comparing the arguments used by these two groups. Then offer your own opinion on whether or not separatism would have been a good choice for blacks during the struggle for civil rights.

5. King was renowned for his reliance upon nonviolence and civil disobedience during the struggle for civil rights. He modeled his

behavior after Mohandas Gandhi, who used similar techniques to secure India's independence from Great Britain. Write a report comparing the lives of these two men. How were their experiences and accomplishments similar? How were they different?

 For More Information

BOOKS

Fradin, Dennis Brindell, and Judith Bloom Fradin. *The Power of One: Daisy Bates and the Little Rock Nine*. New York: Clarion Books, 2004.

King, Martin Luther, Jr., and Clayborne Carson. *The Autobiography of Martin Luther King*. New York: Warner Books, 1998.

Klarman, Michael J. *From Jim Crow to Civil Rights: The Supreme Court and the Struggle for Racial Equality*. New York: Oxford University Press, 2004.

Levine, Ellen S. *Freedom's Children: Young Civil Rights Activists Tell Their Own Stories*. New York: Puffin Books, 2000.

Morris, Aldon D. *The Origins of the Civil Rights Movement*. New York: The Free Press, 1984.

Vollers, Maryanne. *Ghosts of Mississippi*. New York: Back Bay Books, 1995.

Wells-Barnett, Ida B. *On Lynchings*. Amherst, NY: Humanity Books, 2002.

Williams, Juan. *Eyes on the Prize: America's Civil Rights Years, 1954–1965*. New York: Penguin Books, 1987.

WEB SITES

Civil Rights Movement Veterans. *We'll Never Turn Back: History and Timeline of the Southern Freedom Movement*. http://www.crmvet.org/tim/timhome.htm (accessed on December 5, 2009).

The NAACP. "History." http://www.naacp.org/about/history/index.htm (accessed on December 5, 2009).

chapter two *The Arts*

1842 White performer Edwin P. Christy debuts his hugely successful minstrel show, in which the white cast wears black makeup and performs stereotypical portrayals of Southern slaves.

1852 Stage adaptations of Harriet Beecher Stowe's antislavery novel *Uncle Tom's Cabin* appear throughout the Northern states.

1871 A group of students from Fisk University become the Fisk Jubilee Singers and tour the country performing both popular songs and traditional African American spirituals.

1893 Poet Paul Laurence Dunbar publishes his first collection of poetry, *Oak and Ivy.*

1893 Artist Henry Ossawa Tanner completes his famous painting of African American life, *The Banjo Lesson.*

1899 September 18 Scott Joplin publishes his first successful ragtime composition, "Maple Leaf Rag," which becomes the first instrumental sheet music to sell over one million copies.

1900 February 12 The song "Lift Ev'ry Voice and Sing," written by James Weldon Johnson and his brother John Rosamond Johnson, is first performed in Florida at a celebration in honor of Abraham Lincoln's birthday. The song is later recognized as the official song of the NAACP and the "Negro national anthem."

1901 Leading intellectual and educator Booker T. Washington publishes his popular autobiography, *Up From Slavery.*

1902 Bert Williams and George Walker's *In Dahomey* becomes the first black musical performed on Broadway.

1903 Author and activist W. E. B. Du Bois publishes *The Souls of Black Folk,* his landmark collection of essays about race relations in the United States.

1911 Scott Joplin publishes *Treemonisha,* the first grand opera written by an African American. The music for the opera is later lost for over fifty years.

1912 September "The Memphis Blues," a song by W. C. Handy, is published, marking the first commercial recognition of blues music.

1913 The African American historical stage pageant *The Star of Ethiopia,* written by W. E. B. Du Bois, premieres.

1916 Photographer James Van Der Zee opens his first photography studio in Harlem, New York City.

1925 *The New Negro,* an anthology of African American writing edited by Alain Leroy Locke, appears and is recognized as the defining work of the Harlem Renaissance.

1925 Author Zora Neale Hurston becomes the first African American admitted to Barnard College in New York City.

1925 Dancer and singer Josephine Baker arrives in Paris and quickly becomes the most popular American performer in Europe.

1926 Poet Langston Hughes publishes his first poetry collection, *The Weary Blues.*

1927 Duke Ellington becomes the leader of the house band at the Cotton Club, a renowned establishment that broadcasts a popular live radio show.

1928 Actor and singer Paul Robeson stars as Joe in the London production of the musical *Show Boat.*

1931 William Grant Still's *Afro-American Symphony* becomes the first symphonic work written by an African American to be performed by a major symphony orchestra.

1933 Blues singer Billie Holiday makes her first recordings for Columbia Records.

1935 October 10 The George Gershwin musical *Porgy and Bess,* featuring a primarily black cast, premieres on Broadway.

1936 November 23 Delta blues musician Robert Johnson begins the first of

only two recording sessions during his lifetime, resulting in some of the most influential blues songs ever recorded.

1940 Charles Alston and other artists complete murals for the Harlem Hospital Center, despite early objections from hospital administrators that the works are "overly Negro."

1940 March 1 Richard Wright's novel *Native Son* is published as an official selection of the Book of the Month Club.

1943 Artist Charles White completes the mural *The Contribution of the Negro to Democracy in America* at Hampton Institute.

1950 Gwendolyn Brooks wins the Pulitzer Prize for her poetry collection *Annie Allen* (1949).

1950 Actor and activist Paul Robeson is barred from leaving the United States for eight years due to suspected un-American activities.

1952 Dancer Janet Collins makes her debut as the first African American prima ballerina at the Metropolitan Opera House in New York.

1953 Author Ralph Ellison wins the National Book Award for his novel *Invisible Man* (1952).

1958 Dancer Alvin Ailey forms the Alvin Ailey American Dance Theater in New York City, one of the most influential modern dance companies in the country.

1959 **March 11** The play *A Raisin in the Sun* by Lorraine Hansberry premieres, becoming the first Broadway play written by an African American woman.

1960 **April 14** Berry Gordy Jr. founds the recording label Motown Records in Detroit, Michigan.

1961 **January 27** Leontyne Price becomes the female lead singer for the Metropolitan Opera in New York, and is the first African American opera star to earn as much money as her white peers.

Overview

African American participation in the arts was all but nonexistent prior to the Civil War (1861–65). The abolition of slavery and gradual integration as full citizens in American society changed that over the next century. By 1965, nearly every field of artistic endeavor had been shaped by African American influences. The artistic traditions of African Americans were often substantially different from those of Americans of European descent. Works by African Americans therefore breathed new life and innovation into existing fields. Indeed, much of what modern Americans consider to be their unique artistic identity—from music to dance to literature—exists because of African American contributions during this period.

African American contributions to the arts were slow to come at first. Millions of blacks were still coming to terms with their newfound freedom. Many whites, especially in the South, were not yet ready to accept African Americans as creators of art, which they viewed as a mark of "civilized" people. Still, white audiences lined up to attend minstrel shows, in which white performers would wear black makeup and offer stereotypical portrayals of Southern blacks. These portrayals were not entirely negative; many characters in a typical minstrel show were sympathetic figures, and the dances and songs were heavily inspired by actual African American creations. Still, it was not until 1871 that an African American performing group would successfully offer their own versions of traditional African American songs. The group was the Fisk Jubilee Singers, created in an effort to secure funding for the all-black Fisk University. They were so successful that after completing a tour of the United States—which included a performance for President Ulysses S. Grant (1822–85)—they went on two tours of Europe and Asia.

The music of traditional African American slave songs was fundamentally different from music from Europe. It utilized different musical scales and rhythms more commonly found in Africa. These unique qualities found their way into mainstream music first by way of ragtime. Ragtime music was a piano-based variation on popular American march music, and its lively rhythms and unexpected melodies became a hit in dance halls across the country. One of the greatest innovators of ragtime music was Scott Joplin (1867–1917), whose "Maple Leaf Rag" (1899) was the first instrumental sheet music to sell over one million copies.

The first significant works of art and literature by African Americans— other than slave narratives—appeared in the 1890s and early 1900s. Poet Paul Laurence Dunbar (1872–1906) was an immediate success, and wrote in both a formal style and one that reflected black dialect at the time.

Charles W. Chesnutt (1858–1932) wrote novels in which characters wrestled with their mixed-race heritage, much like the author himself. Booker T. Washington (1856–1915), already famous as an educator and leading African American spokesman, released his popular autobiography *Up from Slavery* in 1901. W. E. B. Du Bois (1868–1963) published his influential collection of essays about race relations, *The Souls of Black Folk,* in 1903. In the realm of visual arts, painter Henry Ossawa Tanner (1859–1937) became the most popular American artist in Paris at this time.

The first black Broadway musical, with lyrics written by Dunbar, also debuted in 1903. By this time, a significant number of African Americans were achieving financial security through improving career opportunities, especially in the northern United States. This development enabled black consumers to afford to attend Broadway shows and nightclubs. The music found in these nightclubs was generally jazz or blues, both of which developed in the South from earlier African American music. It was in New York, however, that jazz music was refined and popularized in the 1920s by musicians like Louis Armstrong (1901–71) and Duke Ellington (1899–1974). This was the time of the Harlem Renaissance, a flowering of the arts that was largely based in the Harlem area of New York City. In addition to jazz music, the Harlem Renaissance saw significant works from poets like Langston Hughes (1902–67) and Countee Cullen (1903–46), as well as advances in the fields of drama and photography. Outside of Harlem, Josephine Baker (1906–75) left New York for Paris, and became the most successful American performer in France.

The Great Depression, with its massive unemployment, brought an end to the Harlem Renaissance, but not to African American artistic endeavors. Government-funded programs like the Federal Art Project (FAP) allowed African American artists to make major contributions through murals, stage dramas, and other media. Paul Robeson (1898–1976) earned a place as one of the most popular dramatic actors of American and European theater. William Grant Still (1895–1978) wrote the *Afro-American Symphony* (1931), the first symphonic piece by a black American to be performed by a major symphony orchestra. In literature, Zora Neale Hurston (1891–1960) scored success with both an original novel and a collection of African-influenced folktales.

Beginning in the 1940s, African American writers enjoyed broader recognition from mainstream readers and from critics. Richard Wright's novel *Native Son* (1940), considered controversial by both blacks and whites for its depiction of a black man who accidentally kills a wealthy young white woman, nonetheless became a best-seller. In 1950, poet Gwendolyn Brooks (1917–2000) became the first African American to win a Pulitzer Prize for her collection *Annie Allen* (1949). Ralph Ellison's *Invisible Man* (1952) won the National Book Award, and earned praise not just as a glimpse of African American struggles but as a work of literary art. In 1959, Lorraine Hansberry's *A Raisin in the Sun* became the first Broadway production written by an African American woman. In the classical realm, Janet Collins (1917–2003) became the first prima ballerina for the Metropolitan Opera in 1952, and Leontyne Price (1927–) served as the lead female singer in over a dozen operas for the Met beginning in 1961.

By the 1960s, nearly every form of popular music showed the influence of jazz or blues. This influence expanded with the creation of Motown Records in 1960, which released over one hundred top-ten pop songs by African American performers over the next decade. The unique sound associated with Motown became recognized around the world. While many African American artists and performers focused on the struggle for civil rights throughout the 1960s, their efforts continued to form a growing part of the unique artistic identity of the United States.

Headline Makers

★ LOUIS ARMSTRONG
(1901–1971)

Louis Armstrong was a singer and musician best known for his association with jazz music. His distinctive singing voice and trumpet playing were important in the spread of jazz into the mainstream music scene during the 1920s and 1930s. Armstrong enjoyed a reputation as the best-known jazz musician of his time, gaining fame from his numerous television and film appearances.

Armstrong was born in New Orleans, Louisiana, in 1901, though he often stated later in life that he was born on July 4, 1900. He was raised by his mother and grandmother after his father, a factory worker, left the family while Armstrong was still an infant. His family was very poor, and as a child Armstrong worked various odd jobs to help support the family. Armstrong was surrounded by music while working and playing in the streets of New Orleans. Since he could not afford an instrument, he learned to sing, and joined a vocal quartet that performed on street corners for spare change.

Armstrong's musical career took an unusual turn after he was apprehended by a police officer for firing his stepfather's gun into the air on New Year's Eve. The incident landed the young boy in a juvenile detention center for boys. While there, Armstrong met Peter Davis, the music instructor at the center. He became a member of a brass band there, and learned to play the cornet, which is an instrument very similar to the trumpet. Armstrong's musical talent led to his becoming the band's leader, and he led the group in parade performances around the city.

When he was released from the detention center, Armstrong continued playing cornet in clubs around his neighborhood. He met and learned from master musicians like Joe "King" Oliver (1885–1938) and Bunk Johnson (1879–1949). While still in his teens, he became a well-known and successful horn player, mastering the trumpet in addition to the cornet. Despite his success, he still worked a day job at a coal yard to help support his family. In 1918, he married a young woman named Daisy Parker, and soon after he took a job playing music on a traveling riverboat. The marriage did not last.

In 1922, Armstrong's mentor Joe "King" Oliver invited him to move to Chicago and join a jazz band. He accepted, and began a relationship with a pianist named Lil Hardin (1898–1971). The two married in 1924. Hardin felt that Armstrong's talents were too great to be wasted playing in

Oliver's band, and she encouraged him to find a way to better showcase his own unique style. He took a position in the Fletcher Henderson Orchestra, one of the most prestigious jazz bands in New York City. However, he soon returned to Chicago and began to make recordings as the leader of his own band. In addition to his impressive, improvised horn solos, Armstrong also began to sing on some tracks. His recordings sold very well, and he became known across the country. One of these recordings was "West End Blues" (1928), which features a famous trumpet solo by Armstrong.

In 1929, Armstrong returned to New York City and became the leader of his own orchestra. He was equally successful as a musician and as a singer. By the early 1930s he began appearing in films as well. Successful recordings from this time period include "Stardust" (1931) and "Lazy River" (1931). Many of the works Armstrong recorded were originally written by others, but he reshaped them with his own unique style and personality. His versions of popular works usually sold better than other versions. One of his signature techniques was the use of "scat," or using his voice as an instrument instead of singing actual words.

In 1936, Armstrong appeared in the Bing Crosby musical *Pennies from Heaven*. Like Crosby, Armstrong was quickly being recognized not just as a musician or singer but as a celebrity. He appeared on national radio shows, and in 1938 divorced Hardin to marry another woman. Though he continued to make recordings, the bulk of his time was spent touring the country and performing live. In 1943, he divorced, and then married for the fourth time.

Big bands were no longer enjoying the popularity they once did as the 1940s progressed. This trend led Armstrong to break up his orchestra in 1947 and form a smaller jazz band featuring many of the most talented performers of the day. The group, known as Louis Armstrong and the All-Stars, would continue with various other members throughout the rest of his life.

Armstrong typically did not involve himself in the civil rights movement, but he did famously criticize President Dwight Eisenhower (1890–1969) in 1957. At the time, schools in Little Rock, Arkansas, had been required to end segregation, or the separation of black and white students into separate schools. Nine African American students were registered to attend Little Rock Central High School, a formerly all-white school. The governor of the state blocked the students from entering, using National Guard troops to keep them out. Armstrong spoke harshly of Eisenhower's failure to help the students. His comments were notable because of his fame and because of his usual reluctance to make such comments. Within three weeks, Eisenhower sent federal troops to protect the students and ensure the integration of the school.

Armstrong recorded famous versions of many popular songs, including "Mack the Knife" (1955) and "Hello, Dolly!" (1964). This last song reached number one on the *Billboard* pop charts, an amazing feat for a man over sixty years old. The song also earned two Grammy Awards. Armstrong is perhaps best remembered for his rendition of "What a Wonderful World" (1968), which has appeared in films as diverse as *Good Morning, Vietnam* (1987) and *Twelve Monkeys* (1995). Armstrong remained an active musician and singer up until his death from a heart attack in Queens, New York, in 1971.

★ JOSEPHINE BAKER (1906–1975)

Josephine Baker was a singer, dancer, and actress who achieved greater fame in her adopted home of France than in the United States, her native land. During World War II (1939–45), she participated in the French Resistance, earning herself the Croix de Guerre (Cross of War), France's highest military honor. Baker did not often return to the United States because of the unequal treatment of African Americans there. However, she made a notable appearance at the 1963 March on Washington for Jobs and Freedom in Washington, D.C., a landmark demonstration in the struggle for civil rights.

Baker was born Freda Josephine McDonald in St. Louis, Missouri, to a woman named Carrie McDonald who had previously worked as a stage performer. After giving birth, Carrie became a laundry worker. Josephine's father is officially listed as Eddie Carson, another African American stage performer. However, Josephine and some members of her family expressed doubts about this paternity, believing that her father was actually a white man who was Carrie's previous employer. As a child, Josephine worked as a maid for a white family, where she was often mistreated and even physically abused. She also attended school, but was not an academic success.

Josephine got a job as a waitress at a local club at the age of thirteen. Fascinated by the stage performers, she convinced a local troupe to let her join. She performed both on stage and in the street for money. Her first success was as a comic performer, though her dancing skills were not limited to silly routines. She earned a position in a touring group called the Jones Family Band, ending up in Philadelphia. There, she met and married Willie Baker. Though she was only fifteen, this was already her

Josephine Baker.
Gilles Petard/Redferns

second marriage. The marriage lasted only three years. She continued working as a cabaret dancer and singer at a local club, but soon became a dancer in a successful New York show called *Shuffle Along* (1921). Providing both comic relief and exceptional dancing talent, she was an immediate hit. She went on to star in the Broadway show *Chocolate Dandies* (1924) and a revue called *Blackbirds* (1925).

In 1925 she took a position in a new show opening in Paris, earning $250 per week—double her salary with her previous show. Soon she was receiving star billing at the Folies Bergère, one of the most famous music halls in Paris. She also devoted much of her time and effort to charitable work for the Parisian poor, never forgetting her own childhood spent in poverty.

By 1930, Baker had become fluent in French, and achieved some success as a singer. Her most popular song was "J'ai Deux Amours" ("I Have Two Loves," 1931), which reflected her conflicted feelings about the United States and its treatment of African Americans. The two "loves" of the song are Paris and "my country," referring to her native United States. The equality she enjoyed in Europe made Baker realize that the unequal treatment of African Americans in the United States was not inevitable, nor was it acceptable to her. She returned to the States in 1936 to star in a production of the *Ziegfeld Follies*. While there, she encountered racism and segregation far worse than she remembered when she had left a decade before. She also received brutal reviews for her performance. A reviewer for *Time* magazine called her "a Negro wench" and "just a slightly buck-toothed young Negro woman whose figure might be matched in any night-club show, and whose dancing and singing might be topped almost anywhere outside of Paris." After returning to Paris in 1937, she married a French businessman named Jean Lion and officially became a French citizen.

By 1939, Europe was on the verge of war. German troops led by Adolf Hitler (1889–1945) invaded Poland. The following year, the German army took over much of France. During this time, Baker participated in the French Underground, a resistance movement to support Allied forces and drive the Nazis from France. She risked her life by transporting secret information between agents and spies. Her heroism led to her being honored with three different medals: the Croix de Guerre, Légion d'honneur (the Legion of Honor), and the Medal of the Resistance.

In 1947, Baker married yet again. She was unable to have children of her own, so in 1954 she began adopting unwanted children from various places around the world that she visited. By 1964, she had acquired twelve children of various ethnic backgrounds. She referred to them as her "Rainbow Tribe."

Baker did not participate directly in most of the civil rights struggles taking place in the United States in the 1950s and 1960s. However, during a tour of the United States in the early 1950s, she demanded that all audiences for her performances be integrated, with both black and white attendees. This was virtually unheard-of at the time. In 1963, Baker was also the only woman asked to speak at the March on Washington for Jobs and Freedom in Washington, D.C. This event, at which Martin Luther King Jr. (1929–68) delivered his famous "I Have a Dream" speech, is considered by some to be the most important civil rights demonstration of the era.

Baker lived out the last years of her life in France, launching a highly successful retrospective show in 1975. She died of a cerebral hemorrhage just days after the premiere of her new show, on April 12, 1975.

★ JAMES BALDWIN
(1924–1987)

James Baldwin was a novelist and activist who drew from his own life experiences to create works about African American life in the United States. Prejudice and unequal treatment for blacks in the United States pushed him to develop his writing skills in Europe. When he returned, Baldwin focused on using his talents to portray and support the struggle for civil rights in the United States.

Baldwin was born in Harlem, New York, the first of nine children in the family formed by his mother and his adoptive father, who was a Pentecostal preacher. Baldwin himself was ordained as a preacher at the age of fourteen, though his true interest always lay in books. One early influence was the poet Countee Cullen (1903–46), who was also a teacher at Baldwin's junior high school. In 1944, he met Richard Wright (1908–60), author of *Native Son* (1940) and one of the most acclaimed African American writers of the era. Wright became a friend and mentor to Baldwin, and helped him secure the Rosenwald Fellowship in 1948. The money from this fellowship allowed Baldwin to travel to Europe, where he would live for over nine years.

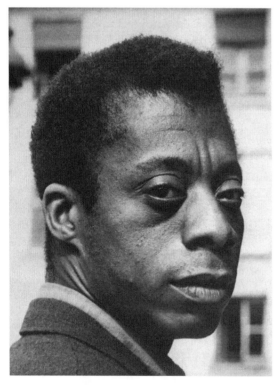

James Baldwin.
© *Bettmann/Corbis*

Baldwin began to establish a name for himself as an essayist, publishing work in *Partisan Review, Commentary,* and *The Nation.* One of his essays, "Everybody's Protest Novel" (1948), criticized Wright's *Native Son,* asserting that the work failed as art because its characters were not believable. This essay damaged Baldwin's friendship with Wright. While in Switzerland, Baldwin wrote his first novel, *Go Tell It on the Mountain* (1953). The book is largely autobiographical, telling the tale of an African American boy growing up in Harlem under the strict rule of his stepfather, who is a preacher. Baldwin used the details from his life to describe the role religion plays in the lives of African Americans.

The novel was followed by a collection of essays, *Notes of a Native Son* (1955), which focused on issues of race in the United States and Europe. Baldwin's second novel, *Giovanni's Room* (1956), again drew upon details of his own life. The book tells the story of a young American living in France who discovers love with an Italian man, even though he cannot come to terms with the fact that he is gay. Though this seems to reflect the author's complicated feelings about his own sexuality, the main character in the book is not African American, and Baldwin received some criticism for not focusing on the African American experience.

Baldwin returned to the United States in 1957, and resumed writing stories and essays that reflected black life in the country, particularly life in Harlem. The neighborhood had grown increasingly slum-like over the years, and Baldwin felt that this was a clear sign of race relations throughout the country. After meeting civil rights leaders such as Martin Luther King Jr., Baldwin decided to use his writing as a way to help the struggle for civil rights. He wrote the collection *The Fire Next Time* (1963), consisting of two extended essays on race relations in the United States. His short story collection *Going to Meet the Man* (1965) also dealt mainly with race, and included one of his most well-known stories, "Sonny's Blues" (1957).

Baldwin actively participated in civil rights demonstrations and attended the March on Washington for Jobs and Freedom in 1963. He became friends with several important figures in the civil rights movement, including Medgar Evers (1925–63) and Malcolm X (1925–65). Both of these men were shot and killed for their civil rights activism, and in 1968 King was also killed. Baldwin later wrote about these experiences in the nonfiction work *No Name in the Street* (1972). He decided to return to France, where he continued writing about different aspects of the African American experience. Although he died in France in 1987 due to stomach cancer, his body was brought back to the United States, and he was buried in Harlem.

★ GWENDOLYN BROOKS
(1917–2000)

Gwendolyn Brooks was the first female African American poet to earn recognition equal to that of male writers like Langston Hughes (1902–67) and James Weldon Johnson (1871–1938). She was also the first African American to win a Pulitzer Prize, for her poetry collection *Annie Allen* (1949). In many of her works, she captured African American life in Chicago in much the same way earlier black writers had captured the African American experience in Harlem.

Gwendolyn Brooks.
© *Bettmann/Corbis*

Brooks's family was from Chicago, Illinois, but she was born in Topeka, Kansas, while her mother Keziah was visiting relatives. Keziah was a former schoolteacher, and provided early encouragement for her daughter's educational pursuits. Her father, David Anderson Brooks, worked manual labor jobs to support his family, but kept many books in the home and often read classics aloud to his children. Gwendolyn received her first library card at the age of six, and at seven years of age she wrote her first poem. By the time she was thirteen, her first published poem had appeared in *American Childhood* magazine.

Brooks attended Wilson Junior College, completing her studies after two years in 1936. Unable to find permanent work as a writer, she briefly became a maid, and then took a position as a typist for a "spiritual advisor" who sold charms and healing medicines. She next worked for the National Association for the Advancement of Colored People (NAACP) Youth Council, where she became the group's publicity director. There she met Henry Blakely, whom she married in 1939. She became a homemaker, but never stopped writing poetry about her experiences and observations of the world around her.

In 1941, Brooks signed up for a poetry class at the local community center. The class was run by Inez Stark, who worked as an editor for *Poetry* magazine. After the class, Brooks dedicated herself to perfecting her poetic talents. In 1943, she was awarded the top prize in a contest sponsored by the

Midwestern Writers Conference. Through this organization, she met an editor at Knopf, a publishing house, who was interested in publishing a collection of her works. However, when the editor told Brooks that she only wanted to publish Brooks's poems about African American themes—which made up only a small part of her poetry—Brooks took offense and rejected the offer.

She eventually came to realize the importance of her African American–themed works, and began to create more of them. Another publisher accepted her new collection, and it was published as *A Street in Bronzeville* in 1945. The collection earned rave reviews. In 1946 Brooks was granted a Guggenheim Fellowship, which eased her family's financial burdens as she continued to work on her poetry. Her second book was *Annie Allen* (1949), a collection focused on a young African American girl coming of age. It uses complex poetic structures modeled after Italian sonnets, and features an extended piece inspired by epic poetry, an ancient form of oral storytelling devoted to the deeds of heroes and gods. Brooks received the Pulitzer Prize for Poetry for this work in 1950. She was the first African American writer, male or female, to win a Pulitzer Prize in any category.

Her next work was her only novel, *Maud Martha* (1953), which received positive reviews. Like *Annie Allen, Maud Martha* is a woman's coming-of-age tale. Instead of telling the story through poems, it is told through vignettes, or scenes taken from different points throughout the woman's life. Brooks returned to poetry with a collection for children titled *Bronzeville Boys and Girls* in 1956, and another collection about African American life in Chicago titled *The Bean Eaters* in 1960. *The Bean Eaters* contains one of Brooks's most famous poems, "We Real Cool" (1960). The short poem sums up the reckless, dead-end life of a group of young African American men at a local pool hall.

Brooks continued to write about Chicago in her collection *In the Mecca* (1968), and wrote about famous African American cultural figures in *Malcolm X* (1968) and *Black Steel: Joe Frazier and Muhammad Ali* (1971). Beginning in the 1960s, Brooks taught creative writing at several colleges in Chicago and New York. She continued to write poetry throughout her later life, and served as poet laureate of Illinois as well as poetry consultant to the Library of Congress. She died in 2000 at the age of eighty-three.

★ JANET COLLINS
(1917–2003)

Janet Collins was a ballet dancer who became the first African American prima ballerina for the Metropolitan Opera in New York in 1951. She was also an innovator in modern dance, combining classical music, her Creole heritage, and Negro spirituals. Despite her enormous talent, she had to overcome racial prejudice to earn her place in the spotlight.

Collins was born in New Orleans, Louisiana, to a tailor and a seamstress. The family relocated to Los Angeles, California, in 1921, when Collins was four years old. She began to study dance at a young age. Since her family could not afford to pay for lessons, her mother sewed outfits and costumes for the dance troupe in exchange for her daughter's participation. She proved to be a success at ballet. At the age of fifteen, she auditioned for the highly prestigious Ballet Russe de Monte Carlo (Russian Ballet of Monte Carlo). The director, Léonide Massine (1895–1979), was impressed by Collins's talent. He asked her to join the company, but only if she would be willing to wear white makeup to cover her dark complexion. She declined.

Collins pursued a career as an artist, attending college as an art major, but continued to study dance. She found success with modern dance in companies led by Katherine Dunham (1909–2006) and Lester Horton (1906–53). She and her partner Talley Beatty (1923–95) were featured in a short film called *Flamingo* (1942) with Duke Ellington (1899–1974) and Herb Jeffries (1913–), both jazz legends. She was one of the dancers featured in the film *Stormy Weather* (1943), and also appeared in *The Thrill of Brazil* (1946). In 1945, she received a fellowship from the Rosenwald Fund that allowed her to attend the San Francisco School of Ballet. In 1948, she choreographed her own show for a Los Angeles theater that was inspired by Negro spirituals and her own New Orleans heritage. It was well received, but she still had to rely on her talents as a painter to earn money.

Janet Collins.
*Sam Falk/New York Times
Co./Getty Images*

In 1949, Collins relocated to New York. She had very little money and virtually no reputation in the East Coast dance community. She was also thirty-two years old—an age at which many dancers are beginning to consider retirement. However, Collins started from the ground up, auditioning for local concerts. She also obtained a position teaching modern dance at the School of American Ballet. Her immediate success led to a role in a Broadway musical called

Out of this World (1950). She earned rave reviews as the character of Night in a production that was otherwise regarded as mediocre. Collins won a Donaldson Award for her work, and attracted the attention of Zachary Solov (1923–2004), the ballet master of the Metropolitan Opera in New York. Solov wanted to hire her, but no African American had ever been employed as a full-time member of the Met's dance company. Solov asked the organization's general manager, who approved. She joined the company in 1951. Collins made her debut at the Metropolitan Opera in its production of *Aida* (1952).

Over the next two years, Collins performed in the Metropolitan Opera's productions of *Carmen* (1952), *La Gioconda* (1952), and *Samson and Delilah* (1953). When the dance company toured the country, Collins encountered segregation and racism that were in stark contrast to her experiences in New York. In the South, Collins was not allowed to perform because she was black. Instead, her understudy took her place.

She decided to leave the Metropolitan Opera in 1954. She performed a series of solo concerts across the country, and then began teaching dance at two Catholic colleges in New York. She also returned to choreography, creating a religious dance piece called *Genesis* (1965) that featured original music by Brazilian composer Heitor Villa-Lobos (1887–1959). She also choreographed the opera *Nobucco* (1970) for the San Francisco Opera. Her *Canticle of the Elements* (1974) was performed in New York by the Alvin Ailey Dance Company. After 1974, Collins focused her attention on painting. She died in Fort Worth, Texas, at the age of eighty-six.

Langston Hughes.
MPI/Getty Images

★ LANGSTON HUGHES (1902–1967)

Langston Hughes is a writer and poet closely identified with the Harlem Renaissance, a flowering of the arts among African Americans in the 1920s. Although best known as a poet, Hughes wrote short stories, novels, plays, essays, and children's books as well. His poetry is notable for its use of rhythm and musical techniques borrowed from jazz, as well as its often stark depiction of the African American condition.

Hughes was born in Joplin, Missouri, to James Nathaniel Hughes and Carrie Langston. His parents separated while he was still an infant, and he spent much of his childhood being raised by his grandmother in Lawrence, Kansas. He entered his first library at the age of five, and was immediately captivated by the world of books. In 1910, his grandmother died, and he spent several years in the care of family friends. In 1914, he rejoined his mother and her new family in Lincoln, Illinois. Together, they moved to Cleveland, Ohio, the following year.

Hughes became an academic and athletic success while attending high school in Cleveland. He began to focus his attention on poetry, particularly the works of Carl Sandburg (1878–1967) and African American poet Paul Laurence Dunbar (1872–1906). Both of these authors shared Hughes's Midwestern upbringing. After graduating from high school, Hughes went by train to visit his father, who had moved to Mexico. Hughes's crossing of the Mississippi River on that trip inspired him to write a poem titled "The Negro Speaks of Rivers" (1921). Its publication in the magazine *The Crisis,* edited by civil rights activist W. E. B. Du Bois (1868–1963), announced the arrival of a major new voice in African American literature.

Hughes returned to the United States and attended Columbia University in New York City. His father had agreed to pay his tuition, but only if Hughes agreed to study engineering. Hughes accepted, and spent a year following this plan. The cultural life of New York distracted him, however, and his increasing success as a poet led him to drop out of Columbia. He spent much of his time in Harlem, writing poems that captured the commonplace scenes of the neighborhood. In 1923, Hughes began traveling as a crew member on a merchant ship. He visited Africa and Europe, and decided to remain in Paris, France, in 1924.

Hughes worked as a busboy in Paris and continued to write poetry. He returned to the United States at the end of 1924, as poor as when he had left. His financial fortunes took a turn for the better when one of his poems—"The Weary Blues" (1925), published in the magazine *Opportunity*—earned him first prize in the magazine's poetry contest. Supported by writer and patron Carl Van Vechten (1880–1964), Hughes gathered some poems for a collection. The collection was published in 1926 as *The Weary Blues,* and it earned mostly positive reviews. Many of the poems in this collection reflect the rhythms and techniques of jazz music, a distinctly African American musical form growing in popularity at the time. In particular, Hughes uses unusual line lengths and words as musical sound effects to illustrate the spontaneous nature of jazz. Many of Hughes's poems focus on jazz clubs, musicians, dancers, and audiences to portray night life in Harlem.

That same year, Hughes enrolled at Lincoln University in Pennsylvania. He also wrote an essay for *The Nation* titled "The Negro Artist and the Racial Mountain" (1926), in which he defended his use of "lowly" subject matter and his pride in his African heritage. His second poetry collection, *Fine Clothes to the Jew* (1927), was received much like his first. He also made the acquaintance of a wealthy elderly woman named Charlotte Mason (1854–1946), who offered to support Hughes financially so he would have time to complete his first novel. The result, *Not Without Laughter* (1929), was published soon after he graduated from Lincoln. The book depicts the struggles of an African American family in Kansas, where Hughes himself grew up. It won the Harmon gold medal for literature in 1930.

In the early 1930s, Hughes received a grant from the Rosenwald Fund that allowed him to tour the South, reading poetry at various African American colleges. He spent time in the Soviet Union and Asia after the tour, and then returned to the United States to finish his first short story collection, *The Ways of White Folk* (1934). Upon hearing of his father's death in 1934, Hughes traveled to Mexico, where he learned that he was not even mentioned in his father's will.

In 1935, Hughes wrote the poem "Let America Be America Again." In it, he points out that the American dream of freedom, equality, and justice has never existed for its black citizens. Yet he looks forward to the day in which the United States can truly fulfill the promise of its ideals. This poem shows his interest not only in race relations but also in the gap between social classes. Hughes used the poem to speak for blacks, Native Americans, immigrants, and the poor. Throughout the 1930s, he grew more politically active, supporting the political ideas of socialism (in which the wealthiest members of a society help to support the poorest members) and communism (in which labor and wealth are distributed equally among all citizens).

Hughes also had a growing interest in the theater. He wrote several plays, and founded the Harlem Suitcase Theater in 1938. He also founded the New Negro Theatre in Los Angeles in 1939, and the Skyloft Players of Chicago in 1941. In 1942, he became a newspaper columnist for the black newspaper *Chicago Defender,* writing from the point of view of Jesse B. Semple, also known as "Simple," a working-class black man in Harlem. The columns used humor to attack issues such as segregation; Hughes continued to write them for much of the rest of his life. He also wrote the first volume of his autobiography, *The Big Sea,* in 1940.

In the 1950s, Hughes enjoyed a major resurgence with his collection *Montage of a Dream Deferred* (1951). It includes what is perhaps his most famous poem, which begins with the line, "What happens to a dream deferred?" The entire collection focuses on two topics familiar to Hughes: jazz and relations between blacks and whites. Hughes suggests that if blacks continue to be denied basic civil rights, the situation might turn violent. Hughes himself, however, did not advocate violence from black activist groups.

He continued to write in nearly every category imaginable through the 1950s and 1960s. His successful Simple columns were collected in *Simple Speaks His Mind* (1950), as well as four subsequent volumes. He published the short-story collection *Laughing to Keep from Crying* in 1952. He wrote several children's books, including *The First Book of Jazz* (1954). He wrote nonfiction works such as *Famous American Negroes* (1954), and a second autobiography, *I Wonder as I Wander* (1956). He translated the poems of Spanish-language writers like Federico García Lorca (1898–1936) and Nicolás Guillén (1902–89). He wrote an opera with Jan Meyerowitz (1913–98) titled *Esther* in 1957. He also completed several plays, including *Simply Heavenly* (1957) and *Black Nativity* (1961). In addition to all this, he published *Ask Your Mama: 12 Moods for Jazz,* a new poetry collection, in 1961.

Zora Neale Hurston.
The Library of Congress

Hughes died from complications related to prostate cancer in 1967, at the age of sixty-five. His home in Harlem was preserved and designated as a landmark by the New York City Preservation Commission. In addition to numerous collections of reprinted writings, one new poetry collection, *The Panther and the Lash: Poems of Our Times* (1967), was published after his death.

★ ZORA NEALE HURSTON (1891–1960)

Zora Neale Hurston was an author equally famous for her short stories, her novels, and her collections of black folktales gathered throughout the American South and the Caribbean. She came to prominence during the Harlem Renaissance, a flowering of African American art and culture that took place in New York beginning in the 1920s. Her reputation declined after the 1940s, but then experienced a resurgence in the 1970s as critics reevaluated her work's importance to African American literature.

Hurston's date and place of birth have been the subject of debate, mostly because of Hurston herself. She insisted for many years that she was born in 1901 in Eatonville, Florida, recognized as the first all-black town in the United States. Scholars have determined that she was actually born ten years before in Notasulga, Alabama, where her father John Hurston was a carpenter and farmer. The family moved to Eatonville when she was still quite young. Her father became a Baptist minister there, and was elected mayor in 1897 for the first of three terms.

Hurston was one of eight children, and often displayed an active imagination. Her mother Lucy died when Hurston was nine years old. Her father's relationship with a new woman left Hurston feeling out of place in the family home. She was sent to a boarding school in Jacksonville, Florida, but at the age of fourteen, Hurston took a job with a touring theater troupe and left Florida. She ended up in Baltimore, Maryland, where she spent several years working before completing high school at Morgan Academy.

In 1918, she attended Howard University, where she joined a literary club led by a professor named Alain Leroy Locke (1885–1954). He encouraged her in her writing, and she won two prizes in a literary contest in *Opportunity* magazine. She also earned admittance to Barnard College in New York City, and became the first African American to attend the school in 1925. She continued to publish stories in various magazines. They showed the influence of her childhood in Eatonville and the folktales she heard there. She also took a job working for Fannie Hurst (1885–1968), a popular novelist at the time, who helped her pay for her schooling.

Hurston studied anthropology at Barnard, and earned her degree in 1927. She continued her studies at Columbia University, and began traveling throughout the American South and the Caribbean collecting tales of black folklore. This resulted in her landmark work *Mules and Men* (1935), which gathered together the folklore she had collected. This was followed by another collection of folklore, *Tell My Horse,* in 1938.

At the same time, Hurston began writing novels. Her first, *Jonah's Gourd Vine,* was published in 1934. Her second and most famous novel, *Their Eyes Were Watching God,* was published in 1937. She completed a third novel, *Moses, Man of the Mountain,* in 1939. Her first two novels were inspired largely by her own life and family experiences in Eatonville. *Jonah's Gourd Vine,* for example, is about a man named John who has a wife named Lucy (the same as her parents) and becomes a successful Baptist minister in a Florida town. *Their Eyes Were Watching God* focuses on a young woman who lives in Eatonville, Florida, in the early twentieth century.

In the 1940s, Hurston continued to publish short stories and articles in various magazines, including *The Saturday Evening Post*. She also wrote an autobiography, *Dust Tracks on a Road* (1942), and a fourth novel, *Seraph on the Suwanee* (1948). However, her popularity suffered a steady decline. She moved back to Florida and wrote occasional articles and essays for various newspapers. In her final years, she supported herself by working as a maid. She died of a stroke in 1960, at the age of sixty-nine.

★ SCOTT JOPLIN
(1867–1917)

Scott Joplin was considered the key creative force behind ragtime music, a popular type of dance music that borrowed heavily from the rhythms of traditional African American songs. His complex and energetic songs made him the most successful composer of popular music at the turn of the twentieth century. Despite his success, Joplin failed in his quest to be recognized as a creator of artistic and culturally significant work during his lifetime.

Scott Joplin.
MPI/Getty Images

Joplin was born in Linden, Texas, not far from the borders of Louisiana and Arkansas. His exact birth date is unknown, but it is believed that he was born sometime between June 1867 and January 1868. His father, Giles Joplin, was a railroad worker who had been a slave just five years before his son was born. His mother, Florence Givens Joplin, was a laundry worker and maid. They relocated to Texarkana, Texas, while Scott was still young. The Joplins were a musical family, and Giles had grown up on Negro spirituals and work songs sung by slaves to keep their spirits raised. The first instrument Scott learned to play was the banjo.

His mother's employment in the home of a white lawyer gave Scott access to a piano. At the age of eleven, he started taking piano lessons from a German tutor named Julius Weiss. Weiss was impressed by Scott's natural talent, and taught him free of charge. Joplin left home as a teenager and worked as a musician in various bars and clubs across the country.

Joplin became one of the main innovators of a type of music called ragtime. One of the key features of ragtime is its use of a melody that has a lively rhythm, similar to songs popular among African Americans and inspired by traditional African rhythms. Ragtime was considered dance music, and many African American dance-hall musicians played their own brand of ragtime during the 1890s. Joplin, however, was unique among these musicians. He had received classical training from Weiss, and he also knew how to transcribe his works to sheet music. Piano playing had become a popular pastime in the homes of many Americans, and sheet music allowed amateur players to try to re-create popular tunes on their own.

In the mid-1890s, Joplin settled in Sedalia, Missouri. There, he studied music at the George R. Smith College for Negroes, and performed at various venues around the town. Joplin also made the acquaintance of John Stark, a publisher of sheet music. Joplin had achieved limited success with published sheet music, but one piece in particular—the "Maple Leaf Rag"—caught Stark's attention. Joplin had written the piece in 1897 to honor a local nightclub of the same name. Even though the piece was very complex, Stark saw potential in its sales. Joplin's "Maple Leaf Rag" became a huge success, and was the first instrumental sheet music piece to sell over one million copies.

Joplin moved to St. Louis in 1901 and continued creating popular ragtime songs, including "The Entertainer" (1902). His works showed increasing sophistication, and Joplin was eager to make the transition from being a writer of "popular" music to being recognized as a creator of artistic music. He began working on an opera concerning a 1901 meeting between Booker T. Washington (1856–1915) and President Theodore Roosevelt (1858–1919), titled *A Guest of Honor* (1903). Although the opera was performed by a touring company, the tour ended abruptly when the proceeds from one show were stolen and Joplin was left without performers or equipment. No copies of the score for this opera were known to exist as of 2010.

Undeterred, Joplin began working on an opera of even grander scale called *Treemonisha* (1911). He moved to New York City in 1907, and continued to write other popular works like "Gladiolus Rag" (1907) and "Euphonic Sounds" (1909). But much of his time, effort, and money was poured into completing *Treemonisha*, a tale set in Texarkana that featured elements of his own life and a heavy influence of traditional African American folktales. Joplin completed the piano and voice score for the opera, and tried to get several different publishers interested in the massive work. They all rejected it. He published it at his own expense in 1911, and arranged for a stripped-down performance of the opera in

Harlem in 1915. He had hoped the performance would convince investors to fund a full-scale production of the opera, but investors left unimpressed.

Joplin's health began to decline around this time due to his having syphilis that had advanced beyond treatment. For two years, Joplin continued to deteriorate, unable to create new music. Eventually, he was unable to play music at all. He died in 1917 from the disease. Although some of his best-selling works remained well known, ragtime music fell out of favor, and his operas were lost. A copy of the piano and vocal score for *Treemonisha* was discovered in 1970, just as historians were rediscovering Joplin's contributions to American music. The first full production of the opera—which Joplin had hoped would be his crowning achievement—debuted in 1972, more than six decades after he wrote it. In 1976, Joplin was awarded a special Pulitzer Prize in recognition of his accomplishments.

★ JACOB LAWRENCE
(1917–2000)

Jacob Lawrence was one of the most significant African American painters to arise from Harlem in the 1930s. His unique style relied on simple shapes and bold colors. He often painted a series of works all connected by a single subject, usually related to African American history or life in Harlem.

Lawrence was born in Atlantic City, New Jersey, but moved with his mother and siblings to Harlem in New York City, when he was thirteen. His mother worked as a single parent, so Lawrence and his siblings spent time in day care at Utopia House. It was there that he first received training and encouragement in art.

Lawrence dropped out of school as a teenager so that he could work and help his mother support the family. Although regular classes did not interest him, he made the effort to attend evening art classes taught by some of the most distinguished artists in Harlem, including Charles Alston (1907–77) and Augusta Savage (1892–1962). Alston even let Lawrence set up his own work space in Alston's studio. In 1937, Lawrence earned a scholarship to the American Artists School, which he attended until 1939. He received a grant from the Rosenwald Fund, established to help benefit African American arts and culture. The grant allowed him to establish his own studio in Harlem. In 1941, Lawrence married another artist named Gwendolyn Knight (1913–2005).

Lawrence's success grew when the Downtown Gallery in New York displayed his series of paintings titled *Migration of the Negro* (1940–41).

Jacob Lawrence.

Robert W. Kelley/Time & Life Pictures/Getty Images

The series focuses on the millions of African Americans who moved from the South to the urban centers of the North during the 1920s and 1930s, searching for economic prosperity and greater equality. Many of Lawrence's works were created in series rather than as stand-alone pieces. Essentially, Lawrence told stories through groups of paintings sharing a common theme or subject. Many of his works concerned African American life in Harlem.

The United States entered World War II at the end of 1941, after Japanese forces bombed the American base at Pearl Harbor in Hawaii. Lawrence joined the United States Coast Guard in 1943 to help with the war effort. He traveled to various locations around the world, and continued to create art during his service. He even became a combat artist as his official job duty. After the war, he received a Guggenheim Fellowship so that he could create a series of paintings based on his experiences during the war. Lawrence was also given a solo exhibition of his paintings at New York's Museum of Modern Art.

Lawrence also spent his time teaching art at various schools, including Black Mountain College, Brandeis University, and the University of Washington. He received many awards and honors over the course of his career, including the Spingarn Medal from the National Association for the Advancement of Colored People (NAACP) and membership in the American Academy of Arts and Letters. In later life, he focused on creating large-scale murals for permanent display. His final major work was a mural for the Times Square subway station in New York, installed in 2001. Lawrence died in 2000, at the age of eighty-two. One of his paintings, *The Builders* (1947), was purchased for display in the White House in 2007, and is part of its permanent collection.

★ PAUL ROBESON
(1898–1976)

Paul Robeson was an actor and singer who was equally renowned for his significant role as an activist for the rights of oppressed people around the world. His career as a stage and film star was severely damaged by accusations that he was disloyal to the United States government. Although he did not recover his reputation while he was alive, he was recognized as an important force in the struggle for civil and workers' rights after his death in 1976.

Paul LeRoy Bustill Robeson was the youngest of eight children born to William Drew Robeson, a former runaway slave who had become a minister, and Anna Louisa Robeson, a schoolteacher. He was born in Princeton, New Jersey, and raised in various cities around the state. His mother died in a fire when he was just six years old. Despite this loss, Paul was an exceptional student and athlete at Somerville High School, and earned a scholarship to Rutgers College (now Rutgers University) in New Brunswick, New Jersey.

Robeson was only the third African American ever admitted to Rutgers. He excelled there, becoming a member of the prestigious Phi Beta Kappa fraternity and graduating first in his class in 1919. He was also chosen as an All-American football player two years in a row. After graduating, he moved to Harlem, a neighborhood in New York City, and attended Columbia University to study law. His skills as a college athlete also secured him a position as a professional football player, which helped him earn money to pay for school. Robeson also enjoyed his first success as an actor while at Columbia. He starred in a production of *Simon the Cyrenian*, staged by the Harlem Young Men's Christian Association (YMCA) in 1921, and in the play *Taboo* in 1922. For a brief time he was a cast member of the hit Broadway musical *Shuffle Along* (1922). During

OPPOSITE PAGE
Paul Robeson.
*Sasha/Hulton Archive/
Getty Images*

this time, he met chemist Eslanda Cardozo Goode, whom he married in 1921.

Robeson graduated with his law degree in 1923, passed the bar exam to become a lawyer, and took a job with a law firm in New York City. He quit after experiencing discrimination from other employees at the firm. Instead, he decided to pursue a career as an actor and a singer. He became a member of the Provincetown Players, and earned a starring role in the Eugene O'Neill play *The Emperor Jones* in 1924. That same year, Robeson starred in another O'Neill play, *All God's Chillun Got Wings* (1924), as a black law student who marries a white woman. A reviewer for *Time* magazine called his performance "brilliant," though the play aroused controversy for its depiction of an interracial marriage—something that was illegal at the time in many states. Robeson was also gaining fame for his vocal stage performances of Negro spirituals, which are traditional African American religious songs.

Robeson's breakout role came in the musical *Show Boat* in 1928. The role of Joe—who sings what is perhaps the show's most famous song, "Ol' Man River"—was written for Robeson and his deep, rich bass voice. Scheduling conflicts, however, prevented Robeson from starring in the show's premiere run on Broadway in 1927. He assumed the role during the show's London production, and starred as Joe in the successful film adaptation made in 1936.

Robeson followed his successful run in *Show Boat* with an acclaimed performance as the title character in Shakespeare's *Othello* (1930), which ran in London. He also starred in a major Broadway production of the play in 1943. For most of the 1930s, he remained in England, where he starred in British films such as *Song of Freedom* (1936) and *The Proud Valley* (1940). Robeson was able to portray serious, three-dimensional African American characters in these films, the likes of which did not exist in American films at that time.

Robeson also grew politically active while in Europe. He supported poor Welsh coal miners who protested poor working conditions, and opposed the racist policies of the Nazis in Germany. In 1937, he helped create the Council on African Affairs (CAA), a group that supported efforts to free colonial territories in Africa from the European countries that ruled them.

Robeson returned to the United States and became especially active in the struggle for African American civil rights. He founded the American Crusade Against Lynching in 1946, which sought to end the murder of African Americans at the hands of white mobs operating outside the law. His support of the political theories of socialism (in which the wealthiest members of a society bear a duty to help support the poorest) and communism (in which all members of a society share equally in the distribution of work and benefits) brought him scrutiny from the United States government. At the time, many Americans feared the spread of communism, and the Federal Bureau of Investigation (FBI) kept a close watch on anyone suspected of supporting Communist causes. From 1950 until 1958, Robeson was denied a passport and could not leave the United States. He was also blocked from performing in large-scale stage productions because of pressure from anti-Communist activists. His status as an All-American player for Rutgers was even removed from the official school record.

In 1958, Robeson was finally given permission to travel abroad. His only book, *Here I Stand,* was published in England in that same year. The book contains autobiographical information as well as detailed explanations of his political and moral beliefs. Robeson performed two shows in Carnegie Hall, and then toured the world for several years. In 1963, he returned to the United States in poor health. He spent a few years in New York City and then moved to Philadelphia, Pennsylvania, where he remained in the care of his family. He died of a stroke in 1976, at the age of seventy-seven. During his lifetime, his reputation never fully recovered from the vicious attacks leveled at him by anti-Communist activists, many of whom were part of the United States government. However, in subsequent years, Robeson was honored by the United States Postal Service, which issued a stamp with his image in 2004, and the College Football Hall of Fame, where he was inducted in 1995.

★ HENRY OSSAWA TANNER (1859–1937)

Henry Ossawa Tanner was the first African American painter to gain worldwide fame for his work. His works depicting African American life during the late nineteenth century offer a unique perspective that influenced later artists like Norman Rockwell (1894–1978).

Tanner was born in Pittsburgh, Pennsylvania, to Benjamin Tucker Tanner and Sarah Elizabeth Miller. His unique middle name was derived from the town of Osawatomie, Kansas, site of a famous battle between John Brown (1800–59), an activist who supported the abolition of slavery, and proslavery forces. In 1868, the family relocated to Philadelphia, Pennsylvania, where Benjamin worked as a minister and the editor of a Christian magazine. Tanner's choice of schools in Philadelphia was limited since African American students were taught separately from white students. Tanner graduated at the top of his class in 1877, but was not able to receive training in the field he loved most: art.

Henry Ossawa Tanner.
Hulton Archive/Getty Images

He was inspired to become a painter after seeing an artist creating a painting in a park near his home. He painted on his own throughout his teenage years, and was accepted into the prestigious Pennsylvania Academy of the Fine Arts in 1880. One of his instructors was the painter Thomas Eakins (1844–1916), who redesigned the classes at the school to emphasize the study of live models and human anatomy. Through these methods, Eakins encouraged students to depict their subjects as realistically as possible.

Tanner studied at the academy for five years. He also took a job at a family friend's flour mill to earn a living while mastering his craft. He sold some pen and ink drawings to magazines, the most notable being an illustration for *Harper's Young People* that earned him fifty dollars in 1888. He moved to Atlanta in 1889 and opened a photography gallery, believing that it would be the best way to use his artistic skill to support himself. The gallery was a failure, but Tanner was able to make a modest living as a professional photographer. He spent some time in the Blue Ridge Mountains of North Carolina, meeting poor Southern blacks who lived a life quite different from the one he had known in Pennsylvania. These impressions of African American life in the South would inform some of his most famous later works. Tanner was offered a position as an art teacher for Clark University in Atlanta, and he began teaching in the fall of 1889. Though he seemed to be a well-regarded teacher, Tanner's greatest desire was to travel to Europe and develop his talents. He finally earned enough money to make this dream a reality by selling several of his paintings to a few wealthy patrons. In 1891, he left the United States for Europe.

Tanner fell in love with Paris. He studied there until 1893, when a serious case of typhoid sent him back to the United States to recover. That same year, Tanner completed one of his most famous works, *The Banjo Lesson*. The painting features an elderly African American man teaching a young boy to play the banjo in a modest, fire-lit cabin. Tanner lived in the South only briefly, but the painting remains one of the most significant depictions of life in the American South by a black artist. Another major painting that depicts African American life, *The Thankful Poor* (1894), shows a grandfather and grandson praying over a modest meal.

Tanner returned to Paris, where his work was accepted for the Salon, the most prestigious art exhibition in the world. He also began to focus on religious subjects in his paintings. Some of his most famous religious works include *Daniel in the Lions' Den* (1896), *The Raising of Lazarus* (1896), and *The Annunciation* (1898). One Philadelphia patron who admired Tanner's religious paintings paid for the artist to travel to Egypt and Palestine so that he could see the locations of so many biblical stories firsthand. Tanner made two trips to the Middle East, while gaining great fame back in Paris. In 1899, Tanner married Jessie Macauley Olssen, who had served as the model for Mary in his painting *The Annunciation*. By 1900, he was considered the most popular American artist in Paris.

After 1900, Tanner gained fame in the United States, being featured in many exhibitions across the country. However, he and his wife—who gave birth to their only child in 1903—chose to continue living primarily in France. He was awarded the French Légion d'honneur (Legion of Honor), one of the nation's highest awards, in 1923. In 1927, he became the first African American chosen as a full member of the National Academy of Design in New York. Tanner died in Paris in 1937. One of his early paintings, *Sand Dunes at Sunset, Atlantic City* (c. 1885), was purchased and placed in the White House during the presidency of Bill Clinton (1946–). It is now a part of the White House's permanent collection.

★ JAMES VAN DER ZEE
(1886–1983)

James Van Der Zee was one of the most celebrated African American photographers of the first half of the twentieth century. He was well known for his photographs of famous figures related to the Harlem Renaissance, the flowering of art and culture that took place in Harlem in the 1920s. Van Der Zee was equally famous for his portrayals of typical Harlem residents, which capture the mood and spirit of the era.

Van Der Zee was born in Lenox, Massachusetts, to John and Elizabeth Van Der Zee. His parents worked for President Ulysses S. Grant as a butler and a maid. James learned both the piano and the violin as a child, and as a teenager he received his first camera. Van Der Zee moved to the Harlem neighborhood of New York City after graduating from high school. He held odd jobs and played in bands with musicians like Fletcher Henderson (1898–1952).

In 1915, Van Der Zee got a job as a darkroom assistant in a Newark, New Jersey, portrait studio. He eventually became a successful portrait photographer, and opened his own studio, called Guarantee Photo Studio, in Harlem soon after. At the time, many important African American cultural figures lived in the Harlem area. Among the famous people photographed by Van Der Zee were the poet Countee Cullen and African rights leader Marcus Garvey (1887–1940). Van Der Zee was even named the official photographer of the Universal Negro Improvement Association (UNIA), created by Garvey.

Most of his customers were middle-class African Americans— something relatively new in American culture. African Americans had finally achieved some acceptance in mainstream society in the northern United States, and many held professional jobs alongside whites. Van Der Zee's photographs document this new segment of the middle class, depicting young, educated black men and women in ways that highlighted their beauty, optimism, and pride. He photographed not just couples and families but also social organizations like church groups and fraternities. He was known for his use of elaborate backdrops, costumes, props, and photographic "touch-ups" to remove flaws or add clever double-images to

OPPOSITE PAGE
James Van Der Zee.
Nancy R. Schiff/Hulton Archive/Getty Images

a scene. His studio was so successful that in 1932 he expanded to a larger space which he called GGG Studios.

His studio operated for several decades with moderate success and little fame beyond the Harlem community. That changed in 1968 when the Metropolitan Museum of Art created an exhibition that focused heavily on Van Der Zee's photographs of Harlem and its residents. The exhibition was called "Harlem on My Mind," and it brought him almost immediate fame. He continued photographing Harlem residents and celebrities like comedian Bill Cosby (1937–) and singer Lou Rawls (1933–2006) well into his nineties. He died in 1983 at the age of ninety-six.

❖ MINSTREL SHOWS EVOLVE INTO MORE SERIOUS THEATER

Stage portrayals of black life in the United States underwent a drastic change between 1865 and 1920. Prior to 1865, African American representation on stage had been limited to minstrel shows. Minstrel shows consisted of white performers in black makeup who offered broad stereotypes of African Americans in an attempt at humor. Portrayals of black life and culture grew increasingly sophisticated after the end of the Civil War in 1865, offering unique insight into African American life for black and white audiences alike.

Minstrel Shows a Uniquely American Success

Minstrel shows first arose in the 1830s, as American entertainers struggled to develop shows that did not rely heavily upon European traditions. Some white performers applied blackface, or black makeup made from grease paint or burnt cork, and imitated the African American dialects they heard throughout the South among slave populations. The most successful of these was Thomas Dartmouth Rice (1808–60), who reportedly bought the clothes off an old African American man in Louisville in order to copy his appearance and manner. He performed a song-and-dance routine called "Jim Crow" to enthusiastic white audiences, often merely as an interlude to another stage show.

The next innovator of the minstrel show was Edwin P. Christy (1815–62), who developed modest blackface routines into a full-fledged musical stage production. Virtually all other minstrel shows followed the basic structure he employed, which began with all the performers parading onto the stage, followed by numerous songs and variety acts, and ending with a full-cast musical number. From its debut in 1842, Christy's minstrel show was a huge success, especially in the northern United States. The characters featured in minstrel shows were stereotypes of African Americans, raucous folks who would rather sing and dance than work. The characters often dispensed commonsense wisdom and poked fun at mainstream American culture, however, leading the audience to identify sympathetically with them.

The heyday for minstrel shows was in the 1840s and 1850s, but they remained popular throughout the nineteenth century. Many African Americans even began performing in minstrel shows after the Civil War (1861–65). They were often ex-slaves billed as typical plantation "darkies" whose stage performances recreated their old lives in the South. These later minstrel shows generally provided music and dance far more authentic to

African American culture than early minstrel shows. They still perpetuated some negative ideas about African Americans, but also offered the first opportunities for African American performers to earn money and fame for portraying elements of their cultural heritage.

At the same time, more serious attempts to portray African American life began to appear. The first successful play in this regard was an adaptation of *Uncle Tom's Cabin* (1852), based on the antislavery novel by Harriet Beecher Stowe (1811–96). Though the tale features several sympathetic African American characters, these roles were usually played by white actors in blackface. Also, many unofficial adaptations of the book combined aspects of the story with elements from minstrel shows, lessening the antislavery message of the novel.

African American Portrayals Evolve

Minstrel shows had a lasting effect on American entertainment even after their decline at the end of the nineteenth century. The more "genuine" minstrel shows, featuring African American performers and authentic black spiritual songs, led to the acceptance and popularity of African American musical traits. These traits led to the development of ragtime music in the 1890s, Dixieland music in the early 1900s, and jazz soon after. The more traditional minstrel shows were combined with the musical variety shows known as vaudeville, which expanded the characters and music beyond

African American vaudeville performers Bert Williams and George Walker created successful stage shows in the early twentieth century.
© *Bettmann/Corbis*

their African American focus. Still, many of the traits of the minstrel show remained, especially the emphasis on stereotyped comic portrayals. African American vaudeville performers like Bert Williams (1875–1922) and George Walker (1873–1911) built on their fame and created their own successful stage shows, including *In Dahomey* (1902), which was the first black musical to be performed on Broadway. Their efforts led to other successful musicals featuring African American performers, such as *Shuffle Along* (1921).

The tradition of stage plays as tools of African American activism—as with *Uncle Tom's Cabin*—also continued in the twentieth century. One notable stage show was *The Star of Ethiopia* (1913), written by author and civil rights activist W. E. B. Du Bois (1868–1963). The production offered a sprawling history of African American culture, from ancient Africa through slavery in the American South and beyond. Also important were dramas meant to condemn lynching—the episodes of white mob violence against blacks that had become epidemic in the South—and other types of discrimination. Angelina Weld-Grimké (1880–1958) was one of the first successful African American female playwrights. She created a play called *Rachel* in 1916 that focuses on a black woman who rebels against the discrimination she witnesses around her. May Miller (1899–1995) also achieved success with her plays about the modern struggles of blacks, such as *The Bog Guide* (1925) and *Scratches* (1929). Miller became the most widely published African American female playwright of her time, and her work was a clear indication of just how far stage portrayals of blacks had advanced in the decades following the Civil War.

❖ BLACK AUTHORS GAIN FAME IN THE EARLY TWENTIETH CENTURY

African American writing in last decades of the nineteenth century showed a unique blend of folk traditions, dialects, and historical and social concerns. By the turn of the twentieth century, African Americans had gone from having virtually no voice in American culture to publishing significant works in a variety of categories. In some cases, however, important works of literature by African Americans did not receive recognition from white scholars until many years later.

The Pre-War Tradition of African American Literature

The scope of written African American literature was severely limited before the Civil War (1861–65) by the practice of slavery in the South and by widespread racism even in parts of the United States where slavery was illegal. Slaves were not permitted to read and write, and therefore had no written literature. Slaves did, however, have a strong oral (spoken) literary tradition composed of folktales and fables that combined elements of African folklore with the direct experience of slavery in the United States. This oral tradition in African American literature would have a major influence on African American writers of the twentieth century.

The only type of written literature by African Americans to achieve widespread attention before the Civil War was the slave narrative. Firsthand accounts of former slaves were a major part of the movement to abolish (end) slavery in the 1840s and 1850s. There were dozens of slave narratives published as books or pamphlets in the years before the war. Most were narrated to white abolitionists. Famous exceptions include *Narrative of the Life of Frederick Douglass* (1845), written by the prominent abolitionist and former slave Frederick Douglass; *Narrative of William W. Brown, Fugitive Slave, Written By Himself* (1847); and *Incidents in the Life of a Slave Girl* (1860), by Harriet Jacobs.

Washington and Du Bois Create Literature of Social Change

The abolition of slavery preoccupied black writers of the pre–Civil War era. Race relations and the living conditions of African Americans remained a central focus of the literature written by African Americans in the last decades of the nineteenth century. The most memorable nonfiction works created by African Americans during this time period are those that dealt with the issue of race in the United States. These were in many ways an outgrowth of the slave narratives popular before the war. However, where slave narratives were often sensational and written with the expressed intent of ending slavery, this new literature aimed to bring independence and equality to free blacks. The two authors most closely associated with this type of literature were Booker T. Washington (1856–1915) and W. E. B. Du Bois.

Washington emerged as a leader in black education in the decades following the Civil War. He was a slave in Virginia until he was nine years old, but rose from these humble beginnings to become the first head of the Tuskegee Institute in Alabama. His first major literary work was *The Future of the American Negro* in 1899. The book combined the history of African American culture with the author's own past, as well as a discussion about the issues that were most critical to African American advancement at the time. He is best known for his autobiography *Up from Slavery* (1901), which emphasizes hard work, patience, and a demonstration of one's value as the best ways to become accepted in mainstream American society.

Du Bois, born into freedom in Massachusetts, also wrote works based on his own experiences and on African American history. His major works include a study on the African slave trade to America, a biography of abolitionist John Brown, and a study of the period after the Civil War known in the South as Reconstruction. His most famous work is *The Souls of Black Folk* (1903), a collection of essays that includes autobiographical tales mixed with the author's thoughts on the current and future state of African Americans in the United States. Du Bois felt that Washington's strategy for blacks—which involved waiting for acceptance from white Americans—was not sufficient. Du Bois wanted African Americans to demand equality, and to take positive action to secure their own rights.

Dunbar and Chesnutt Set the Literary Bar

While Washington and Du Bois made their literary mark with nonfiction, Paul Laurence Dunbar (1872–1906) and Charles W. Chesnutt (1858–1932) created significant works of poetry and fiction. Dunbar and Chesnutt were trailblazing writers, but they enjoyed limited mainstream success during their lifetimes. Their work was largely ignored for decades after their deaths. These authors were often praised or criticized by their contemporaries and by later critics for reasons that had as much to do with race as with the quality of their writing.

Dunbar was raised in a relatively tolerant Ohio community, far removed from the struggles his parents had known as slaves before he was born. As an artist and an intellectual, Dunbar was well respected by blacks and whites alike. His first collection of poetry was *Oak and Ivy,* published in 1893. He wrote his second collection, *Majors and Minors* (1895), with a voice recognizable as a black dialect. He was equally comfortable writing in a more mainstream voice, but found that many editors preferred his poems and stories that sounded "black." At first he obliged out of a desire to earn money and to satisfy critics.

Paul Laurence Dunbar created popular "dialect" poetry in the late nineteenth century. *The Library of Congress*

Dunbar returned to writing in the style he preferred after learning that he was ill with tuberculosis. Tuberculosis is an infectious disease, usually affecting the lungs. Dunbar published several collections of short stories, poetry, and even novels, though these works did not receive the praise of his earlier "dialect" works. Dunbar died of tuberculosis in 1906, at the age of just thirty-three. His work was largely forgotten in mainstream literary circles soon after, but it had a profound effect on a new generation of African American artists. Many of these young writers became key figures in the

Harlem Renaissance, a flowering of African American arts in New York City in the 1920s.

Chesnutt was a man many would have considered white, based on his appearance. During this time period, a person was classified as black, regardless of his appearance, if he had even a single great-grandparent who was black. Chesnutt identified with his African American heritage, and wrote stories inspired by African American folktales. His works relied heavily upon black dialect to create an air of authenticity for white readers. Chesnutt published two story collections in 1899, *The Conjure Woman* and *The Wife of his Youth, and Other Stories of the Color Line.* Both collections were praised by noted critic William Dean Howells (1837–1920). Chesnutt lost the support of white scholars like Howells when his later works like *The Marrow of Tradition* (1901) offered negative views of whites' treatment of African Americans. With the exceptions of Dunbar and Chesnutt, African American writers remained largely shut out of literary circles until the 1920s, when the authors of the Harlem Renaissance would finally gain critical acceptance for their work.

❖ AFRICAN AMERICAN MUSICAL TRADITIONS RESHAPE AMERICAN MUSIC

African American music underwent dramatic transformations after the end of the Civil War (1861–65). Songs that had been known only to slave populations in the South became hugely influential in the development of new American musical styles. Their unique rhythms and musical scales arose from African musical traditions. These stood out from the European traditions that had previously been the models for American music. The merging of these two musical traditions resulted in a unique musical identity appreciated by listeners around the world.

Choirs Celebrate the African American Spirit

The first African American music to be recognized and appreciated by mainstream American culture came from the Fisk Jubilee Singers. The group was formed at the historically black Fisk University in 1871 by the school's treasurer, George Leonard White (1838–95). The name comes from a biblical reference to a time called the "year of jubilee," when all slaves are set free. Some of the songs they performed were religious spirituals that had been sung by slaves on plantations across the South less than ten years before. The choir toured the northern United States to raise money for the school, offering both black and white audiences a glimpse into a world largely unknown by people in that part of the country. Minstrel shows had become popular, but they usually featured white performers wearing black makeup and performing stereotypical routines

The Fisk Jubilee Singers, c. 1875. The group achieved such fame that they were invited to sing for the queen of England. © Hulton-Deutsch Collection/ Corbis

that misrepresented true African American culture. The Fisk Jubilee Singers were so successful that they were invited to perform at the White House for President Ulysses S. Grant (1822–85) in 1872. They embarked on two tours of Europe that included a performance for the queen of England, and earned over one hundred thousand dollars to create permanent campus buildings at Fisk. They later toured Asia, and audiences around the world responded enthusiastically to their authentic spirituals.

Negro spirituals were a unifying force among African Americans in the South. They spoke of the hardships and struggles of African Americans before the Civil War. But none of these stood alone as an encompassing theme for the African American experience. In 1900, poet James Weldon Johnson (1871–1938) and his brother John Rosamond Johnson wrote a song to be performed at a celebration in honor of Abraham Lincoln's birthday, which took place on February 12. The brothers wanted to honor Lincoln for helping African Americans achieve freedom, but did not want to dismiss the struggles that still lay ahead. The song they created was called "Lift Ev'ry Voice and Sing" (1900), and it was first performed by a choir of five hundred schoolchildren in Jacksonville, Florida.

Like the slave spirituals before it, "Lift Ev'ry Voice and Sing" spread throughout the African American community and grew in popularity, especially in the South. Its message of strength in the face of violence held special meaning for Southern blacks, who lived each day under the threat of harm from terrorist groups like the Ku Klux Klan. It was originally written as a song for children, so it became a popular choice for African American school choirs. The National Association for the Advancement of Colored People (NAACP) adopted "Lift Ev'ry Voice and Sing" as its official song in 1920, and it remained the most powerful anthem of the African American struggle until the 1960s civil rights movement popularized the song "We Shall Overcome."

African American Performers Feel the Blues

Spirituals and other slave songs inspired other forms of African American music. These songs were substantially different from other American songs, which arose from European musical traditions. African American music used different notes, different rhythms, and different song structures that were all based on African traditions. One significant feature in African American music is the pattern known as "call and response." In call and response, a musical phrase—which can be played or sung—is followed by another musical phrase related to the first but coming from a different musician or singer. The second performer might even be an entire group of people, as in some traditional African ceremonies. Call and response is a feature commonly found in jazz music. Another important trait that carried over from the days of slavery was the subject matter: Songs told of hardship, struggle, weariness, and loneliness. This formed the core of what came to be called blues music.

Among the earliest performers of blues music was W. C. Handy (1873–1958). Born in Alabama, Handy spent much of his musical career playing in minstrel shows, which were usually not authentic portrayals of African American culture. He returned to the songs of his roots in 1909 and adapted their unusual musical scales for a broader audience. His song "The Memphis Blues" (1912) is generally regarded as the first published example of blues music. He became known for his contribution of "blue notes," which are a key part of the musical scale he adapted from more traditional African American songs. In technical terms, a blue note is a note sung or played a semitone (half tone) or less lower than the major scale.

Handy was not the only black musician to make use of blue notes, and even he acknowledged hearing blues music from unknown performers in the South years before "The Memphis Blues" became a hit. Every region of the South, in fact, gave rise to its own brand of blues. In Delta blues, found in Louisiana near the delta—or mouth—of the Mississippi River, players used an object such as the neck of a bottle to slide up and down the frets of a guitar. This unique way of playing, which made notes "bend" up or down as they were played, was called slide guitar. The most famous Delta blues musician was Robert Johnson (1911–38). His life is poorly documented, and he did not become famous until after his death—probably from poisoning—at the age of twenty-seven. Johnson is known almost entirely from two recording sessions in 1936 and 1937, during which he performed twenty-nine original songs. Some of these recordings were released during his lifetime, but Johnson did not achieve mainstream success until Columbia Records released a compilation of his songs titled *King of the Delta Blues Singers* in 1961.

African American women played an important part in the success of blues music as well. Ma Rainey (1886–1939) was a singer who performed blues songs throughout the South, and was one of the first female blues performers to be recorded by a music label. She had been well known as a live performer, but as a recording artist, Rainey became a star. She recorded almost one hundred songs over a five-year period beginning in 1923, including many that would become classics, like "Bo-Weevil Blues" (1923) and "See See Rider" (1924). She became known as the "Mother of the Blues." Another woman, Bessie Smith (1894–1937), matched Rainey in

Ma Rainey, shown performing with a band in 1923, became known as the "Mother of the Blues." *Frank Driggs Collection/Getty Images*

both fame and acclaim, earning the title "Empress of the Blues." She began her recording career in 1923, the same year as Rainey. Her first record featured the songs "Down-Hearted Blues" and "Gulf Coast Blues," and it sold well. Between her numerous recordings and her live shows, Smith was soon earning more money for her talents than any other African American in the country. However, black musicians in the first half of the twentieth century—including Smith—were not offered a share of the profits from the sale of their records. They were simply given a one-time payment, regardless of how well a record sold.

Jazz Moves North and Makes a Splash

In the first decades of the twentieth century, a new kind of music called "jazz" developed from a combination of blues and ragtime. Ragtime was an energetic type of piano music popularized by black composer Scott Joplin (c. 1867–1917) in the 1880s and 1890s. The music was called ragtime because of its "ragged," or syncopated (with irregularly spaced or stressed beats), rhythm. Ragtime and blues came together in New Orleans, Louisiana, a city famous for its full-band performances featuring brass, woodwind, and string instruments. The result was called Dixieland jazz (now called traditional jazz), and made use of the "call and response" style of earlier African American songs. During a piece, performers would often take turns playing a melody, while other performers would respond with a different but related melody. The musicians were encouraged to improvise, or come up with new variations on the central theme of the song. This became a defining feature of jazz, and live performances of the same song often differed dramatically from one show to the next.

Dixieland jazz moved northward as African American musicians like Louis Armstrong (1901–71) left the South after World War I (1914–18) for greater economic opportunities in Chicago and New York City. It was in Harlem, a predominantly black neighborhood in New York, that jazz became the dominating force in American music. It spread throughout the Harlem nightclubs in the 1920s, even attracting attention from white listeners who traveled to Harlem just to hear this innovative new sound. Venues like the Cotton Club—which catered exclusively to white customers—drew celebrities and radio hosts to the area, and helped to popularize the jazz sound among white artists and performers.

One of the most important performers at the Cotton Club was Duke Ellington (1899–1974), who led the band there from 1927 until 1932. Originally from Washington, D.C., Ellington had come to jazz by way of ragtime. He played the piano for his band, and wrote the songs with the specific talents of his other band members in mind. The exposure they received at the Cotton Club resulted in a successful tour of the

United States during the middle of the Great Depression in the 1930s—an economic downturn that severely limited the average American's ability to pay for a live show or a jazz record. Among Ellington's hits were "It Don't Mean a Thing If It Ain't Got That Swing" (1932) and "Sophisticated Lady" (1932). The success of Ellington and others meant that African American musicians were as popular among mainstream listeners as their white counterparts for the first time in American history.

Like Ellington, Billie Holiday (1915–59) found her first great success in Harlem. Although she was looking for a job as a dancer, a chance audition as a singer landed her a position as a performer in a Harlem nightclub in 1932. Her emotionally moving, soulful performances earned her immediate attention, as well as the name "Lady Day." In 1933, white musician Benny Goodman (1909–86) asked her to perform on two songs for Columbia Records. She went on to co-write hits such as "God Bless the Child" (1939) and "Lady Sings the Blues" (1956). Another notable recording was the musical adaptation of a graphic poem about lynching in the South by Abel Meeropol, titled "Strange Fruit" (1939).

From Swing and Bebop to Motown Pop

Several other varieties of music evolved as jazz and blues gained popularity among mainstream listeners. Jazz itself became bigger in the 1930s and 1940s, utilizing such large groups of musicians that the period came to be known as the "big band era." Goodman and other bandleaders like Count Basie (1904–84) relied more on a full orchestral sound than the lean improvisations of earlier jazz bands. At the same time, African American groups like the Ink Spots were pioneering an entirely new kind of band sound. Each member of the small group played an instrument such as a guitar or bass, and they contributed harmonizing vocals to support one lead singer. The Ink Spots scored popular hits with songs like "If I Didn't Care" (1939) and "Don't Get Around Much Anymore" (1942). Individual performers like Harry Belafonte (1927–) achieved fame by bringing other African-influenced music styles like calypso, which originated in the Caribbean, to wider audiences in the 1950s.

Perhaps as a reaction to the swing music made popular by big bands, bebop music offered a wilder and more improvisational spin on jazz in the 1940s. In some respects, bebop was a return to the spirit of earlier jazz. The rhythms and melodies of bebop were unpredictable, and the band size was once again small. Musicians like Dizzy Gillespie (1917–93) and Charlie Parker (1920–55) were pioneers in the development of bebop. Famous bebop recordings include Gillespie's "Salt Peanuts" (1942) and Parker's "Billie's Bounce" (1945).

Where bebop was deliberately challenging to the listener, other African American performers used jazz sounds to create more commercial songs that nonetheless stayed true to their traditional musical roots. Rhythm and blues, as the name suggests, paired the musical style of blues with a heavier beat. Very often, though, the term was applied broadly to more mainstream African American music. Soul music of the 1960s combined rhythm and blues with more traditional African American religious music, featuring energetic vocals similar to the gospel music heard from church choirs throughout the South. Ray Charles (1930–2004) and Aretha Franklin (1942–) are considered pioneers of soul music, with Franklin's version of the song "Respect" (1967) being a prime example.

One of the most important factors in the success of African American popular music was the creation of Motown Records in 1960. Berry Gordy Jr. (1929–) formed the company in Detroit, Michigan, and attracted the most talented black performers of the era, including Smokey Robinson (1940–), Stevie Wonder (1950–), and Diana Ross (1944–). The label developed a signature style and sound, relying on a small group of songwriters and studio musicians to create songs for many of the different Motown acts. Because of this, some have viewed Motown as a commercial success more than an artistic success. In any case, popular music in the 1960s was one of the few realms in which African Americans performed as equals with white artists thanks largely to Motown Records, which remained a major force in popular music into the 1980s.

Success in the Classical Realm

Accomplishments for African American musicians and performers were not limited to popular music. William Grant Still (1895–1978), raised in Arkansas, found success as a composer in New York. Still began his career in music in the early 1920s as an arranger for noted blues and jazz composers W. C. Handy and Eubie Blake (1887–1983). Beginning in the late 1920s, Still chose to create music for a more classical form, although he also enjoyed jazz. His compositions applied blues and jazz influences to full orchestra pieces, with the hope that the resulting works would sound uniquely American and would show that African American music was worthy of being called art. In 1931, his *Afro-American Symphony* was the first symphony written by an African American to be performed by a major symphony orchestra. Likewise, his 1949 opera *Troubled Island* was the first traditional opera written by an African American to be performed in a major opera house. The opera tells the tale of a Haitian of African descent who led a revolution in his country and became its leader.

Another African American success in the classical realm was Leontyne Price (1927–). Like Still, Price grew up in the South, where segregation severely limited her chances of pursuing a career in the arts. Her parents saw her talent at a young age, however, and committed themselves to helping her achieve her artistic potential. She attended Wilberforce College in Ohio at the same time as Betty Allen (1927–2009), who would also go on to become a successful opera singer. From there she attended the Juilliard School in New York City, and soon landed roles on Broadway, including the female lead in the 1952 production of *Porgy and Bess*. She joined the Metropolitan Opera in 1961, and became the first African American leading lady to earn a salary comparable to white performers. She performed lead roles in more than a dozen operas for the Met, and over the course of her career won nineteen Grammy Awards, the most ever awarded to any classical singer.

❖ HARLEM BECOMES CENTER OF ARTISTIC RENAISSANCE

The Harlem Renaissance was a flourishing of the arts that occurred in the Harlem neighborhood of New York City during the 1920s and into the 1930s. The movement was reflected in literature, music, drama, dance, and the visual arts. It is also associated with a renewed recognition of the African American struggle for equality and fairness in mainstream American society.

Setting the Stage for a Cultural Renaissance

One key factor in the Harlem Renaissance was the Great Migration. The Great Migration is the term used to describe the flow of millions of African Americans out of the South and into the urban centers of the North between 1910 and 1930. After the end of the Civil War, former slaves were no longer required to labor on plantations in the South. Some remained to work as sharecroppers, or farmers who tend land owned by someone else. But a large number of African Americans traveled northward to seek employment in the factories there. Neighborhoods of mostly black residents formed in the major northern cities. The largest of these was Harlem, a neighborhood in New York City.

African Americans were able to find jobs at better wages than were available to them in the South. They began to form a powerful segment of the middle class—people who were financially secure, though not wealthy. The financial security resulted in improved education and a greater interest in the arts. Many African American musicians were among those who moved northward during the Great Migration. They brought with them a new musical style that combined elements of traditional African American songs with a more modern sound. The music was called jazz, and it formed the core of a new artistic lifestyle in Harlem.

Living the Jazz Lifestyle

Jazz clubs became wildly popular throughout Harlem after World War I, and the music began to draw audiences from the rest of New York City and beyond. This increased interest in African American music led to an increased demand for African American performers—not just musicians, but also dancers and singers. Among these performers were Fletcher Henderson (1897–1952) and Duke Ellington (1899–1974), who first became famous as bandleaders at clubs in Harlem, and later achieved great fame as composers. Jazz was known for allowing musicians to showcase their talents on just about any instrument through improvised solo parts during each song. Soloists became closely identified with their trademark instruments: Louis Armstrong (1901–71) and his trumpet; Chick Webb (1905–39) and his drums; Lonnie Johnson (1899–1970) and his guitar; and Sidney Bechet (1897–1959) and his saxophone. Singers such as Ella Fitzgerald (1917–96) and Cab Calloway (1907–94) even became famous for using their voices as musical instruments in a style known as "scat singing," where words are replaced by nonsense syllables in improvised melodies.

The development of new forms of dance went hand-in-hand with the evolution of jazz music. Harlem became New York's hotspot for the young and culturally adventurous. Ballrooms like the Savoy and the Cotton Club drew dancers from throughout the region. The Cotton Club featured leading African American performers, but catered exclusively to white customers. The Savoy allowed both whites and blacks to dance together. Many of the most popular dances to sweep the country, such as the lindy hop, were first popularized in Harlem.

The music of Harlem also served to reinforce and revitalize other art forms; for example, jazz clubs and their performers became the subjects of paintings and poems. Poet Langston Hughes (1902–67) even used the rhythms and themes of jazz and blues in his poetry.

Exploring the Black Experience through Literature

Two prominent black educators—Alain Leroy Locke (1885–1954) and James Weldon Johnson—were driving forces behind the literary achievement of the Harlem Renaissance. Locke grew up in middle-class Philadelphia, and achieved great success as a scholar at Harvard and later as a teacher. He served as a professor of English and philosophy at Howard University in Washington, D.C., one of the premier African American schools in the country. Locke was a champion of the new generation of thinkers and artists who were living and studying in the northeast at that time. He saw the flourishing of the arts in Harlem perhaps earlier than anyone. He created an anthology of writing and art that reflected this new movement in 1925. The book was called *The New Negro*, and it contained works by nearly every major writer of the Harlem Renaissance, including Langston Hughes, Zora Neale Hurston, Countee Cullen, Claude McKay (1889–1948), and W. E. B. Du Bois. James Weldon Johnson, whose poetry appeared in Locke's *The New Negro*, edited influential collections of African American literature as well, including *The Book of American Negro Poetry* (1922) and *The Book of American Negro Spirituals* (1925). Johnson also published a major work of his own poetry during this Harlem Renaissance period: *God's Trombones: Seven Negro Sermons in Verse* (1927).

Langston Hughes was perhaps the best known of the Harlem Renaissance writers, succeeding as a poet with *The Weary Blues* (1926), as a novelist with *Not Without Laughter* (1930), and as a dramatist with a series of plays throughout the 1930s. Like other writers of the Harlem Renaissance, his work focused on the African American experience, documenting the details and sentiments of the Harlem community at the time he wrote. Other writers of the movement also enjoyed success by focusing on life in the Harlem area. Claude McKay enjoyed great success with his novel *Home to Harlem*, which offered a controversial depiction of Harlem's rowdy nightlife. Poet Helene Johnson (1906–95) became most famous for her poem "Bottled" (1928), which describes a black man dancing to jazz on the streets of Harlem.

Some writers associated with the Harlem Renaissance dealt with the black experience on a broader scale. Nella Larsen (1891–1964) wrote *Passing* (1929), the first novel to address the conflicts that existed between light-skinned and dark-skinned African Americans. Zora Neale Hurston first gained fame by writing a collection of black folktales—*Mules and Men* (1935)—and then by publishing a largely autobiographical novel about her youth in the South, *Their Eyes Were Watching God* (1937). Jean Toomer (1894–1967) also wrote about African American life in the South in his influential novel *Cane* (1923), and also included vignettes about urban black life in Washington, D.C. Countee Cullen wrote poems dealing with race and racism, such as "Incident" (1925), yet he used a more traditional style and formal language that relied upon classical literary models, and did not wish to be categorized as simply a "Negro poet."

A Renaissance in Visual Arts

As with music and literature, the visual arts were revitalized by African American artists who achieved success by introducing their own unique perspectives into their work. This focus on African American culture was apparent in both style and subject matter. Sargent Claude Johnson (1888–1967) was noted for his sculpture, which showed distinct African influences. Jacob Lawrence (1917–2000) grew up in Harlem in the 1920s, and studied in the Harlem Art Workshop. His paintings are marked by strong color and simple shapes. Sculptor Augusta Savage (1892–1962), who taught art to students in Harlem, was known for her depictions of Harlem residents both famous (like Marcus Garvey) and anonymous (as with *Gamin*, her well-known bust of a neighborhood child). Muralists like Charles Alston (1907–77) and Aaron Douglas (1899–1979) captured people and events significant to African American culture in large-scale works that still adorn public buildings across the country.

The Great Depression of the 1930s, a period of economic hardship for people worldwide, brought an end to the excitement surrounding the Harlem Renaissance. Some of the artists who contributed to the movement relocated to different cities, or traveled in search of paying work. Many of these artists continued to create, however, and they also served to inspire newer artists who found a growing acceptance from white audiences, even as they dealt with themes of racial injustice. In this way, the Harlem Renaissance continued to influence the American arts for decades after its conclusion.

❖ BLACK THEATER ACHIEVES BREAKTHROUGHS IN MID-CENTURY

Up until the 1930s, stage portrayals of African American life had been, for the most part, less than authentic. They relied on comedy and music instead of offering realistic and sympathetic portrayals of African American struggles. Even more serious works were often focused upon a single cause or issue, such as lynching, and were more concerned with delivering a message than providing genuine insight into African American culture. In the decades that followed, however, African American stage productions grew increasingly sophisticated and drew more fully upon the experiences of blacks in their search for dramatic truth.

African American Musicals Achieve Breakthroughs

African American musicals had already achieved success by the 1930s, most notably *Shuffle Along* (1921). *Shuffle Along* was the first all-black musical on Broadway. It was written, directed, produced, and performed by African Americans, and ran for more than 500 performances, making it a landmark production in the history of African American theater. *Shuffle Along* was a lighthearted comedy that appealed to white and black audiences. It paved the way for several more African American musicals in the years immediately following. These included: *Strut Miss Lizzie*, *Plantation Review*, *Oh Joy!*, and *Liza* (1922); *How Come?* and *Runnin' Wild* (1923); and *The Chocolate Dandies* and *Dixie to Broadway* (1924).

Porgy and Bess and *Anna Lucasta* Are Successful, but Not Authentic

Porgy and Bess (1935) brought stage portrayals of African American life and music to a new artistic depth and range. The musical, written by composer George Gershwin (1898–1937) and author DuBose Heyward (1885–1940), was based on Heyward's 1925 novel *Porgy*. It tells the tale of a disabled black man and the slum neighborhood in which he lives. The slum is called Catfish Row, and is based on an actual neighborhood in Charleston, South Carolina, where Heyward lived. Although Heyward was white, his portrayal of life among poor blacks was considered sympathetic and believable by many critics, including African American author Langston Hughes.

Gershwin considered the work to be a uniquely American opera. His music drew heavily upon jazz and blues, and the cast consisted of highly trained African American performers. Gershwin had previously won a Pulitzer Prize for the musical *Of Thee I Sing* (1931), and *Porgy and Bess* would be his last major creation for the stage. Despite the popularity of several of its songs, however, the production was not entirely well received, and was not truly a work of African American culture. White audiences at the time were ill-prepared for a musical in which nearly every character is African American. Some black audiences considered the characters—which include a beggar, a killer, and a drug dealer—to reflect poorly on African Americans as a whole. The musical remained controversial in its many subsequent revivals, as well as its 1959 film adaptation by Otto Preminger.

Although black musicals did not disappear entirely after *Porgy and Bess,* stage works by and for African Americans became increasingly dramatic in nature. Many playwrights associated with the Harlem Renaissance wrote plays that tackled social injustice. The Harlem Renaissance refers to the flowering of the arts beginning in the 1920s in the New York City neighborhood of Harlem. Langston Hughes opened several theaters, including the Harlem Suitcase Theater, where his political play *Don't You Want to Be Free?* (1938) appeared. Between 1935 and 1939, the Federal Theatre Project (FTP) provided funding for productions of classical stage works featuring African American casts. FTP-funded projects included a 1936 production popularly called the "Voodoo *Macbeth*," a production of William Shakespeare's *Macbeth* set in Haiti. The play, directed by Orson Welles (1915–85), featured an all-black cast. Other FTP-funded plays include a play by Arna Bontemps (1902–73) and Countee Cullen called *The Conjure Man Dies* (1936) and George MacEntee's *The Case of Philip Lawrence* (1937).

The greatest success of the FTP was the play *Anna Lucasta* (1944), about a reformed prostitute who finds love—much to the dismay of her scheming family. The play, by Philip Yordan (1914–2003), was originally written with

Lafayette Theater in Harlem during the Harlem Renaissance.
© Bettmann/Corbis

the main characters being of Polish descent. The FTP version featured an African American cast with adaptations by Abram Hill (1911–86), and became a success without the original author even knowing about it. It opened at the American Negro Theater in Harlem, but quickly moved to Broadway, where it was a resounding success. Like *Porgy and Bess,* however, the play clearly originated from a white author, and a film adaptation in 1949 even recast the characters as whites, as in the original version. Despite its success, *Anna Lucasta* could not shake its white roots, and the theater world was left waiting for its first major drama written by an African American.

Inspired by True Life, Hansberry Strikes Gold

African American playwright Lorraine Hansberry (1930–65) gained fame as the creator of the drama *A Raisin in the Sun* in 1959. The play became the first Broadway production written by an African American woman, and the first Broadway production directed by an African American. She based the play on her family's experiences integrating the neighborhood of Woodlawn.

Porgy Songs Recorded Widely

Despite the controversy surrounding the characters in *Porgy and Bess* and the fact that the musical was written by two white men, few critics had anything negative to say about George Gershwin's music. The score of *Porgy* is generally considered a masterpiece. Songs such as "Summertime," "I Loves You Porgy," and "It Ain't Necessarily So" have been widely recorded by African American jazz and opera singers, including Ella Fitzgerald, Louis Armstrong, Leontyne Price, William Warfield, and Nina Simone. Jazz composer and musician Miles Davis released an instrumental interpretation of *Porgy and Bess* in a 1958 album that is widely regarded as one of the greatest jazz albums of all time.

Hansberry was the daughter of a successful real-estate broker in Chicago. Throughout Chicago in the 1920s and 1930s, predominantly white neighborhoods had adopted covenants, or agreements between all the neighbors, stating that they would not sell to black families. However, two factors led to inconsistent enforcement of these covenants. The first was the Great Depression, during which many Americans were unemployed and property owners were willing to rent or sell to anyone who could afford it, regardless of race. The second was the Great Migration, in which millions of African Americans moved from the South to the urban centers of the northern United States, including Chicago.

The Hansberry family purchased a home in Woodlawn, a mainly white area covered by one of these covenants. The local property owners' association attempted to prevent the family from moving in, and threatened the family in an attempt to scare them out of the neighborhood. A lawsuit over the covenant eventually reached the United States Supreme Court in 1940, which ruled that the Hansberrys could not be kept out of the home. Lorraine grew up amid this turmoil, shunned by her white neighbors and cut off from any other members of the African American community.

Hansberry relocated to New York City to become a writer in 1950. *A Raisin in the Sun* was her first play. The drama was a critical and popular success, and Hansberry won the New York Drama Critics Circle Award for best play. In addition to establishing the careers of African American stage performers like Sidney Poitier (1927–) and Ruby Dee (1924–), the play

Sidney Poitier performs in the stage play *A Raisin in the Sun*, along with Ruby Dee (left) and Diana Sands (right), c. 1954.
© *Bettmann/Corbis*

paved the way for future African American playwrights to portray black life in the United States through their own eyes.

❖ THE FEDERAL ART PROJECT FUNDS BLACK MURALISTS

Murals are large-scale works of art that are applied directly to the surface of a building or other structure. Murals are often found on the walls of public buildings, and usually depict a single grand scene. Some murals show a progression through time from one end to the other, displaying the history of a place or organization. Murals became popular in the first decades of the twentieth century as a way to beautify neighborhoods and to express cultural identity.

The FAP Helps Artists Find Their Voices

During the 1930s, the United States was in the grip of the Great Depression. As many as one in four able-bodied American workers could not find a job. This economic downturn hit especially hard in African American communities in the northern United States, where millions of black workers had migrated to find jobs. Unemployment rates among blacks were about twice as high as the national average. The federal government created the Works Progress Administration (WPA; later called the Work Projects Administration) as a way to provide jobs to Americans and to fund projects with lasting cultural benefits. The effects of the WPA were especially helpful in areas like Harlem, a largely African American neighborhood in New York City.

One project backed by the WPA was the Federal Art Project (FAP), which funded the creation of murals on government buildings around the country during the 1930s. A handful of artists were already experienced mural painters at the time. One of these was Aaron Douglas, an African American artist who created some murals in Harlem and in Nashville, Tennessee, during the 1920s and early 1930s. Douglas found himself in constant demand, painting murals in North Carolina, Texas, Illinois, and New York. Many other artists also took up mural painting, even though they had previously worked on a much smaller scale.

Aaron Douglas was a popular muralist during the 1930s. *Schomburg Center/Art Resource, NY*

Charles Alston was one of these artists. He had become famous as an illustrator, working on book covers for Langston Hughes and jazz album covers. Alston was one of several artists commissioned to create murals for the Harlem Hospital Center in 1935. After the artists' sketches had been approved by the FAP, the superintendent of the hospital raised objections to the overly Negro subject matter of the works. The artists received an outpouring of community support, causing the hospital to change its position. Work on the murals began. Alston's two murals, *Magic in Medicine* and *Modern Medicine,* were not completed until 1940. The murals feature both white and African American figures working together, expressing a hope for integration that was ahead of its time. *Magic in Medicine* contains many elements significant to African American culture, including African sculpture and traditional spiritual healers.

White and Biggers Carry the Movement Beyond the FAP

Charles White (1918–79) was an artist who began his career as a sign painter, so mural work suited his talents and experience. He had studied the work of Mexican muralist Diego Rivera (1886–1957), which often contained political messages. His first mural project for the FAP was *Five Great American Negroes* (1939), which sought to call attention to significant African American historical figures whom White felt had been ignored by white historians. His subsequent murals remained highly political, depicting figures like abolitionist John Brown (1800–59), who led a revolt to end slavery before the Civil War. White's mural *The Contribution of the Negro to Democracy in America* (1943) is often cited as his masterwork of the mural form. Created for the Wainwright Auditorium of Hampton Institute (now Hampton University), the work depicts historic instances of black resistance to white oppression. It also includes images of notable contemporary African Americans, including actor Paul Robeson (1898–1976).

One Hampton student who watched White create his famous mural was John Biggers (1924–2001). Biggers would himself carry on the tradition of African American mural art. Biggers was chosen to create a new department of art at Texas Southern University in Houston in 1949. There, he co-created a mural painting program that involved students in the production of art throughout their community. Biggers's most famous mural is *The Contribution of Negro Women to American Life and Education* (1952), which features historical figures such as Phyllis Wheatley (1753–84), Sojourner Truth (1797–1883), and Harriet Tubman (1822–1913). Even in his murals that did not specifically address African American history, such as *Birth from the Sea* (1966), Biggers uses mainly African American figures and incorporates elements of African culture. The work combines the European myth of the birth of Venus with a legend the painter himself heard from locals in Ghana during a visit there.

Mural art saw a renewed popularity in African American communities during the late 1960s and 1970s. Chicago's Organization of Black American Culture (OBAC), for example, produced its famous Wall of Respect in 1967. This large mural celebrated African American leaders of the civil rights movement. The Wall of Respect inspired similar murals in major cities across the United States.

❖ NOVELS OF PROTEST HIGHLIGHT RACISM

A protest novel is a work in which an author calls attention to a negative aspect of society and takes a stand against it. By the 1940s and 1950s, African American literature had developed to the point that black writers could impact white society with fiction that protested the treatment of blacks in the United States. The three major African American protest novels of this era were *Native Son* (1940) by Richard Wright, *Invisible Man* (1952) by Ralph Ellison, and *Go Tell It on the Mountain* (1953) by James Baldwin.

Wright Exposes the Frustration of Black Americans

Richard Wright's *Native Son* was the first novel written by an African American to make a significant impact on white American culture. The novel tells the tale of Bigger Thomas, a young black man who lives with his family in a rat-infested slum. He gets a job as a chauffeur for a wealthy white family named the Daltons, but finds their kindness confusing, since his previous experiences with white people had been negative. The daughter of the family gets drunk one night with her boyfriend, and Bigger drives her home and carries her up to her room. When the girl's blind mother enters the room, Bigger is afraid that she will discover him there and accuse him of harming her daughter. In order to keep the drunken daughter quiet, he puts a pillow over her face. He ends up suffocating her.

Bigger tries to blame the murder on the girl's boyfriend, Jan, who nonetheless tries to help Bigger receive fair treatment from the justice system. Although the initial killing was an accident, Bigger then rapes and kills a black female friend. He ends up being arrested and sentenced to death, and never admits to the first, accidental killing.

The message of the novel is that most African American men are given no chance to distinguish themselves in life, except through violence or crime. Bigger does not feel that he has an identity at all until he becomes a killer. The book also points out how surface-level kindness toward African Americans often masks fear, mistrust, and scorn. The Dalton family, for example, are polite and friendly to Bigger, yet they also own the rat-infested building in which his family lives. They seem to show no consideration for the African American people who live in the building they own.

The book was a great success, and opened a dialogue about the cultural gap between black and white Americans. However, some criticized the book for depicting black men as uncontrollably violent and dangerous. Wright justified his portrayal in an essay called "How 'Bigger' Was Born" (1940), noting that Bigger was inspired by several people he knew throughout his life. They had all rebelled against the white power structure in some way, and although most were eventually killed or jailed, their rebellious actions had given them identity and purpose. Wright's novel gave voice to a generation of African Americans frustrated by their inability to fulfill their own potential.

Ellison Creates an Invisible Narrator

Ralph Ellison's *Invisible Man* also has a main character who faces obstacles to success. Like Bigger, the unnamed narrator of *Invisible Man* has no identity because he is essentially "invisible" to society as a whole. Ellison's narrator lives in the basement of a whites-only apartment building, and taps into the building's electricity for his own use. He relates the events of his life that led him to this point.

The narrator of *Invisible Man* is highly educated; he's at the top of his class in high school. Before he is given a college scholarship, however, he is forced to fight several other black boys in a ring while blindfolded, all for the amusement of white onlookers. He is later expelled from college because of the actions of a wealthy white donor. The president of the college even destroys the narrator's chances of finding decent employment by writing sealed letters of "recommendation" that actually warn potential employers not to hire him. The narrator works at a factory until he is injured in an explosion, caused when he follows the directions of a devious white coworker. The narrator later becomes involved in workers' rights activism, but is hounded by a violent black rights group that believes he is just a puppet for white leaders. In the end, a race riot erupts in the streets, and the narrator finds refuge in his secret basement home. However, after telling his story, he appears ready to reenter society.

Ralph Ellison's novel *Invisible Man* expressed the frustrations of African Americans in the mid-twentieth century. *Ben Martin/Time & Life Pictures/ Getty Images*

The novel was well received by readers and critics, and won the National Book Award in 1953. Many people—including the author—regard it as more of an artistic work than a novel of protest, though the book clearly expresses the frustrations felt by millions of African Americans in the 1950s.

Baldwin Tackles Religion and Race

James Baldwin's *Go Tell It on the Mountain* is a book about African American identity, though its elements of social protest are far less obvious than those in Richard Wright's *Native Son* or Ellison's *Invisible Man*. The novel tells of several members of a Harlem family who search for answers in religion, but are often held back by their own shortcomings and by mistreatment from whites. In the book, the character of John is a young man dominated by his strict stepfather, who is a preacher. This parallels

"Everybody's Protest Novel"

During the 1940s, James Baldwin befriended Richard Wright, whose work he greatly admired. Their friendship ended, however, when Baldwin published what is now considered one of the most important essays on African American fiction in the twentieth century: "Everybody's Protest Novel" (1949). In the essay, Baldwin takes aim at Harriet Beecher Stowe's classic abolitionist protest novel *Uncle Tom's Cabin* (1852), calling it a bad novel because its characters and plot had been made shallow and obvious in order for the novel to serve as a blunt protest against slavery. He said that *Native Son*, another protest novel, suffered from the same problem for the same reason. Baldwin argued that black writers needed to move beyond the conventions of protest fiction in order to reach their potential as literary artists.

Baldwin's own early life. The author famously criticized Wright's *Native Son* for its focus on a message of protest and its lack of believable characters. Baldwin thought that any protest novel should succeed first as a work of literature, and only second as a message of protest. For this reason, Baldwin drew inspiration from his life and wove these autobiographical elements into his story.

The brutal actions of white characters are brief and mostly exist at the margins of the tale. A black girl from the neighborhood is raped by several white men, and the description of the event is deliberately vague. The aftermath of the crime is violent but ends quickly. Later, a black man is beaten by white police officers during an interrogation about a crime he did not commit. Even this action is viewed more as a comment on religious belief than on race relations. The beaten man wonders aloud why Jesus does not protect him, since he is innocent.

Native Son, Invisible Man, and *Go Tell It on the Mountain* are all novels that protest the conditions of African Americans during the middle of the twentieth century. They served as important entry points for white Americans seeking to better understand black culture. They also provided common points of reference for activists across the country who were just beginning to work together in the struggle for civil rights.

❖ ALVIN AILEY INFLUENCES MODERN DANCE

New York City was viewed as the cultural center for African American dance and other arts during the middle of the twentieth century. By the 1940s, the most popular forms of dance in the United States were variants of swing, inspired by African American movements and music that originated in Harlem. The world of classical dance was just beginning to open up to African American performers like Janet Collins (1917–2003), who would become the first permanent African American member of New York's Metropolitan Opera ballet company. At the same time, a few African American innovators were making strides in expanding the realm of modern artistic dance.

Alvin Ailey (1931–89) was raised in a dance tradition far removed from New York. Born in a small town in central Texas, Ailey relocated to Los Angeles with his mother when he was eleven years old. His early experience with dance came from many sources, but mainly Hollywood films in which white performers danced routines that were often inspired by African American performers. As a teenager he became involved with a dance studio run by Lester Horton, a film choreographer. Working with Horton exposed Ailey to a wide variety of dance types, and he followed Horton's emphasis on using the full body in dance rather than just the arms and legs.

It was also through the Horton dance troupe that Ailey eventually traveled to New York to perform in 1953. Ailey could tell that the New York dance scene was much livelier than the one he had known in California. He took charge of the Horton dance troupe's choreography when Horton died in 1953. Ailey found success as a creator as well as a performer. In 1954, he returned to New York to work on Broadway, and in 1959, he opened his own dance studio there. The dances he created were a blend of more formal styles like ballet and grand Hollywood musical routines he learned from Horton, and the popular dances associated with jazz and other African American musical styles. He utilized blues music in many of his works, which were frequently themed around African American life. He also made use of spirituals, traditional African American religious songs that had originated during the days of slavery.

His audiences were largely African American, and though they were familiar with much of the music he used, they were not accustomed to artistic dance. Ailey and his dance troupe managed to succeed despite the audience's lack of familiarity. His most acclaimed work was *Revelations* (1960), which relates the history of the African American religious spirit in the United States, from slavery to modern times. The company toured the United States as well as Asia and Australia throughout the early 1960s.

Alvin Ailey (center) greatly influenced modern dance through his innovative use of dance forms associated with African American musical traditions. *Hulton Archive/Getty Images*

Ailey offered opportunities to African American dancers, but his company never excluded talented dancers of any race.

Ailey was not the only African American to make an impression on modern dance. Katherine Dunham (1909–2006) also ran a dance studio in New York, and her academic work studying Caribbean cultures had a direct impact on her dances. She incorporated traditional dance movements she saw performed in Haiti and Martinique, among other places. These dances featured more dramatic movements of the torso and limbs than is usually seen in classical dance. Pearl Primus (1919–94), originally from the island of Trinidad, also brought a Caribbean influence to modern dance. Primus was known for creating dance routines that reflected other significant works of African American culture. For example, in 1944, she created a dance performance for the Langston Hughes poem, "The Negro Speaks of Rivers" (1921). In 1945, she created a routine based on the poem and song "Strange Fruit" (1936) by Abel Meeropol (1903–86), which depicts a lynching in the South.

LANGSTON HUGHES REMEMBERS THE HARLEM RENAISSANCE (1940)

The Harlem Renaissance was the flowering of art and culture that swept through the African American community in the 1920s. It was a time when African American culture came into greater acceptance with whites, particularly in urban communities that had substantial black populations. African American musical forms like jazz were all the rage, and it was stylish for white people to travel to nightclubs in the Harlem neighborhood of New York City to watch black performers. The popularity of African American culture, however, did not translate into greater equality for African Americans. The end of the popularity of African American culture coincided with the end of American economic prosperity during the Great Depression in the 1930s. African Americans would have to struggle to obtain equal rights for another forty years.

Langston Hughes was one of the most celebrated authors of the Harlem Renaissance. In the following excerpt from his 1940 autobiography *The Big Sea*, Hughes describes the time "when the Negro was in vogue," noting the artistic excellence and success of many black performers and artists. But the very phrase "in vogue" indicates the superficial nature of this success, which Hughes also describes.

....

WHEN THE NEGRO WAS IN VOGUE

The 1920's were the years of Manhattan's black **Renaissance.** It began with *Shuffle Along, Running Wild*, and the Charleston. Perhaps some people would say even with *The Emperor Jones,* Charles Gilpin, and the tom-toms at the Provincetown. But certainly it was the musical revue, *Shuffle Along,* that gave a scintillating send-off to that Negro **vogue** in Manhattan, which reached its peak just before the crash of 1929, the crash that sent Negroes, white folks, and all rolling down the hill toward the Works Progress Administration.

Shuffle Along was a honey of a show. Swift, bright, funny, rollicking, and gay, with a dozen danceable, singable tunes. Besides, look who were in it: The now famous choir director, Hall Johnson, and the composer, William Grant Still, were a part of the orchestra. Eubie Blake and Noble Sissle wrote the music and played and acted in the show. Miller and Lyles were the comics. Florence Mills skyrocketed to fame in the second act. Trixie Smith sang "He May Be Your Man But He Comes to See Me Sometimes." And Caterina Jarboro, now a European **prima donna,** and the internationally celebrated Josephine Baker were merely in the chorus. Everybody

Renaissance
A flowering of the arts and other cultural areas

Vogue
Fashion or style; to be "in vogue" means to be fashionable or popular

Prima Donna
The lead female singer in an opera company

Innumerable

More than can be counted

was in the audience—including me. People came back to see it **innumerable** times. It was always packed.

To see *Shuffle Along* was the main reason I wanted to go to Columbia. When I saw it, I was thrilled and delighted. From then on I was in the gallery of the Cort Theatre every time I got a chance. That year, too, I saw Katharine Cornell in *A Bill of Divorcement,* Margaret Wycherly in *The Verge,* Maugham's *The Circle* with Mrs. Leslie Carter, and the Theatre Guild production of Kaiser's *From Morn Till Midnight.* But I remember *Shuffle Along* best of all. It gave just the proper push—a pre-Charleston kick—to that Negro vogue of the '20s, that spread to books, African sculpture, music, and dancing.

Put down the 1920's for the rise of Roland Hayes, who packed Carnegie Hall, the rise of Paul Robeson in New York and London, of Florence Mills over two continents, of Rose McClendon in Broadway parts that never measured up to her, the booming voice of Bessie Smith and the low moan of Clara on thousands of records, and the rise of that grand comedienne of song, Ethel Waters, singing: "Charlie's elected now! He's in right for sure!" Put down the 1920's for Louis Armstrong and Gladys Bentley and Josephine Baker.

White people began to come to Harlem in droves. For several years they packed the expensive Cotton Club on Lenox Avenue. But I was never there, because the Cotton Club was a Jim Crow club for gangsters and monied whites. They were not cordial to Negro patronage, unless you were a celebrity like Bojangles. So Harlem Negroes did not like the Cotton Club and never appreciated its Jim Crow policy in the very heart of their dark community. Nor did ordinary Negroes like the growing **influx** of whites toward Harlem after sundown, flooding the little **cabarets** and bars where formerly only colored people laughed and sang, and where now the strangers were given the best ringside tables to sit and stare at the Negro customers—like amusing animals in a zoo.

Influx

An inward flow of something to a certain point or location

Cabarets

Clubs that featured shows combining dance, song, and theatrical routines

The Negroes said: "We can't go downtown and sit and stare at you in your clubs. You won't even let us in your clubs." But they didn't say it out loud—for Negroes are practically never rude to white people. So thousands of whites came to Harlem night after night, thinking the Negroes loved to have them there, and firmly believing that all Harlemites left their houses at sundown to sing and dance in cabarets, because most of the whites saw nothing but the cabarets, not the houses.

Grievous

Obviously incorrect or deliberately meant to cause grief

Some of the owners of Harlem clubs, delighted at the flood of white patronage, made the **grievous** error of barring their own race, after the manner of the famous Cotton Club. But most of these quickly lost business and folded up, because they failed to realize that a large part of the Harlem attraction for downtown New Yorkers lay in simply watching the colored customers amuse themselves. And the smaller clubs, of course, had no big floor shows or a name band like the Cotton Club, where Duke Ellington usually held forth, so, without black patronage, they were not amusing at all.

Some of the small clubs, however, had people like Gladys Bentley, who was something worth discovering in those days, before she got famous, acquired an **accompanist,** specially written material, and conscious vulgarity. But for two or three amazing years, Miss Bentley sat, and played a big piano all night long, literally all night, without stopping—singing songs like "The St. James Infirmary," from ten in the evening until dawn, with scarcely a break between the notes, sliding from one song to another, with a powerful and continuous underbeat of jungle rhythm. Miss Bentley was an amazing exhibition of musical energy—a large, dark, masculine lady, whose feet pounded the floor while her fingers pounded the keyboard—a perfect piece of African sculpture, animated by her own rhythm.

But when the place where she played became too well known, she began to sing with an accompanist, became a star, moved to a larger place, then downtown, and is now in Hollywood. The old magic of the woman and the piano and the night and the rhythm being one is gone. But everything goes, one way or another. The '20's are gone and lots of fine things in Harlem night life have disappeared like snow in the sun—since it became utterly commercial, planned for the downtown tourist trade, and therefore dull.

The **lindy-hoppers** at the Savoy even began to practice acrobatic routines, and to do absurd things for the entertainment of the whites, that probably never would have entered their heads to attempt merely for their own effortless amusement. Some of the lindy-hoppers had cards printed with their names on them and became dance professors teaching the tourists. Then Harlem nights became show nights for the Nordics.

Some critics say that this is what happened to certain Negro writers, too—that they ceased to write to amuse themselves and began to write to amuse and entertain white people, and in so doing distorted and over-colored their material, and left out a great many things they thought would offend their American brothers of a lighter complexion. Maybe—since Negroes have writer-racketeers, as has any other race. But I have known almost all of them, and most of the good ones have tried to be honest, write honestly, and express their world as they saw it.

All of us know that the gay and sparkling life of the so-called Negro Renaissance of the '20's was not so gay and sparkling beneath the surface as it looked. Carl Van Vechten, in the character of Byron in *Nigger Heaven,* captured some of the bitterness and frustration of literary Harlem that Wallace Thurman later so effectively poured into his *Infants of the Spring*—the only novel by a Negro about that fantastic period when Harlem was in vogue.

It was a period when, at almost every Harlem upper-crust dance or party, one would be introduced to various distinguished white celebrities there as guests. It was a period when almost any Harlem Negro of any social importance at all would be likely to say casually: "As I was remarking the other day to Heywood—," meaning Heywood Broun. Or: "As I said to George—," referring to George Gershwin. It was a period when

Accompanist
A musician who plays with another performer, often a singer, who is considered the star of the show

Lindy-Hoppers
Dancers who performed a variation of the Charleston known as the Lindy Hop, which usually involved dramatic physical movements such as spins and flips

local and visiting royalty were not at all uncommon in Harlem. And when the parties of A'Lelia Walker, the Negro heiress, were filled with guests whose names would turn any Nordic social climber green with envy. It was a period when Harold Jackman, a handsome young Harlem school teacher of modest means, calmly announced one day that he was sailing for the Riviera for a **fortnight,** to attend Princess Murat's yachting party. It was a period when Charleston preachers opened up shouting churches as sideshows for white tourists. It was a period when at least one charming colored chorus girl, amber enough to pass for a Latin American, was living in a pent house, with all her bills paid by a gentleman whose name was banker's magic on Wall Street. It was a period when every season there was at least one hit play on Broadway acted by a Negro cast. And when books by Negro authors were being published with much greater frequency and much more publicity than ever before or since in history. It was a period when white writers wrote about Negroes more successfully (commercially speaking) than Negroes did about themselves. It was the period (God help us) when Ethel Barrymore appeared in blackface in *Scarlet Sister Mary!* It was the period when the Negro was in vogue.

Chauve-Souris

Literally, "The Bat"; a
touring show from
Russia that was briefly
popular in the United
States in the early
1900s

I was there. I had a swell time while it lasted. But I thought it wouldn't last long. (I remember the vogue for things Russian, the season the **Chauve-Souris** came to town.) For how could a large and enthusiastic number of people be crazy about Negroes forever? But some Harlemites thought the **millennium** had come. They thought the race problem had at last been solved through Art plus Gladys Bentley. They were sure the New Negro would lead a new life from then on in green pastures of tolerance created by Countee Cullen, Ethel Waters, Claude McKay, Duke Ellington, Bojangles, and Alain Locke.

Millennium

A period of time one
thousand years long;
also used to refer to a
time of happiness and
peace that some
believe will arrive
sometime in
the future

I don't know what made any Negroes think that—except that they were mostly intellectuals doing the thinking. The ordinary Negroes hadn't heard of the Negro Renaissance. And if they had, it hadn't raised their wages any. As for all those white folks in the **speakeasies** and night clubs of Harlem—well, maybe a colored man could find *some* place to have a drink that the tourists hadn't yet discovered.

Speakeasies

Establishments that
secretly sold alcohol
during Prohibition,
the period during
which the sale
and consumption of
alcohol was illegal in
the United States

BILLIE HOLIDAY SINGS THE BLUES (1956)

Billie Holiday was one of the most famous blues singers of the twentieth century. Her ability to convey powerful emotion with her singing was the hallmark of her career from the 1930s until her career was cut short by her death in 1959. In this excerpt from her 1956 memoir *Lady Sings the Blues*, Holiday recounts her first break as a singer in a Harlem club.

• •

By the time mom and I had got together and found us a place of our own in Harlem the Depression was on. At least, so we heard tell. A depression was nothing new to us, we'd always had it. The only thing new about it was the bread lines. And they were about the only thing we missed.

We moved into an apartment in 139th Street, and not long after, for the first time since I could remember, Mom was too sick to make Mass on Sunday. For her, that was really sick. Give her coffee every morning and Mass every Sunday, and she thought she could go on working forever. But she had to quit working out as a maid. She couldn't even walk, her stomach was so shot. She just had to stay put in bed.

What little money we had saved started running out and she was getting panicky. She had worked for most of her life, and it was beginning to tell on her. For almost half of that time she had been grieving over Pop. This didn't help any . . . .

About that time Fletcher Henderson's band was working downtown at the Roseland Ballroom. It was the first Negro band to work there, and Pop Holiday was with them on the guitar. Sick as she was, Mom was too proud to turn to Pop and ask his help with the rent money. But not me.

I used to go right down there and haunt him. Pop was in his early thirties then, but he didn't want anyone to guess it—especially the young chicks who used to hang around the entrance waiting for the musicians.

I was around fifteen then, but I looked plenty old enough to vote. I used to wait for him down in the hallway. I'd try to catch his eye and call out to him, "Hey, Daddy." I soon found out just waving at him would make him feel like forty-five, and he didn't like that. He used to plead with me.

"Please," he'd say, "whatever you do, don't call me Daddy in front of these people."

"I'm going to call you Daddy all night unless you give me some damn money for rent," I'd tell him. That would do it.

I'd take the money home to Mom, proud as all get out. But I couldn't hurt her feelings by telling her where it came from. If she kept worrying me about it, I'd finally tell her I stole it. Then we'd have a fight and she'd tell me I was going to end up in jail again.

One day when the rent was overdue, she got a notice that the law was going to put us out on the street. It was in the dead cold of winter and she couldn't even walk.

I didn't know they did things like that up North. Bad as it was down South, they never put you out on the street. When we were due to get set out on the street the next morning, I told Mom I would steal or

Billie Holiday singing in a club in 1942. *Gjon Mili/Time & Life Pictures/Getty Images*

murder or do anything before I'd let them pull that. It was cold as all hell that night, and I walked out without any kind of coat.

I walked down Seventh Avenue from 139th Street to 133rd Street, busting in every joint trying to find a job. In those days 133rd Street was the real swing street, like 52nd Street later tried to be. It was jumping with after-hours spots, regular hour joints, restaurants, cafés, a dozen to a block.

Finally, when I got to Pod's and Jerry's, I was desperate. I went in and asked for the boss. I think I talked to Jerry. I told him I was a dancer and I wanted to try out. I knew exactly two steps, the time step and the crossover. I didn't even know the word "audition" existed, but that was what I wanted.

So Jerry sent me over to the piano player and told me to dance. I started, and it was pitiful. I did my two steps over and over until he barked at me and told me to quit wasting his time.

They were going to throw me out on my ear, but I kept begging for the job. Finally the piano player took pity on me. He squashed out his cigarette, looked up at me, and said, "Girl, can you sing?"

I said, "Sure I can sing, what good is that?" I had been singing all my life, but I enjoyed it too much to think I could make any real money at it. Besides, those were the days of the Cotton Club and all those glamour pusses who didn't do nothing but look pretty, shake a little, and take money off tables.

I thought that was the only way to make money, and I needed forty-five bucks by morning to keep Mom from getting set out in the street. Singers were never heard of then, unless it was Paul Robeson, Julian Bledsoe, or someone **legit** like that.

So I asked him to play "Trav'lin' All Alone." That came closer than anything to the way I felt. And some part of it must have come across. The whole joint quieted down. If someone had dropped a pin, it would have sounded like a bomb. When I finished, everybody in the joint was crying in their beer, and I picked thirty-eight bucks up off the floor. When I left the joint that night I split with the piano player and still took home fifty-seven dollars.

I went out and bought a whole chicken and some baked beans—Mom loved baked beans—and raced up Seventh Avenue to the house. When I showed Mom the money for the rent and told her I had a regular job singing for eighteen dollars a week, she could hardly believe it.

As soon as she could get out of bed she came down to see for herself and became my biggest booster. In those days they had five or six singers in the clubs and they called them "ups." One girl would be "up" and she would go from table to table singing. Then the next one would be "up" and she'd take over. I was an "up" from midnight every night until the tips started thinning out, maybe around three o'clock the next morning.

In those days, too, all the girls took money off the tables, but I broke that up. With my first loot I got me a pair of fancy drawers with little rhinestones on them. But I didn't like the idea of showing my body. There was nothing wrong with my body, I just didn't like the idea. When the time came to take those bills off the table, I was always messing up.

One night a millionaire came in the joint and put out a twenty-dollar bill on the table. I wanted that twenty-dollar bill so bad. I really tried, but I dropped it so many times he got disgusted and said, "Why, you're nothing but a punk kid. Get the hell away from here."

When I finished my "up" he must have felt sorry for me. Anyway, he asked me to come back and have a drink with him. When I did, he gave me the twenty-dollar bill in my hand. I figured, if a millionaire could give me money that way, everybody could. So from then on I wouldn't take money off tables. When I came to work the other girls used to razz me, call me "Duchess" and say, "Look at her, she thinks she's a lady."

I hadn't got my title Lady Day yet, but that was the beginning of people calling me "Lady."

Research and Activity Ideas

1. African American scholars became increasingly interested in documenting and researching their cultural heritage during the Harlem Renaissance of the 1920s. Zora Neale Hurston, for example, spent time in the Caribbean collecting folktales told by locals of African descent. Dig into your own cultural heritage to find a similar type of story. It can be a story passed down within your own family, or it can be a tale familiar to people in the region where you live. Write down your own version of the tale. Try to keep the main details intact, but feel free to add your own creative touch.

2. African American artists received federal funding to create murals for government buildings across the country during the Great Depression of the 1930s. These murals often captured a specific event in African American history, or celebrated African American contributions to a certain field such as medicine. Using poster board or construction paper, create your own mural commemorating a significant event from the history of African American arts. You can use the chronology included in this chapter for ideas.

3. Blues and jazz music have been credited with introducing a number of unique elements into popular music. For example, jazz used rhythms that had not been heard in European-style music, and blues made use of the "blue notes" for which it was named. Create a list of all the characteristics you can identify that jazz and blues introduced to American popular music. Then find examples of each of these traits in modern songs. Do some elements seem more common than others in modern music?

4. James Baldwin criticized Richard Wright's novel *Native Son* because he felt that, while it made a compelling statement about race relations in the United States, it was not successful as a work of art. Many significant literary works by African Americans in the early twentieth century are concerned with political or social messages. Langston Hughes was an author who frequently presented political viewpoints in his poems. Read several of Hughes's poems that contain political messages, such as "Harlem" or "Let America Be America Again." In your opinion, does the political message get in the way of the poem's qualities as art? Why or why not? Write a short essay expressing your view.

5. Early twentieth-century stage productions that featured African American themes and casts tended to be either light-hearted comedies or dramas that focused on a particular issue, often at the expense of character development. African American theater became more

sophisticated as the century wore on, resulting in such important stage works as Lorraine Hansberry's *A Raisin in the Sun* in 1959. *A Raisin in the Sun* had psychologically complex characters while also exposing the racism of restrictive housing covenants that kept black families from buying into white neighborhoods. Think of an issue faced by African Americans during the time period between 1865 and 1965. Write a synopsis (an outline of the plot) of a play you would create to illustrate this issue.

 For More Information

BOOKS

Armstrong, Louis. *Satchmo: My Life in New Orleans.* Cambridge, MA: Da Capo Press, 1986.

Barnwell, Andrea D. *Charles White.* Rohnert Park, CA: Pomegranate Communications, 2002.

Berlin, Edward A. *King of Ragtime: Scott Joplin and His Era.* New York: Oxford University Press, 1994.

Dorinson, Joseph, and William Pencak, eds. *Paul Robeson: Essays on His Life and Legacy.* Jefferson, NC: McFarland, 2002.

Haugen, Brenda. *Langston Hughes: The Voice of Harlem.* Minneapolis, MN: Compass Point Books, 2006.

Hutchinson, George, ed. *The Cambridge Companion to the Harlem Renaissance.* New York: Cambridge University Press, 2007.

Jules-Rosette, Bennetta. *Josephine Baker in Art and Life: The Icon and the Image.* Urbana-Champaign, IL: University of Illinois Press, 2007.

Mathews, Marcia M. *Henry Ossawa Tanner: American Artist.* Chicago: The University of Chicago Press, 1994.

PERIODICALS

Garland, Phyl. "Gwendolyn Brooks: Poet Laureate." *Ebony,* vol. 23, no. 9 (July 1968): 48–56.

"James Van Der Zee: New life, new wife at age 94." *Ebony,* vol. 36, no. 7 (May 1981): 150–152.

WEB SITES

Alvin Ailey American Dance Theater Web site. "History and Timeline." http://www.alvinailey.org/page.php?p=stat&t;=h5&sec;=aaadt (accessed on January 1, 2010).

The Columbia University Institute for Research in African-American Studies. "Harlem Hospital WPA Murals." http://www.columbia.edu/cu/iraas/wpa/index.html (accessed on January 1, 2010).

chapter three *Business and Industry*

1867 February 22 The Pullman Company, a manufacturer and operator of luxury railroad sleeping cars, is founded and immediately institutes a policy of hiring only African Americans to work as porters.

1893 May 17 Frederick M. Jones, a gifted inventor who would go on to receive sixty-one patents over the course of his lifetime, is born in Covington, Kentucky.

1900 August 23 Booker T. Washington founds the National Negro Business League to promote African American business and entrepreneurship. The league eventually includes more than three hundred chapters throughout the United States.

1902 Annie Turnbo Malone begins selling hair straighteners, skin-care products, and other cosmetics designed for African American women through a company named Poro Systems based in St. Louis, Missouri.

1903 November 2 Maggie Lena Walker opens the St. Luke Penny Savings Bank and serves as its president. She is the first African American founder or president of a bank.

1905 Madame C. J. Walker, a former employee of Annie Malone's Poro Systems, goes into business for herself, selling hair straighteners, creams, and other styling products designed specifically for African American women.

1908 A'Lelia Walker goes to work for her mother, C. J. Walker, and is immediately responsible for running the company's Pittsburgh, Pennsylvania, office and overseeing the operation of the company's cosmetology school.

1910 The rise of sharecropping as a common method of farming increases the number of farms in the South to 3,097,547 from 672,313 in 1860.

1910 C. J. Walker moves the headquarters of her cosmetics business, the Madame C. J. Walker Manufacturing Company, from Denver, Colorado, to Indianapolis, Indiana, so that the company's mail-order business will be more centrally located.

1912 August Madame C. J. Walker takes the stage at the National Negro Business League's national convention in Chicago and criticizes Booker T. Washington, the organization's founder, for not inviting any women to speak to the convention.

1915 Henry Ford offers African Americans jobs in his automobile production facilities for the same wages and on the same terms that the jobs are offered to white employees.

1917 The number of African American–owned businesses in the United States increases to fifty thousand from four thousand in 1867, thanks in large part to credit and financing provided by black-owned banks.

1917 Annie Malone opens Poro College, the first school in American history to specialize in providing training in African American cosmetology, in St. Louis, Missouri.

1917 The Madame C. J. Walker Manufacturing Company has annual revenues of approximately five hundred thousand dollars, making it the largest African American–owned business in the United States.

1918 The Federal Division of Negro Economics is established. Its first mission is to mobilize African American labor in the war effort (the United States had just entered World War I), but it later becomes an employment opportunity agency.

1919 May 25 A'Lelia Walker becomes the president of the Madame C. J. Walker Manufacturing Company after Madame C. J. Walker dies unexpectedly at the age of fifty-one.

1920 Forty-six percent of all female domestic employees working in the United States are African American.

1925 August 25 A. Philip Randolph agrees to help railroad porters employed by the Pullman Company organize a union. The union becomes known as the Brotherhood of Sleeping Car Porters.

1926 Poro Systems has more than seventy-five thousand sales agents working in the United States and around the world.

1928 A'Lelia Walker oversees the opening of the Walker Building at 617 Indiana Avenue in Indianapolis, Indiana, the new world headquarters of the Madame C. J. Walker Manufacturing Company.

1930 Maggie Lena Walker merges the St. Luke Penny Savings Bank with two other black-owned banks to form the Consolidated Bank and Trust Company. The bank continues to operate in the twenty-first century, making it the oldest continuously operating African American–owned bank in the United States.

1936 January Sharecroppers and their families are evicted from their homes in Parkin, Arkansas, as punishment for having become members of the Southern Tenant Farmers' Union.

1937 April 25 The Brotherhood of Sleeping Car Porters becomes the first all-black union in American history to negotiate a labor agreement with a major corporation when it enters into a collective bargaining agreement with the Pullman Company.

1940 Of the 10,000 Americans working in the pre–World War II aircraft industry, just 240 (less than one-fifth of 1 percent) are African Americans.

1941 June 25 President Franklin D. Roosevelt signs Executive Order 8802, making it illegal for government agencies and private companies that do business with the government to refuse to hire African Americans.

1945 The percentage of female domestic employees working in the United States who are African American rises to 60 percent.

1946 Ophelia DeVore, one of the first African American fashion models in U.S. history, helps found the Grace Del Marco Agency, which is the only New York modeling agency that is willing to employ nonwhite models.

1960 African Americans hold approximately 16 percent of all jobs in the American automobile industry.

1960 Membership in the Brotherhood of Sleeping Car Porters declines from a peak of about fifteen thousand to approximately three thousand as planes replace railroads as the primary mode of passenger travel.

 *Overview*

African Americans made important progress in business and industry between 1865 and 1965. The end of slavery gave many African Americans the chance to participate in the economy for the first time. Racial discrimination, however, made it difficult for many African Americans to have successful careers. In the late 1800s, most African Americans lived in or close to poverty. There were some notable exceptions. African Americans began to find better opportunities in the early twentieth century. World War II (1939–45) and favorable changes to the law helped African Americans break into new professions and earn higher wages in the middle and latter part of the twentieth century.

Most jobs that were available to African Americans in the years immediately after the end of slavery involved farming, household service, or unskilled labor. The farming system of sharecropping emerged in the South almost as soon as the Civil War (1861–65) was over. In many ways, sharecropping took the place of slavery. Sharecropping is a method of farming in which a family farms land that is owned by someone else. The family pays the landowner half of what they make from selling their crops in exchange for using the land. More than 80 percent of African Americans in the South worked as sharecroppers in the late 1800s. Most sharecroppers earned very little money. Sharecropping remained common until the 1940s.

Many African Americans, especially women, also worked as domestic employees. Domestic employees do paid work in someone else's home. African American women made up a large portion of all domestic employees for the entire period from 1865 to 1965. The work of a domestic employee is physically taxing. In the late 1800s, domestic employees were expected to live with the family they worked for and work very long hours. Wages and hours improved in the early 1900s. Many African American women were able to get nondomestic jobs in industry during World War II because so many men who would otherwise fill the jobs were in the military. However, once the war was over, many of these women were forced to return to domestic employment.

African American leaders in the late 1800s worked hard to provide their fellow African Americans with better opportunities for education and employment. Booker T. Washington (1856–1915) was the most famous African American leader of the late 1800s. Washington believed that the best way for African Americans to improve their fortunes was to learn trade skills. Washington helped found the Tuskegee Normal and Industrial Institute in Alabama in 1881. The Tuskegee Institute provided its all-black student body with practical, hands-on job training. Another famous African

American leader, W. E. B. Du Bois (1868–1963), took a different strategy. He encouraged the best African American students to attain an education and become political leaders.

Some African Americans were able to find success in business despite the system of racial segregation in place throughout the South in the late 1800s and early 1900s. A large number of African American–owned businesses opened in the South during this time. They provided the goods and services African Americans needed but often could not get from white-owned businesses. African American banks were especially important at this time. They loaned money to other African American business owners and helped build a business community. Newspapers that specifically targeted an African American audience also met with great success.

Booker T. Washington aided the spread of African American businesses by founding the National Negro Business League in August 1900. The league promoted the commercial and financial success of black-owned businesses. League members did business with each other. They also shared information and strategies for how to succeed. The National Negro Business League had more than three hundred chapters in cities throughout the United States by 1907.

African American women made important inroads into the business world during this time. Annie Turnbo Malone (1869–1957) was one of the earliest African American women to own a successful business. She founded a company called Poro Systems that sold cosmetics and hair-care products to African American women. One of Malone's first employees, Madame C. J. Walker (1867–1919), founded a cosmetics company of her own. Malone and Walker were the first two African American women ever to become self-made millionaires. Walker's daughter, A'Lelia Walker (1885–1931), also became a successful businesswoman as well as a patron of the arts in the African American neighborhood of Harlem in New York City.

African Americans' economic fortunes began to improve in the early twentieth century. One example was the case of railroad porters. The Pullman Company, which manufactured and operated luxury railroad cars, had long employed African American men as porters. Pullman porters were well respected, but they worked long hours and earned low wages throughout the late 1800s and into the early 1900s. The porters tried for years to organize into a labor union. They finally succeeded in 1925. After twelve years of negotiations, they were able to sign a contract with the Pullman Company in 1937 that allowed them to work on more favorable terms. It was a major economic victory for African Americans.

The automobile industry was also a source of economic opportunity and advancement for many African Americans. The vast majority of African

Americans living in the United States in the late 1800s and early 1900s lived in the South. However, cities in the North and the West began to develop industrially in the early 1900s. Many African Americans left the South and moved to these cities in search of work between 1910 and 1930. Industrial jobs were often hard to get. However, the automobile industry, led by Henry Ford (1863–1947), began employing African Americans in the late 1920s. The number of African Americans employed in the automobile industry increased dramatically during World War II. Many African Americans retained their auto industry jobs even after the war ended. These jobs were many families' road to the middle class.

World War II itself also provided economic opportunities for many African Americans. In 1941, President Franklin D. Roosevelt (1882–1945) made it illegal for companies that worked for the government to practice racial discrimination in hiring. This was a very important change to the law because so many companies did business with the government during World War II. The war enabled many African Americans—including African American women—to obtain skilled, high-paying industrial jobs for the first time. The war helped African American men make permanent inroads into the industrial workforce. For African American women, however, the opportunities in the industrial sector the war provided largely proved to be temporary.

⭐ **Headline Makers**

•••

⭐ **OPHELIA DEVORE**
(1922–)

Madame Ophelia DeVore (1922–) was a famous African American fashion model in the first half of the twentieth century. She was the first African American model to achieve mainstream, commercial success. Later in her career, DeVore founded the Grace Del Marco Agency. The Grace Del Marco Agency played a critically important role in helping African American models to break into the fashion industry. DeVore developed and promoted the careers of many famous African American models. She spent much of her career working to make the world of fashion and beauty more hospitable to African American women. DeVore was a true pioneer in a field that long refused to make room for women of color.

A Mother Instills Values

Emma Ophelia DeVore was born on August 12, 1922, in Edgefield, South Carolina. Edgefield is a small town in the southwest corner of South Carolina about thirty miles from the Georgia border. She was one of ten children born to John Walter DeVore and Mary Emma Strouther. Her father owned his own business. The business frequently required him to travel away from home. DeVore's mother was a major influence in her life. She worked as a teacher and played the organ at her church. She firmly stressed the value of education and the arts. She also believed that appearances and social graces played a big role in determining who would be successful in life. She taught Ophelia to be polite, to dress nicely, to take pride in her appearance and grooming, and to speak properly.

DeVore was of mixed-race descent. Her father was white and her mother was part Native American and part African American. DeVore was light-skinned. As a result, she could often "pass" for white. This means that even though she considered herself African American, her appearance often led others to conclude that she was white. The ability to "pass" was a valuable social asset for African Americans in the early twentieth century. Light-skinned African Americans who could "pass" often faced less discrimination and enjoyed better professional success than darker-skinned African Americans. According to DeVore, many people whom she met assumed that she was either Spanish or Italian.

DeVore grew up in the South during the era of segregation. Segregation is the practice of using the law to force members of different races to live apart from each other. The schools and businesses of South

Carolina were segregated during DeVore's childhood. DeVore's mother refused to let her children go into any of the segregated businesses in the town where she lived. DeVore's mother taught her daughter not to think of herself as a victim of racism. She also taught her to refuse to let the world dictate to her what she could and could not do. DeVore would put these lessons into practice throughout her professional life.

New York Presents Modeling Opportunities

DeVore left South Carolina when she was nine years old. She moved to Winston-Salem, North Carolina, to live with her uncle and attend school. Two years later, at the age of eleven, she moved to New York City to live with her great-aunt. DeVore remained in New York for the rest of her education. She graduated from the racially integrated, all-girls Hunter College High School in Manhattan sometime in the late 1930s. She then attended college at New York University, where she studied math and foreign languages. In 1941, she married a man named Harold Carter. Carter was a firefighter in New York. He and his brothers were some of the first African American members of what had once been an all-white fire department.

DeVore began modeling when she was sixteen years old and still in high school. Her friends and relatives encouraged her to try it because they thought she had a good chance to become a successful model. However, the Great Depression was still going on in the late 1930s. It was very hard for models to find work. DeVore's career started slowly. It began to turn around when she attended the Vogue School of Modeling in 1938. The Vogue School was the most elite school for models in New York at the time. It also was supposed to be an all-white school. DeVore's light-colored skin enabled her to enroll in the school. Her training at the Vogue School enabled DeVore to become one of the first African American models to attain mainstream commercial success.

DeVore worked as a model in the late 1930s and the early 1940s. Her success was unusual. It was still difficult for African American women to find work as models. DeVore was determined to do something to make it easier for women of color to break into the modeling business. She decided to open her own modeling agency. Modeling agencies work with fashion designers, magazines, and other businesses who hire models. The agency's job is to try to convince these businesses to hire the models the agency represents. One of the reasons that so few African American women worked as models is that many modeling agencies refused to represent them. In 1946, DeVore and four of her friends founded the Grace Del Marco Modeling Agency to represent African American models.

Helps Create Opportunities in Fashion

The Grace Del Marco Agency began recruiting young African American women from prominent New York families and from all-black sororities at nearby colleges and universities. DeVore and her colleagues quickly discovered that the young women they were recruiting needed training and preparation before they were ready to work as models. Therefore, DeVore opened the Ophelia DeVore School of Self-Development and Modeling in 1948. The school and the agency worked together to find jobs for African American models. Many of the agency's models found work in advertisements that would appear in *Ebony* magazine and other publications targeted toward an African American audience.

DeVore worked tirelessly on behalf of the models she represented. For example, one problem African American models encountered was a lack of suitable makeup. Most professional makeup artists in the late 1940s and early 1950s had never worked with African American models. They did not have products suitable for women with darker skin tones. DeVore created a line of cosmetics for her models to use. DeVore's hard work did not immediately translate into profits. Late in 1948, the four friends with whom she had founded the Grace Del Marco Agency had to leave the agency because they were not making enough money. DeVore persevered. She found affordable office space in the African American neighborhood of Harlem and continued to run the agency.

DeVore built up her business slowly but surely throughout the 1950s. One of the new techniques she used was the promotional fashion show. Clothing designers pay models to appear in fashion shows. This is the primary source of income for many models. DeVore hosted promotional fashion shows at her agency. She would go to designers and clothing manufacturers and offer to have her models wear the clothes for free. The designers benefited because members of the public saw their clothes. The models benefited because designers could see them in action. DeVore's agency benefited because it could charge admission to the shows. DeVore invented the idea of a promotional fashion show. This innovation helped many African American models to get their start in the fashion business.

DeVore also helped the models whom her agency represented to find work by entering them into beauty contests. DeVore used a beauty contest to help a model named Cecilia Cooper achieve a milestone in 1959. Most beauty contests in the United States were racially segregated in the 1950s. DeVore decided to enter Cooper in the Miss Festival beauty contest at the Cannes Film Festival in Cannes, France. Because the contest was being held overseas, it included white and black models. Cooper won the contest. She was the first African American woman to win a high-profile beauty contest that included contestants of more than one race. Cooper's win was a major breakthrough for African American models in the United States. It showed that African American models could occupy the same stage and perform just as well as their white counterparts.

DeVore's agency and the models it represented finally achieved widespread commercial success in the 1960s. African American models began working for the most famous fashion designers in New York. The agency's models also achieved crossover success in television and film. DeVore continued to advocate on behalf of the models she represented. In 1974, DeVore went to the biggest advertising agencies in New York and told them they should encourage the companies they represented to advertise their products in newspapers and magazines that targeted an African American audience. That same year, an African American model appeared on the cover of the prestigious fashion magazine *Vogue* for the first time.

DeVore remained active in the fashion and business world as of late 2009. The modeling agency that she founded continued to operate under the name "Ophelia DeVore Organization." More than twenty thousand students had attended the Ophelia DeVore School of Self-Development and Modeling by the end of the first decade of the twenty-first century. DeVore was also owner of a newspaper based in Columbus, Georgia, called *The Columbus Times*, and worked as a consultant to various large corporations.

★ FREDERICK M. JONES
(1892–1961)

Frederick M. Jones was a mechanic and inventor who received sixty-one patents during his lifetime. A patent is legal recognition for an invention, and protection of the right to make money off the invention. Jones's most famous and important invention was a portable air-conditioning unit that refrigerated the inside of a trailer pulled by a truck. His invention made it possible to transport perishable foods across great distances even during hot weather. It revolutionized how people eat all over the world. Jones's inventions also made important contributions to the U.S. war effort during World War II (1939–45). Jones was one of the most productive African American inventors in U.S. history at the time of his death in 1961.

Mechanical Aptitude Opens Doors

Frederick McKinley Jones was born on May 17, 1892, in Covington, Kentucky. Covington is a small town that is about two miles from Cincinnati, Ohio, across the Ohio River. His mother was African American and his father was white. Jones's mother died when he was very young. He spent the first seven years of his life living with his father. His father

worked long hours for a railroad company. He was not able to spend a lot of time with his son because of his job. As a result, Jones's father, a devout Catholic, sent him to live at the West Covington Roman Catholic Church and School. His father hoped that living and studying with priests would teach Jones discipline and the value of education.

Jones displayed a mechanical curiosity and aptitude from a young age. He enjoyed taking things apart to see how they worked. However, he was not particularly interested in his schoolwork. When Jones was nine years old and still living at the West Covington Roman Catholic Church and School, his father died. Two years later, when he was only eleven, Jones ran away from the school to live on his own. He moved across the Ohio River to Cincinnati and began looking for work. He eventually found a job in a garage.

Garages of this era mostly focused on repairing carriages that were drawn behind horses. Jones quickly proved himself to be a talented repairman. He received training to be a mechanic at the garage. He was working full-time as a mechanic by the time he was fourteen years old. He was a foreman (a supervisor of a group of workers) at the garage during his late teens. While Jones was working as a foreman at the garage, automobiles were slowly starting to replace carriages as the preferred method of transportation. Gasoline-powered automobiles presented a different set of problems from horse-drawn carriages. Jones quickly became skilled at identifying and solving these new problems.

Inventions Come Pouring Out

Jones eventually left the garage and moved away from Cincinnati. For a while, he worked as a mechanic on a steamboat that traveled up and down the Mississippi River. He took a job with a hotel in Minneapolis, Minnesota, in 1912. His responsibilities at the hotel included performing repairs on the hotel's boiler and other electrical equipment. In 1913, Jones's skills as a maintenance man attracted the attention of a hotel guest named Oscar Younggren. Younggren owned a fifty-thousand-acre farm in Hallock, Minnesota. Hallock was a small farming community just miles from the Canadian border. Younggren offered Jones a job on his farm, repairing and maintaining cars, tractors, and other farm equipment. Jones accepted the job. He lived and worked in Hallock for most of the next eighteen years.

Jones left Hallock to serve in the U.S. Army during World War I (1914–18). He used his mechanical abilities to repair and maintain communications equipment for the U.S. Army. Jones continued his work as a farm mechanic when he returned to Hallock after the war. He also began studying electrical engineering. In addition, Jones took a job as a movie projectionist. It was in his job as a movie projectionist that Jones came up with his first invention. Until the late 1920s, there was no dialogue or sound in movies. Early movie projectors were only equipped to show silent films. In the late 1920s, a technological breakthrough gave birth to "talkies," movies that came paired with a soundtrack. Technology was not yet available that would store the images and the soundtrack on the same medium. These new movies required a separate, expensive machine that could play the soundtrack in time with the film. The movie theater where Jones worked could not afford such a machine.

Jones built a machine that would play the soundtrack in time with the film. He was able to build the machine using spare parts he found in the machine shop on the farm where he worked. Jones's unit was inexpensive, and it was also high in quality. It was reported that his machine actually worked better than the more expensive models. A few years later, when the sound and images of "talkies" began to be stored all on one film, Jones built another machine that could play these new films.

Word of Jones's mechanical aptitude traveled more than 380 miles southeast to Minneapolis, Minnesota's largest city. Joseph Numero was the president of a company in Minneapolis called Cinema Supplies that manufactured and sold various products to movie theaters. Numero offered Jones a job with his company in 1930 after he heard about the machines Jones had built for the movie theater in Hallock. Jones accepted the position and moved to Minneapolis. Numero's decision to hire Jones proved to be a wise one. Cinema Supplies marketed and sold versions of the machines Jones had built in Hallock. Jones also invented the machine for which he would receive his first patent while working for Cinema Supplies. The machine dispensed movie tickets and provided

OPPOSITE PAGE
Frederick M. Jones.
© *Bettmann/Corbis*

change to customers who used it. Jones's application for a patent was granted in 1939. Movie theaters continued to use his machine until the early 1990s.

Invents a Portable Refrigeration System

Numero eventually sold Cinema Supplies to a larger company, and he and Jones began to expand beyond the movie business. The inspiration for Jones's most famous invention came in 1938. That year, Numero had a conversation with a man named Harry Werner, who owned a trucking company, and a man who owned an air-conditioning company. Werner's trucking business often lost money during the summers when it was hired to transport perishable foods across great distances. The summer heat would cause the ice blocks that Werner used to keep the food cold to melt, and the food would spoil. Werner asked the man who owned the air-conditioning company if he could build a refrigeration unit that would attach to trucks and keep the inside of the trailer cold enough to prevent the food from spoiling. The man said it was impossible. Numero joked that he thought he could probably do it. Werner took him seriously. He sent one of his trucks to Numero's company and asked him to fit it with an air conditioner.

Jones accepted the challenge. The most difficult part of the problem was the need to keep the refrigeration compressor stable. The compressor is the part of an air conditioner that cools the inside air. Compressors cannot run unless they are stable and still. This presented a challenge for a mobile refrigeration unit designed to be attached to a moving truck. Several failed experiments gave Jones the idea of mounting the compressor to the front of the truck in a shockproof box. The front is the heaviest part of a truck because it houses the engine. Its weight makes it less likely to jostle and move than other parts of the truck.

Jones was able to stabilize the compressor and create a working mobile refrigeration unit. He invented the unit in 1935. He received a patent for his invention in 1940. He and Numero went into business together selling the unit. They founded a company called the U.S. Thermo Control Company in 1938. The company began operations just as World War II was beginning. Its trucks were used to transport perishable foods across the country for U.S. soldiers. Jones also helped the military develop mobile cooling units for use in the cockpits of airplanes and for use on the battlefield. These units helped preserve perishable medical supplies such as certain medicines and blood for transfusions.

It is no exaggeration to say that Jones's portable refrigeration unit fundamentally changed the way that people eat in the United States. The federal government developed an extensive interstate highway system in the years after World War II. Trucking became the primary way that food was transported. Because of Jones's invention, people in all parts of the country enjoyed fresh eggs, meat, fruits, and vegetables at all times of the year. The frozen foods industry also developed after World War II. Frozen foods last longer than fresh foods and became very popular beginning in the 1950s. It was only thanks to Jones's invention that manufacturers could reliably transport frozen foods to grocery stores without having to worry that the foods would thaw.

Jones continued to work as an inventor and engineer after World War II. He patented sixty-one inventions over the course of his lifetime. Forty of those patents were in the area of refrigeration and cooling. Jones died on February 21, 1961, in Minneapolis at the age of sixty-seven. The company he helped found continued in business under the name of Thermo King into the twenty-first century.

★ ANNIE TURNBO MALONE
(1869–1957)

Annie Turnbo Malone was a pioneering African American business-woman. Malone built a successful business selling cosmetic, hair-care, and beauty products to African American women. Many historians believe she was the first African American woman ever to become a millionaire. Malone was also a great philanthropist, which means she donated a lot of money to various charities. In addition, Malone founded a college in St. Louis, Missouri, that was dedicated to the study and teaching of African American cosmetology (the cosmetic treatment of skin, hair, and nails). She succeeded as a businesswoman during a time when very few African American women were able to do so.

A Thriving Business Is Born

Annie Turnbo Malone was born under the name Annie Minerva Turnbo on August 9, 1869, in Metropolis, Illinois. Metropolis is a small town in the very southernmost part of the state. Malone was the tenth of eleven children born to Robert and Isabella Turnbo. Malone's parents both died while she was still a child. She moved north to Peoria, Illinois, to live with one of her older sisters after her parents died. Malone spent most of her childhood in Peoria.

Malone developed her interest in hair-care products as a child in Peoria. Many African American women's natural hair texture is coarse, curly, or corkscrew-shaped. A woman with coarse, curly hair who wants to wear her hair straight has to use some kind of product to straighten her hair. When Malone was growing up, many African American women would use harsh chemicals such as lye to straighten their hair. This often burned or caused other damage to women's hair and scalps. Malone became interested in finding a product that would allow African American women to straighten their hair without causing pain or damage.

As a young adult, Malone began developing new beauty products for African American women. She formulated several new products while she was in her late twenties. She developed products to help women straighten and grow their hair. She also formulated a skin-care product that was known at the time as a "tetter" relief. "Tetter" was a general term for a skin disease that causes rashes or other irritation. A tetter relief helped relieve the itching and burning caused by such diseases. Malone also invented the pressing iron and comb, which is a device that uses heat to straighten hair. By 1900, Malone had established a successful business, selling these products in her hometown in Illinois.

Malone's success in Illinois prompted her to pursue the business opportunities available in the bigger market of St. Louis, Missouri. She moved to St. Louis in 1902. Malone hired several assistants and began selling her beauty products under the name Poro Systems. "Poro" is a West African term for spiritual and physical growth. Malone and her assistants initially sold her products door-to-door. They won over new clients by providing free samples and demonstrations of Malone's products. Malone's success enabled her to open a store within a few months after moving to St. Louis.

Builds a Business Empire

Malone was a savvy businesswoman. She knew that, at the time, the South was home to more African American women than any other part of the country. She toured the South in 1903 and introduced her products to thousands of potential customers. Malone was also a pioneer in marketing. She took out advertisements in weekly African American newspapers that specifically targeted black customers. Most marketing at the time targeted white customers. Malone also recruited other African American women to sell her products. This gave her an advantage because many other cosmetics companies refused to hire African American women. One of Malone's first employees, Madame C. J. Walker (1867–1919), went on to found her own cosmetics and beauty company. Walker eventually became a self-made millionaire.

Malone's business sense served her well. Her company grew steadily, and by 1910 she had to move her business into a bigger office. Malone continued to expand her business during the 1910s. Her business was so successful that she was able to open Poro College in St. Louis in 1917. Poro College was the nation's first school that specialized in providing training in

African American cosmetology. Poro College was a large, diverse institution. It contained cosmetology classrooms, manufacturing facilities, and an auditorium. It also boasted social and community features such as an ice cream parlor, a barbershop, a theater, and a roof garden. The buildings and facilities alone were valued at more than one million dollars.

Poro College employed almost two hundred people and became a centerpiece of the African American community in St. Louis. It also cemented Malone's status as one of the most successful African American businesswomen in the entire nation. Malone had attained a personal wealth of approximately fourteen million dollars by the early 1920s. She accomplished this despite having been born just four years after the end of the Civil War (1861–65). Malone wanted to use Poro College as a way to put its African American students in a position to succeed just as she had. Poro College taught not only cosmetology but also manners and decorum (standards of good taste and behavior), which Malone believed were an indispensable part of her success.

Malone's business continued to grow. She moved Poro College from St. Louis to Chicago, Illinois, in 1930, where she became almost as famous for her generosity as a philanthropist as she was for her business successes. Malone gave large amounts of money to charities throughout the country. She was especially generous to charities that benefited African Americans. She donated thousands of dollars a year to African American orphanages. Her most famous work was probably at the St. Louis Colored Orphans Home. Malone was herself an orphan, and she worked tirelessly on behalf of African American orphans in the St. Louis area. She donated both time and money. Her generosity was recognized in 1946, when the St. Louis Colored Orphans Home was renamed the Annie Malone Home. She also funded scholarships for multiple students each year at historically black colleges and universities. She made generous contributions to the endowments of schools such as Howard University and the Tuskegee Institute. Endowments are funds that have been donated to a university to support its educational mission. Malone eventually came to be known as the first major African American philanthropist in U.S. history.

A Series of Setbacks Takes Its Toll

Malone's business success created difficulties for her in her personal life. She had married a man named Pope in 1903, but the two divorced very shortly after they were married because Pope wanted Malone to let him run her business. Malone was married for a second time to Aaron Malone in 1921. Once again, Malone's husband tried to interfere with her business. Aaron Malone worked for Poro Systems from 1921 to 1927. His refusal to allow Annie to run the company created tensions in their marriage. These tensions eventually spilled over into the Poro Systems business.

Malone's conflict with her husband Aaron came to a head in 1927 when the two filed for divorce. Aaron Malone claimed during the divorce proceedings that he was entitled to control of Poro Systems. Aaron argued that he, not Annie, had been running the business and that Poro owed its success to his knowledge and contacts in the business community. The divorce was highly publicized. Many leaders in the African American community took Aaron's side. However, Poro Systems marketed and sold its products almost exclusively to women. The National Association of Colored Women's Clubs voiced its support for Annie Malone. Annie eventually had to pay Aaron Malone a settlement of two hundred thousand dollars, but she was able to retain control of the company.

Unfortunately, Malone's divorce proved to be the beginning of her business problems, not the end of them. Malone was confronted with two lawsuits during the 1930s. One was filed by Edgar Brown. Brown was a newspaper editor at the *St. Louis Post-Dispatch*. Brown had supported Aaron Malone during the couple's divorce. The second lawsuit was filed by a former employee of Poro Systems. The employee claimed that Malone had stolen her ideas and that the employee was responsible for Poro's success. Brown's case was dismissed, and Malone settled the employee's case in 1937. Neither lawsuit was a major loss, but both of them cost Malone money. They also distracted her and prevented her from putting all of her energy into running her business.

Poro Systems was also under pressure from both the federal government and the state government because of unpaid taxes. The federal government imposed a 20 percent excise tax on all luxury and cosmetic goods during the early 1900s. An excise tax is a tax that is imposed on the manufacture or sale of a commodity. Malone thought the tax was unfair because it targeted cosmetics. She frequently failed to pay the tax. The government imposed penalties on Malone for her failure to pay. By the early 1940s, she owed the federal government nearly one hundred thousand dollars in unpaid taxes. Malone had also failed to pay property taxes to the state government on the real estate she owned for Poro College.

Malone was never able to overcome her tax troubles. By 1951, she had reduced the amount of back taxes she owed the federal government from one hundred thousand dollars to forty-eight thousand dollars, but she could never pay off the debt entirely. In 1951, the federal government imposed a lien on Poro Systems. A lien is a legal tool that allows the government to take control of valuable property that belongs to someone who owes the government money. The government sold most of Poro Systems's property and assets to generate money to pay the back taxes Malone owed. Malone's personal wealth dropped from a high of fourteen million dollars to approximately one hundred thousand dollars at the time she died. It was a disappointing end for one of America's pioneering African American businesswomen. Malone spent the last years of her life living in Chicago. She died on May 10, 1957, at the age of eighty-seven.

⭐ LEON H. SULLIVAN
(1922–2001)

Leon H. Sullivan was a minister and civil rights activist who fought against racial injustice not only in the United States, but other parts of the world as well. In addition to being a pastor, he focused his career in the United States on creating economic opportunities for African Americans. He worked hard to help African Americans find work opportunities, and he founded an influential organization to provide needed job training. He was the first African American to serve on the board of directors of General Motors. Sullivan is perhaps best known for his "Sullivan Principles," a set of ideals for American businesses conducting business in South Africa.

Leon H. Sullivan.
© *Bettmann/Corbis*

Sullivan was born on October 16, 1922, in Charleston, West Virginia. His parents divorced, and Sullivan lived with his grandmother. He grew up in the segregated American South and developed a passion for racial justice early on. He fought against local business owners who refused to serve him because he was black. In one case, he was refused service at the same local restaurant several times. Angered by this, Sullivan returned to the restaurant and told the owner he would not leave. Instead, he recited the preamble to the Constitution. The owner was intrigued by Sullivan, and he let him eat at the restaurant.

Becomes a Leader

Sullivan became ordained as a pastor around the time he went to college. He attended West Virginia State College, where he was an athlete. He was involved with many campus activities. Sullivan moved to New York City in

1945 at the urging of Adam Clayton Powell Jr. (1908–72), a well-known African American minister and politician. Powell encouraged Sullivan to move to the city, and Sullivan worked for some years at Powell's Abyssinian Baptist Church. That experience reinforced for Powell the idea that black ministers could be important agents of social change and promoters of justice. Sullivan went on to study religion at Union Theological Seminary in New York and to receive a graduate degree from Columbia University.

One important focus for Sullivan was economic opportunity for African Americans. In 1958, he led a successful boycott of businesses in Philadelphia, Pennsylvania, that did not provide opportunities for black workers. Sullivan also discovered that many African Americans lacked the job training they needed to take advantage of job opportunities. He created the Opportunities Industrialization Center (OIC), an organization that provided job training and assistance to African Americans. Soon, there were branches of the OIC all over the country.

Sullivan was unusual among many black activists during his life because he believed that business and corporations could be tools to provide opportunities for blacks. During the 1960s, he developed strong relationships with many people in corporate America. As a result, he was invited to join the board of directors of General Motors (GM), the American automobile giant, in 1971. A board of directors is a group of people, often outside a corporation, who supervise a corporation's operation. Their job is to act in the best interest of the company and its shareholders. Shareholders are people who own a company's stock.

Fights to End Apartheid

During Sullivan's time at GM, he had a chance to visit South Africa. One of GM's largest plants was in South Africa. On that trip, he witnessed firsthand the country's system of apartheid. Apartheid was a system of legal segregation in South Africa. It was similar to segregation in the United States, but it was more severe in many ways. This is because apartheid, which means "separation" in the Afrikaans language, was based on a formal system of laws put into place by the national government. These laws said where blacks could and could not live, work, and travel. The laws set up separate neighborhoods and schools for whites and blacks. Apartheid in South Africa persisted from 1948 until 1994, long after legal discrimination ended in the United States. Sullivan himself became a victim of apartheid while on his visit to South Africa, when he was arrested and harassed by white police officers.

Sullivan was disturbed by what he had seen in South Africa and decided to take action at home. He began talking to American business leaders. He soon won the support of the leaders of GM and International

Business Machines (IBM), two of the country's largest corporations. With the support of many in the business community, Sullivan unveiled what became known as the "Sullivan Principles" in 1977. The Sullivan Principles were a series of ideas about how American companies doing business in South Africa should conduct themselves:

1. Non-segregation of the races in all eating, comfort, and work facilities.

2. Equal and fair employment practices for all employees.

3. Equal pay for all employees doing equal or comparable work for the same period of time.

4. Initiation of and development of training programs that will prepare, in substantial numbers, blacks and other nonwhites for supervisory, administrative, clerical, and technical jobs.

5. Increasing the number of blacks and other nonwhites in management and supervisory positions.

6. Improving the quality of life for blacks and other nonwhites outside the work environment in such areas as housing, transportation, school, recreation, and health facilities.

7. Working to eliminate laws and customs that impede social, economic, and political justice.

The Sullivan Principles were adopted by more than 125 companies, and many ceased doing business in South Africa altogether. Sullivan was discouraged, however, that his principles did not have much of an immediate effect in South Africa. Apartheid persisted throughout the 1980s, and Sullivan believed his principles had failed to cause change. The end of apartheid in 1994 inspired Sullivan to rededicate himself to his principles. In 1999, Sullivan and United Nations Secretary-General Kofi Annan (1938–) developed a new list of "Global Sullivan Principles" designed to support economic and social justice around the world. Sullivan died after a long battle with leukemia in 2001.

★ A'LELIA WALKER
(1885–1931)

A'Lelia Walker was a famous African American businesswoman and patron of the arts. She was the daughter of Madame C. J. Walker (1867–1919), who founded a cosmetics company that catered to African American women. A'Lelia Walker took over her mother's business and ran it successfully for more than ten years. She became well known in New York for her lavish (large and expensive) parties. Walker also made herself into an important supporter of the arts in the African American neighborhood of Harlem in New York City in the 1920s during the period known as the Harlem Renaissance.

A Business Stays in the Family

A'Lelia Walker was born under the name Lelia McWilliams on June 6, 1885, in Vicksburg, Mississippi. She changed her name to A'Lelia when she was an adult. She was the daughter of Moses McWilliams and Sarah Breedlove. Her father was killed by a lynch mob when she was very young. (A lynching is the murder of an individual by a group acting without legal authority. Lynchings of African American males were common in the South in the late 1800s and early 1900s.) She was raised by her mother and grew up in poverty. Her grandparents were former slaves who worked as sharecroppers. Sharecroppers farm land that is owned by someone else. In exchange for being allowed to farm the land, they give half of the money they earn to the landowner. It is difficult, physical labor that pays little. A'Lelia's mother

A'Lelia Walker.
© Underwood & Underwood/Corbis

probably would have had to take work as a sharecropper if she had stayed in Mississippi. Thus, A'Lelia was taken by her mother to St. Louis, Missouri, when she was two years old so that her mother could find better work. Her mother worked mostly as a washerwoman in St. Louis. Working as a washerwoman is also physically demanding and low-paying.

A'Lelia's mother eventually remarried and took the name C. J. Walker. When A'Lelia was about eighteen years old, her mother went into the cosmetics business. Initially, she worked for Poro Systems, the cosmetics company owned by the famous African American businesswoman Annie Turnbo Malone. By the time A'Lelia was twenty years old, her mother had decided to strike out on her own. Madame C. J. Walker opened her own business in 1905, selling cosmetics, hair-care products, hair straighteners, and hair irons. The business became a phenomenal success. Madame C. J. Walker was one of the first African American women to be a self-made millionaire.

A'Lelia Walker joined her mother's business at a young age. She left home after finishing high school to attend Knoxville College, a historically black college in Tennessee. While A'Lelia was in college, C. J. Walker opened two offices. One was in Denver, Colorado, and the other was in

Pittsburgh, Pennsylvania. Her mother also set up a cosmetology (the cosmetic treatment of skin, hair, and nails) school in Pittsburgh that she named Lelia College. A'Lelia Walker graduated from college in 1908, and she went to work for her mother's company at its office in Pittsburgh. A'Lelia was just twenty-three years old, but she was put in charge of running the Pittsburgh office and Lelia College.

A New Chapter Begins in New York

A'Lelia and her mother worked well together as business partners. C. J. Walker would travel the South—which was home to more African American women than any other part of the country—marketing her beauty products. She would recruit new customers who would order the products through the mail. A'Lelia supervised the mail-order aspect of her mother's business out of the office in Pittsburgh. The business grew steadily under their leadership. They moved the headquarters of the company to Indianapolis, Indiana, in 1910. In 1913, the Walkers decided to move again, this time to Harlem.

Harlem was a very exciting place to be in the 1910s. It was rapidly becoming an important center of African American business and culture. The headquarters of Madame C. J. Walker's company remained in Indianapolis, but Walker purchased two townhouses in Harlem so that she could expand her business into New York. A'Lelia helped her mother set up a second cosmetology school in one of the townhouses. The school was called the Walker College of Hair Culture. Between the beauty colleges and her line of hair-care and beauty products, business was booming for C. J. Walker. She was earning enough money to purchase a large, expensive home in New York. A'Lelia was by her mother's side at each step of the way. She provided advice, made public appearances, and ran some aspects of the company.

A'Lelia Walker took on an even more prominent role in the Walker Manufacturing Company after her mother died on May 25, 1919. A'Lelia Walker became the president of the company. The company flourished under her guidance. She had a new building built in Indianapolis in 1928. The building housed the company's business offices and manufacturing facilities, a beauty college, a salon, a barbershop, and even a movie theater. These amenities (attractive features) caused the Walker Building to become a center of local black culture in Indianapolis. The Walker Company used the facilities in the building to maintain its nationwide customer base.

Embraces the Roaring Twenties

A'Lelia Walker also became a well-known socialite (a person of high social status or position) in New York in the years following her mother's death. The decade of the 1920s is often referred to as the "Roaring Twenties" because of the social, artistic, and cultural excitement and changes that were taking place at the time. The mood across the country was optimistic. This feeling was particularly acute in Harlem. An exciting, vibrant community of African American businesspeople, intellectuals, artists, authors, and musicians was coming together in Harlem. The period later would be known as the Harlem Renaissance. Walker became a well-known figure in Harlem during the 1920s.

Walker began hosting parties at the large, expensive home her mother had built before she died. The home had been designed by Vertner Tandy. Tandy was the first African American to be licensed as an architect by the state of New York. The home was known as Villa Lewaro. It was named after A'Lelia. The name combines the first two letters of "Lelia Walker Robinson," which was A'Lelia's name at the time the house was built.

A'Lelia Walker's parties at Villa Lewaro were the talk of Harlem. She would entertain large crowds of houseguests for days at a time. The crowd was a diverse mix of white and black, young and old, artists and businesspeople. Walker was easy to pick out of the crowds. She was six feet tall and often wore turbans covered in jewels. Her personality and the hospitality she provided to her guests prompted the famous poet Langston Hughes (1902–67) to nickname her "The Joy Goddess of Harlem."

Walker also became a well-known patron of the arts. A patron is a person who provides money for artists to live on while they develop their art. In 1927, Walker dedicated to the arts one of the townhouses that she and her mother had purchased when they moved to New York. She renamed the townhouse "The Dark Tower." The name was borrowed from a 1927 poem by Countee Cullen (1903–46), a famous African American poet. "The Dark Tower" was intended to be a salon, which means it was a place where artists and authors could gather to eat, drink, and discuss their work.

Walker's parties became less frequent, and her lifestyle became less lavish, as the 1920s came to a close. The beginning of the Great Depression in 1929 caused a slowdown in business for Walker's cosmetics and beauty supply company. Walker was forced to close "The Dark Tower" just three years after it opened. Walker had also fallen into poor health due to years of excessive eating and drinking. She died on August 16, 1931, when she was only forty-six years old. Fittingly, the last thing she did before she died was to host a birthday party for a friend. Walker was a much beloved figure in Harlem. A large crowd of mourners, including famous authors and artists whom she had supported financially, turned out for her funeral.

★ MADAME C. J. WALKER
(1867–1919)

Madame C. J. Walker was a business owner and entrepreneur who founded the Madame C. J. Walker Manufacturing Company. Walker rose out of a background of poverty and illiteracy to become one of the first African American women in the United States to found, own, and operate her own business. Walker's company produced cosmetics, hair-care, skin-care, and beauty products for African American women. Many historians believe Walker was the first African American woman ever to become a

Madame C. J. Walker.
*Michael Ochs
Archives/Getty Images*

self-made millionaire. Walker's business success allowed her to become a leader of the African American community. She also provided generous support to numerous African American charities. Madame C. J. Walker was truly a pioneer in business and industry.

Poverty and Hardship Come Early

Madame C. J. Walker was born under the name Sarah Breedlove on December 23, 1867, in Delta, Louisiana. Delta is a small town in eastern Louisiana just a few miles across the Mississippi River from Vicksburg, Mississippi. Owen and Minerva Breedlove, Walker's parents, were both former slaves. The Breedloves worked as sharecroppers on the plantation of the same family that had held them as slaves. Sharecropping is a system of farming in which a landowner allows a family to live on and farm his land. In exchange, the family must give the landowner one-half of all the money they make from selling the crops they grow on his land. Sharecropping is an unfair, exploitive labor system. It was commonplace throughout the South after the Civil War.

Most African American families who practiced sharecropping were trapped in lives of grueling physical labor and grinding poverty. The Breedloves were no different. The family shared a one-room shack that had no windows or running water. They slept on the shack's dirt floor. The Breedloves were cotton sharecroppers. In the late 1800s, growing and picking cotton was incredibly labor-intensive. As a result, Walker spent her early childhood working with her parents on the farm. She was not able to attend school or receive an education. She grew up without learning how to read or write.

Walker's parents both died by the time she was seven years old. After her parents' deaths she moved across the river to Vicksburg to live with her older sister Louvenia and her sister's husband. Life did not get any easier. Walker still had to work in the field as a sharecropper. She also suffered from physical abuse at the hands of her sister's husband. Walker left her sister's house at the age of fourteen, when she married a man named Moses McWilliams. In 1885, when Walker was eighteen, she gave birth to her daughter Lelia. Tragedy struck two years later, when Moses McWilliams was killed by a lynch mob. A lynching is the murder of an individual by a group acting without legal authority. Lynchings of African American males were common in the South in the late 1800s and early 1900s.

A Move North Offers a Fresh Start

Walker needed to find a way to financially support herself and her daughter after her husband's death in 1887. Economic opportunities for

African Americans, especially African American women, were limited in the South. Cities in the North and the Midwest offered better employment prospects, so Walker decided to move north. She traveled up the Mississippi River to St. Louis, Missouri. Walker was able to find work in St. Louis in restaurants and laundries. She was not earning a lot of money, but she was earning more than she had been in Mississippi. Her wages were barely enough for herself and her daughter.

Walker was only twenty years old when she moved to St. Louis, but she was already beginning to lose her hair. Her hair loss was caused by the technique she was using to straighten her hair. Many African American women's natural hair texture is coarse, curly, or corkscrew-shaped. There are various techniques and products African American women can use to straighten their hair. A popular technique in the late 1800s was the wrap-and-twist method. Women would tightly wrap string and portions of their hair and then twist the string in the opposite direction from their hair's curls to straighten it out. The wrap-and-twist method places a lot of stress on hair follicles and can cause hair loss and baldness. A follicle is the bottom part of a piece of hair that attaches the hair to the scalp.

Walker's hair loss ultimately would inspire her to start a business. Walker was disappointed to be losing her hair. She wished there was some way she could restore her hair. Walker started experimenting to see if she could come up with a product to re-grow her hair. Eventually, she developed a product that worked. She applied it to her scalp, and her hair started to grow back. She shared the product with some of her friends, and it caused their hair to grow back, too.

A Business Is Born

Walker decided to make more of the hair-growth product and to go into business selling it. She named the product "Wonderful Hair Grower." She developed several additional hair-care products, including a hot comb. A hot comb is a tool that African American women can use to straighten their hair. The hot comb does not require the use of any chemicals, and it does not damage the scalp like the wrap-and-twist method does. Walker began selling her collection of products door-to-door in African American neighborhoods in St. Louis. Walker also went to work for Annie Turnbo Malone, an African American woman from Illinois who also had invented hair-care and skin-care products designed for African American women. Walker worked as a sales agent for Malone for several years in the early 1900s.

Walker's business expanded rapidly after she moved to Denver, Colorado, in 1905. She moved to Denver to live with her sister after her sister's husband died. Walker continued to invent new cosmetic products and sell them door-to-door while she was living in Denver. By 1906, she was earning enough money to quit her job as a domestic employee and concentrate full-time on her hair-products business. Walker also married a man named C. J. Walker while she was living in Denver. This is how she came to be known as Madame C. J. Walker. Her husband was in the newspaper business. As a result, he was familiar with advertising and mail-order businesses. Walker used what she learned from her husband to expand her business even further. However, she and her husband soon grew apart from each other. They divorced just a few years after their marriage. Walker nonetheless continued to use the name Madame C. J. Walker, and she called her business the Madame C. J. Walker Manufacturing Company.

Walker worked hard to grow her business over the next several years. The vast majority of the nation's African American population resided in the South at this time. Walker thus began traveling in the South to expand her business into this large and potentially lucrative market. Her daughter Lelia was in her early twenties by this time, so Walker left Lelia in charge of the business in Denver. Lelia oversaw the manufacturing of the company's products and handled the mail-order business. Walker began recruiting women whom she met during her trips to the South to become agents of her company and sell her products in their communities.

Madame C. J. Walker driving in her car with three other women, c. 1916. Walker's business brought her wealth that was extremely rare for African American women of that time. *New York Daily News Archive/New York Daily News/NY Daily News via Getty Images*

The Madame C. J. Walker Manufacturing Company was expanding rapidly. Walker opened an office and a school of African American cosmetology (the cosmetic treatment of skin, hair, and nails) in Pittsburgh, Pennsylvania, in 1908. She named the school "Lelia College" after her daughter. By 1910, more than five thousand African American women were working as agents of the Walker Company. That same year, Walker relocated her company's headquarters from Denver to Indianapolis, Indiana. She wanted to locate the company in a city that was more geographically central because of her mail-order business.

Becomes a Success Story

Walker was enjoying a level of success that would have been unimaginable for an African American woman just a few years earlier. By 1917, the Madame C. J. Walker Company sold approximately five hundred thousand dollars' worth of beauty products every year. It was the largest African American–owned business in the United States. Walker herself had amassed a substantial personal fortune. Many historians believe she was the first African American woman ever to become a millionaire thanks to her own business efforts. (Walker's former employer, Annie Turnbo Malone, also became a self-made millionaire around this time.) Walker moved to New York City in 1913 to enjoy the fruits of her success. She built a mansion in New York and became a well-known figure around the city.

Walker also became an active philanthropist. A philanthropist is a person who regularly donates money to charities and nonprofit organizations. Walker was a generous supporter of the National Association for the Advancement of Colored People (NAACP). She also donated money to colleges and universities across the country that were dedicated to educating African American students. She spoke out on behalf of women's right to vote and to own and run their own businesses.

Walker died in New York on May 25, 1919. She was only fifty-one years old, but she suffered from hypertension (high blood pressure). She had collapsed while on a business trip to St. Louis shortly before her death. Walker was a generous philanthropist even in death. She bequeathed (made a gift in her last will and testament) two-thirds of all her personal wealth to charities and educational institutions. She left the remaining one-third of her wealth, as well as ownership of the Madame C. J. Walker Manufacturing Company, to her daughter. Her daughter ran the company for the next twelve years until her own death in 1931.

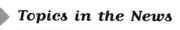

Topics in the News

....

❖ AFRICAN AMERICANS TRANSITION FROM SLAVERY TO SHARECROPPING

The end of the Civil War in 1865 resulted in the freeing of more than four million slaves. Almost all of these former slaves lacked money, property, and education. They had few job prospects. The government's efforts to provide "freedmen" (recently freed former slaves) with land of their own failed. This resulted in the rise of the sharecropping system. Sharecroppers are people who farm land that they do not own. The owner of the land allows them to farm there in exchange for a share of the farm's profits. Though sharecropping can be an arrangement that benefits both the landowner and the tenant, this was not generally the case in the South, where sharecroppers struggled in constant debt and poverty.

The Freedmen's Bureau Fails to Provide Land

The end of the Civil War caused massive changes in the economy and society of the South. More than four million African Americans who had been held as slaves were freed by the passage of the Thirteenth Amendment in 1865. These former slaves wanted to strike out on their own. However, they did not have any economic assets—such as land or cash—that they could use to earn a living. Many faced the prospect of homelessness,

Sharecropping kept African American families in poverty that was little better than slavery. *The Library of Congress*

unemployment, and poverty. President Abraham Lincoln (1809–65) responded to this situation by creating the Freedmen's Bureau. The purpose of the Freedmen's Bureau was to help former slaves earn a living.

The core idea behind the creation of the Freedmen's Bureau was land grants. Lincoln wanted the bureau to confiscate (have the government take away) lands that belonged to people in the South who had joined the Confederate Army or served in the government of the Confederacy. The bureau would then rent these lands to former slaves. Former slaves would farm the land for several years until they had saved enough money to buy the land from the bureau. The system was designed to allow African Americans to acquire property so that they could improve their economic situation. Lincoln had the Freedmen's Bureau set aside approximately eight hundred thousand acres of land for this purpose.

The Freedmen's Bureau never provided the land grants that Lincoln envisioned. Lincoln was assassinated in April 1865. His successor, Andrew Johnson (1808–75), was a former slave owner from Tennessee who was sympathetic to white landowners in the South. Johnson scrapped Lincoln's plan to confiscate their lands and sell them to former slaves. Instead, Johnson allowed former members of the Confederacy to keep their lands so long as they signed an oath swearing they would be loyal to the United States. Almost none of the eight hundred thousand acres of land Lincoln had set aside for the Freedmen's Bureau ended up in the hands of African Americans.

The System of Sharecropping Emerges

The failure of the Freedmen's Bureau to provide African Americans in the South with land resulted in the rise of the system of sharecropping. Slave owners had long prohibited their slaves from learning to read or otherwise getting an education. They had forced their slaves to work long hours on plantations (very large farms). As a result, very few former slaves had any job skills other than as farmers. However, the failure of the Freedmen's Bureau meant that very few former slaves owned any land on which to start a farm. Sharecropping was a response to this situation.

Sharecropping started with a plantation owner breaking his very large farm into a number of smaller parcels of land. The plantation owner would allow an African American family to build a small house on this parcel of land. The plantation owner also provided the family with farming supplies such as seeds, tools, and animals. In turn, the family took responsibility for planting, tending, and harvesting crops on the land. The plantation owner would pay for the supplies he had given the family out of the money generated from selling crops. The family and the landowner divided any remaining profits equally.

Sharecropping became widespread throughout the South in the years following the Civil War. The number of farms in the South increased from 672,313 in 1860 to 3,097,547 in 1910. This increase was caused by plantation owners dividing their land among sharecroppers. Most African Americans in the South were farmers at this time, and almost 80 percent of African American farmers in the South were sharecroppers.

Sharecroppers Struggle to Make Ends Meet

The system of sharecropping was very unfair to African American farmers. The plantation owners would charge African American share-croppers very high prices for the equipment—seeds, tools, and animals—they sold them to use on the farms. The landowners would take money to pay for this equipment out of the proceeds generated by the sale of each year's crops. The plantation owners often charged such unfairly high prices for the equipment that the sale of the crops did not produce enough money to cover the costs of the equipment. This resulted in African American families becoming indebted to the landowners.

Sharecropping thus created a vicious cycle of indebtedness. African American sharecroppers would have to work the next year to pay off their debts from the previous year. A portion of the proceeds from the next year's crop would go to cover the previous year's debt. That resulted in the creation of more debt the next year. Many African Americans thus became trapped as sharecroppers, burdened by debts they could never repay. To make matters worse, many landowners exaggerated the amount of debt that sharecroppers owed to them.

This cycle of indebtedness caused sharecropping to resemble slavery. African American sharecroppers had little chance of building wealth for themselves because they were constantly trying to pay off their debts. Raising more crops was the easiest way to earn more money, so many sharecroppers' children ended up working on the farm instead of attending school. This made it more difficult for these children to get better jobs. Landowners could also use the debt they held to coerce (force someone to do something against their will) African Americans into not voting or otherwise exercising their civil rights.

Sharecropping remained common throughout the South through the 1930s. Several factors combined to bring about its decline. The increasing mechanization (use of machines and mechanical tools to complete tasks previously performed by people) of farming made sharecropping less economical. President Franklin D. Roosevelt's New Deal (the name of a package of economic programs designed in response to the Great Depression) launched policies that provided alternatives to sharecropping. Finally, sharecroppers in the South began joining the Southern Tenant

Farmers' Union, which helped them attain better working conditions. These developments helped bring about the end of the system of share-cropping by the early 1940s.

❖ BLACK-OWNED BUSINESSES EMERGE UNDER SEGREGATION

Many African American–owned businesses emerged throughout the South during the era of segregation. Segregation is the practice of using the law to force members of different races to live apart from each other. Segregation was in place throughout the South from the late 1800s until the 1960s. Southern states enforced segregation by passing "Jim Crow" laws. The purpose of "Jim Crow" laws was to prevent African Americans from enjoying economic and political equality. These laws did so by requiring African Americans to live apart from whites.

The emergence of black-owned businesses was a natural consequence of segregation. Segregation allowed white business owners to refuse to serve African American customers. Segregation also caused African Americans to live in different neighborhoods from whites. Black-owned businesses opened in all-black neighborhoods to provide the services that white businesses refused to provide. The result of segregation was to create two worlds of business in the South. In effect, black-owned businesses and African American consumers made up a separate, self-sustaining economy.

There were both positive and negative aspects of this feature of the Jim Crow system. On the one hand, many African Americans became business owners for the first time. They gained valuable knowledge and experience. Many used part of the money they earned to support the civil rights movement in the 1960s. On the other hand, African American businesses were limited in how successful they could be. They were not able to compete with white-owned businesses and only drew customers from the African American community.

African Americans owned and operated a wide variety of businesses. There were black-owned grocery stores, restaurants, dry cleaners and laundries, beauty salons and barbershops, garment- and shoe-repair companies, funeral homes, and even insurance companies. However, African American businesses achieved particular success in two noteworthy fields: banking and the newspaper business.

African American Banks Fill a Need

White banks refused to provide basic banking services to African Americans. They also refused to lend money to African American families and businesses. Black banks met both of these needs. They provided basic

Employees of the black-owned Dunbar National Bank pose outside of the building, c. 1920. Black banks served the African American community at a time when white banks refused to do so. *Photographs and Prints Division, Schomburg Center for Research in Black Culture, The New York Public Library, Astor, Lenox and Tilden Foundations*

financial services and advice to African American residents in their communities. Historians believe that the willingness of black-owned banks to provide these services gave the African American community confidence that it would be economically secure even in the Jim Crow South.

The willingness and ability of black banks to lend money to African Americans was especially important. The parallel African American economy that developed in the South during the Jim Crow era could not have emerged without the financial support of black banks. Loans from these banks enabled African American families to buy their own homes. They also enabled African American businesses to open their doors and to stay in business during tough times. For example, in Richmond, Virginia, loans from African American banks helped the number of black-owned businesses in the city to increase by 76 percent between 1907 and 1920. Nationwide, fifty-seven black-owned banks opened between 1888 and 1928. The number of black-owned businesses increased from four thousand in 1867 to approximately fifty thousand in 1917.

The number of African American–owned banks declined in the middle part of the twentieth century. This was due to the Great Depression (1929–41), the period following the stock market crash in 1929 that was marked by

Maggie Lena Walker

Maggie Lena Walker (1864–1934) was the first African American woman to found and run a bank. The daughter of a former slave, Walker was raised in Richmond, Virginia. Her mother's husband was killed when she was young, and her mother worked as a laundress to support Maggie and her half brother. When she finished school, Walker started working as a teacher, and she took business courses at night. In 1903, she founded St. Luke Penny Savings Bank and worked as its president. The bank prospered. In 1930, Walker merged the bank with two other black-owned banks to form the Consolidated Bank and Trust Company, of which she was chairman of the board. In addition to running the bank, Walker worked tirelessly for various charities. She was co-founder of the Richmond branch of the National Association for the Advancement of Colored People.

a poor economy and high unemployment. Between 1929 and 1953, only five new black banks opened in the entire United States. A far greater number of existing black banks were forced to close. The Great Depression hit black banks particularly hard. Black banks relied on African Americans to borrow money and conduct other business. However, African Americans were unemployed at a much higher rate than the general population during the Great Depression. In addition, black banks typically had fewer reserves (money deposited in accounts at a bank) than white-owned banks. As a result, they were more vulnerable to a downturn in the economy.

Black banks began to rebound once segregation came to an end. The civil rights movement had a positive impact on the African American business community in general and on banks in particular. The period from 1954 to 1969 saw seventeen new black-owned banks open across the country. These banks continued to serve primarily African American customers. They remained an important source of business capital (money to work with) and personal loans well into the second half of the twentieth century.

African American Newspapers Flourish

Newspapers were an important part of African American culture even before the Civil War. The first black newspaper in American history, *Freedom's Journal*, was founded in New York City in 1827. Only a handful of black newspapers were published before the Civil War. That number exploded after the Civil War ended. Newly freed African American communities were eager to establish their own periodicals. By 1890, the United States was home to 575 black-owned magazines and newspapers.

Black-owned newspapers provided a forum in which African American leaders could speak out on important civil rights issues of the day. Ida B. Wells (1862–1931), a famous African American journalist, used her column in the *Chicago Conservator* to speak out against lynching (a lynching is the killing of an individual by a group acting illegally) and other racial problems in the South.

Black newspapers flourished throughout the North in the early 1900s. New York's *Amsterdam News,* the *Pittsburgh Courier,* the *Chicago Defender,* and the *Baltimore Afro-American* all achieved circulations (the number of people who read a newspaper on a daily basis) of over fifty thousand. All of these papers were owned and operated by African Americans. Newspapers played a central role in American political culture in the early twentieth century. Black newspapers uniquely enabled African Americans to have a voice in the political process during this period.

❖ BLACK WOMEN ENTER JOB MARKET AS DOMESTICS

Many African American women took work in the area of domestic employment from the 1860s to the 1960s. Domestic employment is employment that takes place inside the house or home of a person who is not a member of the employee's family. People who work as maids, butlers, servants, and nannies all work as domestic employees. Domestic employment is often very difficult, demanding work. People who work as domestic employees also tend to get paid very low wages. African American women accepted jobs in domestic employment despite these drawbacks because other jobs were not available to them due to racial and gender discrimination.

The practice of African American women working in domestic employment has its roots in slavery. The majority of slaves in the South worked in the fields of plantations, planting and harvesting cotton and other crops. However, a small number of slaves also worked in plantation houses doing domestic labor. Approximately 15 percent of all slaves in the South performed exclusively domestic labor. Of that 15 percent, the vast majority, probably around 90 percent, were African American women. White slave-owners in the South viewed domestic slaves as status symbols. The use of slaves to perform household tasks was a sign of wealth and power.

Most domestic slaves were African American women for two main reasons. First, many slave-owners believed that African American women were naturally better suited to domestic work than African American men. Slave-owners stereotyped their male slaves as strong, brutish (similar to an animal), and unintelligent. Female slaves were believed to be better capable of performing the delicate, personal work of the domestic sphere. Second, it was a common practice during slavery for slave-owning men to force their female slaves to bear their children. Even though these children were the children of the slave owner, they were still slaves. However, the children, especially the girls, were often put to work in the house because domestic work was easier physically than working in the fields.

The practice of African American women working in houses owned by white people did not end when slavery ended. African Americans, who until recently had been slaves, found themselves in need of employment. Most slave owners had forbidden their slaves from learning to read or otherwise receiving an education. Many former slaves had a hard time finding work. As a result, they often continued doing the same kind of work they had done as slaves. A large number of African American men and families took on farming work as sharecroppers. African American women who had been domestic slaves sought work as domestic servants or household workers.

In the late 1800s, domestic servants often lived in the house of the family they worked for, providing cleaning, cooking, and childcare services. Domestic servants earned very low wages and worked long hours with few breaks and little free time. The practice of employing African American women as domestic servants spread to cities in the North during the Great Migration of the early twentieth century. Millions of African Americans left the South and moved to cities in the North in the years shortly before and after World War I (1914–18). One of the main reasons the Great Migration took place was the lack of employment opportunities for African Americans in the South. African Americans moved north in search of work. Many African American women found work as domestic servants. In 1920, just 46 percent of all female domestic servants nationwide were African American. By the end of World War II in 1945, that number had risen to 60 percent.

African American women were largely limited to work as domestics in white households until World War II opened up opportunities in factories.
© *Bettmann/Corbis*

African American women fared better in domestic employment in the North than they had in the South. One study found that a black female domestic servant working in Chicago in the 1910s could earn as much in one week as she would have earned in three weeks in the South. It was also more common for domestic servants in the North to live in a home of their own instead of boarding with the family that employed them. This helped reduce the number of hours that domestic employees had to work.

The political changes of the 1930s were another major development that helped improve the quality of life for African American women working as domestic employees. Labor unions became increasingly common during the 1930s. Labor unions are groups of employees who have banded together to negotiate with their employers for higher wages and better working conditions. African American women who worked as domestic employees began to join together around this time. By the 1960s, a labor union called the National Conference of Domestic Workers had formed to protect the rights of domestic workers.

The number of African American women working as domestic employees began to decline after World War II. The end of racially segregated education made it possible for African Americans to find jobs in fields that had previously been closed to them. In addition, fewer middle-class families were hiring full-time domestic servants. In 1940, 60 percent of employed African American women were working as domestic employees. By 1967, that number had dropped to 24.5 percent.

❖ THE NATIONAL NEGRO BUSINESS LEAGUE IS FOUNDED

The National Negro Business League was founded in Boston, Massachusetts, on August 23, 1900, by the famous African American leader Booker T. Washington (1856–1915). The league became the largest and most influential African American professional and business organization in the country from 1900 until about 1930. Washington promoted a philosophy of economic self-sufficiency. He argued that the way for African Americans to improve their fortunes was to work hard at jobs in the fields of agriculture, industry, and business. Washington believed that African Americans could obtain civil rights and political equality only after they had become economically productive and successful. He founded the National Negro Business League as a way to help the African American community attain economic self-sufficiency.

The National Negro Business League's mission statement explained that it was established "to promote the commercial and financial development of the Negro." Washington believed that African Americans who owned their own businesses would benefit from being part of a network of fellow African American business owners. Members of the league would be able to exchange information and learn from each other. One of the most valuable functions the league served was bringing these business owners together for conferences and meetings. League members would use these conferences to exchange tips and experiences on how to better run their businesses. The league also used these conferences to compile statistics on black-owned businesses. By 1914, the league reported that there were more than forty thousand African American businesses throughout the United States.

Establishing contacts with business owners in other fields and cities also helped National Negro Business League members grow their businesses. For example, African American store owners sometimes had difficulty buying merchandise for their stores because white-owned wholesalers (businesses that sell goods to stores) refused to deal with a black-owned business. The league put African American business owners in touch with one another so that they could do business together.

The executive committee of the National Negro Business League in the 1910s. Founder Booker T. Washington sits second from the left in the front row. © *Corbis*

A wide variety of business owners and professionals became members of the National Negro Business League. Doctors, lawyers, small-business owners, farmers, industrial workers, and tradesmen all joined the league. The league initially concentrated its work in the South. It slowly expanded over time. The league opened state and local chapters in major cities across the country. Eventually the league had more than three hundred branch offices, including thirteen in Washington's home state of Alabama.

The National Negro Business League expanded its focus in the 1910s and 1920s. It began encouraging businesses owned by other races to do business with African American businesses and to sell their products to African American consumers. The league leaders argued that everyone, including white Americans, benefited from a successful, thriving African American business community. They also pointed out that white-owned businesses that did not try to sell their products to African Americans were missing out on a very large market. The league encouraged these businesses to advertise in newspapers and magazines directed at African American readers.

The National Negro Business League also helped African American women develop vocational and professional skills. The league's willingness to provide encouragement to women who wanted to work was unusual during that era. Most men believed at that time that women should not perform paid labor outside of their own homes. However, Booker T. Washington had long believed that African American women also needed to be able to earn a living. The Tuskegee Institute, the famous all-black school Washington founded in Alabama, had always admitted female students. The league followed Washington's lead and allowed African American women to become members.

Women were always allowed to be members of the National Negro Business League, but on at least one occasion they had to assert their right to be leaders of the organization. The league held its national convention in 1912 in Chicago, Illinois. The convention included a series of speakers. None of the scheduled speakers was a woman. Madame C. J. Walker (1867–1919) was attending the convention that year. Walker was a well-known businesswoman who had started a very successful company selling beauty products to African American women. The lack of female speakers prompted Walker to come down to the front of the room while Booker T. Washington was standing at the podium introducing the next speaker. Walker took the microphone away from Washington and criticized him for not inviting any women to speak at the convention. The very next year, Washington invited Walker to speak at the league's national convention.

The National Negro Business League's influence peaked in the early part of the twentieth century, and declined as African Americans achieved greater integration into American society during the civil rights era of the 1950s and 1960s. Historians credit the league with playing an important role in helping African American–owned businesses to expand and succeed during the 1920s. The league remained in operation into the twenty-first century, with its headquarters based in Washington, D.C. The organization renamed itself the National Business League in 1966.

❖ AFRICAN AMERICANS FIND WORK IN CAR FACTORIES

The automobile industry was an important source of jobs and income for African Americans beginning in the 1910s. Most African Americans still lived in the South in the late 1800s and early 1900s. The promise of work in industrial positions caused many African Americans to move to cities in the North as part of what is known as the Great Migration. Many African Americans were able to find work in the factories that manufactured automobiles. These jobs paid good wages and provided reliable work. The automobile industry helped many African American families attain a middle-class lifestyle.

As late as 1900 almost 90 percent of all African Americans lived in the South. African Americans in the South had very few economic prospects at this time. Most of them worked as sharecroppers. Sharecropping is a system of farming in which a landowner allows a family to farm the land he owns. In exchange, the family gives the landowner a percentage (usually half) of the profits the family makes from selling the crops it raises. In the early part of the twentieth century, most African American sharecroppers in the South were trapped in poverty.

At the same time, a wave of industrialization was taking place in the North. Industrialization occurs when a large number of businesses that previously operated on a small scale use new forms of energy and technology to produce or manufacture goods on a much greater scale. Railroads, steel-making, petroleum production, and numerous other industrial businesses took root across the North and the Midwest in the late 1800s. These industrial businesses required a lot of workers. New jobs were being created in the cities of the North and the Midwest. The automobile industry began to develop in the early 1900s. Henry Ford (1863–1947) created the first mass-produced car, the Ford Model T, in 1909. Even more jobs would soon become available in the automobile industry.

The Great Migration Brings African Americans North

The combination of a lack of economic opportunity in the South and the promise of new industrial jobs in the North caused what is known as the Great Migration. The Great Migration lasted from 1910 to 1930.

An assembly line in a Ford auto factory in 1928. Henry Ford opened up good-paying jobs in his factories to African Americans when few other companies would. *Hulton Archive/Getty Images*

Approximately 1.3 million African Americans left the South and moved to cities in the North, the West, and the Midwest during the Great Migration. African Americans relocated in hopes of finding better work than was available in the South at the time.

Many African Americans found work in sectors of the economy other than industry. Many industrial companies in the North practiced racial discrimination in hiring. They refused to hire African Americans to work alongside white Americans in factories and on assembly lines. However, the white employees who took industrial jobs left behind positions at mills, meatpacking plants, and stockyards. Conditions in these jobs were often better than the conditions African Americans had left behind in the South. However, they were not as desirable as skilled labor positions in factories and manufacturing businesses.

The first industry to hire African Americans in large numbers was the automobile industry. Henry Ford, the founder of Ford Motor Company, needed workers to staff the assembly lines in his plants. Demand was growing for Ford's most popular car, the Model T. World War I was also beginning to cause a labor shortage. As a result, Ford began recruiting African Americans in 1915 to come to work at his plants. Ford promised to pay African Americans the same wage that he paid his white workers. This was a rare opportunity. Ford's offer of employment drew thousands of

African Americans to Detroit, Michigan, where his company was based. Detroit was home to only five thousand African Americans in 1910. By 1930, the city's African American population was one hundred thirty thousand.

African Americans faced challenges in the automobile industry in the early twentieth century. They were often required to work the dirtiest or most dangerous jobs in an automobile plant. In addition, Henry Ford's willingness to hire African Americans proved to be atypical. Most car companies refused to hire African Americans or hired only a small number of black employees. By 1940, only 3 percent of the workforce in the automobile industry was African American.

The Automobile Industry Provides Wages and Security

African Americans were finally able to find employment throughout the automobile industry during World War II. Legal and practical changes made this breakthrough possible. On the legal side, President Franklin D. Roosevelt (1882–1945) issued Executive Order 8802 in June 1941. An executive order is a document signed by the president that gives legally binding instructions on how to comply with the law. Executive Order 8802 made it illegal for any business that sold its products to the federal government to discriminate against African Americans. As a practical matter, as soldiers went overseas to fight in the war, a massive labor shortage developed. Auto manufacturers turned to African American workers to fill the vacant positions.

Many African Americans were able to hold on to their jobs in the automobile industry after World War II ended. By 1960, African Americans made up roughly 16 percent of the workforce in the automobile industry. Jobs in the automobile industry were a boon (a benefit or blessing) to the African American community. African American auto workers earned higher wages than African American workers in other industries. Many African American families that had been living in poverty in the South were able to pull themselves up to a middle-class lifestyle.

❖ THE BROTHERHOOD OF SLEEPING CAR PORTERS IS ORGANIZED

The Brotherhood of Sleeping Car Porters (BSCP) was the first successful all-black labor union in U.S. history. The BSCP represented African American porters who worked in the railroad industry. A porter's job is to handle luggage and provide whatever service and assistance that railroad passengers request. Almost all porters were African Americans during the period from 1865 to 1965. Early in this period, porters faced difficult working conditions. These conditions prompted the porters to try to organize a labor union. Labor unions are organizations that represent large groups of employees as the employees bargain with their employers over wages, hours, and working conditions. The BSCP was the union the porters organized. After years of struggle, the BSCP helped the porters secure much better working conditions.

Porters Encounter Opportunity and Obstacles

The story of the BSCP begins with the Pullman Company. The railroad was the primary way that people traveled around the country in the years following the Civil War. The Pullman Company manufactured special luxury sleeping cars used by railroad companies. The Pullman Company also owned and operated all of the sleeping cars that it built. It also hired porters to work on its sleeping cars. The Pullman Company was founded in 1867, just two years after the Civil War ended. The company decided it would only hire African Americans to work as porters on its sleeping cars. It made this decision for two reasons. First, African Americans would work for lower wages. Second, the founder of the company believed that African Americans were more likely to be polite and deferential to the customers who were using the cars.

A sleeping car porter prepares to collect shoes left out for him to shine. Sleeping car porters worked grueling hours and had to pay for their own supplies, such as shoe polish. *Hulton Archive/ Getty Images*

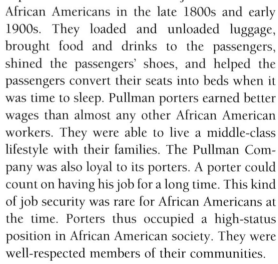

Working as a Pullman porter was one of the best jobs available to African Americans in the late 1800s and early 1900s. They loaded and unloaded luggage, brought food and drinks to the passengers, shined the passengers' shoes, and helped the passengers convert their seats into beds when it was time to sleep. Pullman porters earned better wages than almost any other African American workers. They were able to live a middle-class lifestyle with their families. The Pullman Company was also loyal to its porters. A porter could count on having his job for a long time. This kind of job security was rare for African Americans at the time. Porters thus occupied a high-status position in African American society. They were well-respected members of their communities.

The status that accompanied being a porter came at a high price. Even though porters earned better wages than most African Americans, their wages were not especially high. They also were required to pay for their work supplies, including their uniforms and their shoe polish, out of their own wages. In addition, porters had to spend

The Washing Society Strike

African American laborers had made various attempts to organize and press for better working conditions before the Brotherhood of Sleeping Car Porters was formed. One famous strike happened in Atlanta in July 1881, when the members of the Washing Society—all female and all African American—refused to do the laundry until their demands for higher pay were met. In the 1880s, doing laundry was a difficult, time-consuming task. Labor-saving devices such as mechanical washers and dryers were not available. There were commercial laundries in the North, but in the South, laundry was done the old-fashioned way: Women scrubbed it on wooden boards by hand and hung it out to dry. Laundry was such an unappealing task that any family that could afford to do so sent its laundry out for cleaning, usually to an African American laundress who worked for less than ten dollars a month. More African American women in the South did laundry than any other kind of domestic work.

In July 1881, a group of twenty laundresses, with the support of local black ministers, formed the Washing Society with the goal of demanding higher wages and a standard pay scale. They held meetings in churches across the city of Atlanta and went door to door to recruit new members. In just three weeks, their membership swelled to three thousand. The white community was alarmed by the actions of the Washing Society, and local officials arrested some of the society's members and fined others. In the end, however, the laundresses got what they wanted. Wages went up, and the labor of laundresses was acknowledged as a vital part of the economy of the South.

several hours loading and unloading baggage when the train was in the station. Porters were only paid for time they were on the train, so their work handling baggage was unpaid. Furthermore, porters worked very long hours. They were expected to work four hundred hours a month. By comparison, the average full-time employee today works about 170 hours a month.

A Union Begins to Form

The Pullman porters began trying to organize a union in the early 1900s. However, the Pullman Company refused to allow the porters to organize. Porters who took a leadership role in trying to organize the union

Segregation and Integration in Major Unions

African Americans were barred from many major unions. In part, this was due to racism. It also occurred because white workers interested in pushing for better wages and improved conditions worried that African American workers would hurt their efforts by agreeing to work harder for less. The first major federation of unions, called the American Federation of Labor (AFL), was founded in 1886. It was technically integrated, but in practice it actively discriminated against black workers and women because many of its member unions were segregated. In contrast, the International Workers of the World (IWW) was open to all workers, including women and African Americans. It was founded in 1905 by a group of socialist, anarchist, Communist, and otherwise politically radical workers who opposed the policies of the AFL. The Knights of Labor, founded in 1869, also welcomed African American members starting in 1878. However, the IWW and the Knights of Labor were not as influential as the AFL. In 1938, a new union federation, the Congress of Industrial Organizations (CIO), was founded by ten former member unions of the AFL. The CIO, which was open to women and African Americans, had the support of President Franklin D. Roosevelt. The CIO actively battled racism in its member unions, sought to educate its members about race relations, and supported the Roosevelt administration's efforts to end race discrimination in wartime industries. The AFL and CIO battled for dominance for years, and then finally merged in 1955. The newly formed AFL-CIO welcomed African American members and became an active supporter of the growing civil rights movement.

were fired. The porters' efforts to form a union remained unsuccessful until 1925. That year, they decided to ask someone who was not a porter to organize their union. They reasoned that someone who was not employed by the Pullman Company would be less vulnerable to pressure and intimidation. The porters decided to ask A. Philip Randolph (1889–1979), a well-known journalist and political activist from the African American neighborhood of Harlem in New York City, to organize their union.

Randolph agreed to help the Pullman porters form a union called the Brotherhood of Sleeping Car Porters. He announced the creation of the BSCP to a meeting of five hundred porters in New York on August 25,

1925. The BSCP faced an uphill fight in its early stages. The Pullman Company did everything it could to break up the BSCP. The company refused to negotiate with the union or recognize its existence. Any porter who was known to be a member of the union was fired. There were even reports of porters who joined the union being assaulted and beaten.

The BSCP also faced resistance within the African American community. The Pullman Company had provided jobs for many African Americans. Some black leaders opposed the BSCP because they thought it might cause the Pullman Company to stop hiring African Americans. Other African Americans were opposed to the idea of a labor union. Most American unions at this time were all-white and refused to admit African American members. This pattern of racial discrimination had caused many African Americans to conclude that organized labor could not be of any benefit to them.

Gains Are Finally Won

These difficulties were not enough to prevent a steadily increasing number of porters from joining the BSCP. By 1928, just three years after the BSCP was formed, 46 percent of all Pullman porters belonged to the union. The BSCP had two main goals. First, it wanted to decrease the number of

A. Philip Randolph and other labor leaders participate in the 1939 Labor Day parade in New York City. © *Joseph Schwartz/Corbis*

hours that porters were required to work every month from 400 to 240. Second, it wanted to increase the porters' wages from an average of $67 to $150 per month. The Pullman Company refused to recognize the BSCP. That means the company did not acknowledge that it had a legal duty to negotiate with the union. The BSCP responded with a public relations campaign designed to put pressure on the company.

The election of President Franklin D. Roosevelt in 1932 was the beginning of a breakthrough for the BSCP. Roosevelt supported unions. He had Congress pass a law that required companies such as Pullman to recognize worker-run unions. The law passed in 1933. The Pullman Company finally recognized the BSCP and began negotiations. The company and the union signed a labor agreement on April 25, 1937. It was the first time in American history that an all-black union had negotiated a labor agreement with a major corporation.

The 1937 agreement significantly improved working conditions for porters. It increased both the minimum and maximum wage, decreased the number of hours worked per month, and required the company to pay the porters for the time they spent loading and unloading luggage. The BSCP continued to represent porters for the next forty years. It peaked in size in the 1940s, when it had fifteen thousand members. As airplanes began to replace the railroad as the preferred method of passenger travel, the BSCP began to decline in size. By the 1960s, it had just three thousand members. The BSCP merged with another union in 1978.

❖ WORLD WAR II CREATES NEW JOBS FOR AFRICAN AMERICANS

World War II (1939–45) brought about massive changes in the American economy. The Great Depression had created widespread unemployment and a shortage of jobs between 1929 and 1941. American involvement in World War II reversed that situation within a few years. Seemingly overnight, there was a shortage of qualified workers for the available jobs. African Americans benefited from the jobs created by the war. They also made important contributions to the war effort by playing important roles in the industrial sector. African American women uniquely benefited from the job opportunities created by World War II. Industrial jobs in factories that made military equipment gave many African American women their first chance to work in skilled, high-paying jobs.

Military Buildup Sparks Industrial Production

The United States did not become involved in World War II until 1941, but the war was under way in Europe in the late 1930s. The beginning of the war in Europe prompted the United States to begin ramping up industrial production of military supplies. These supplies were then sold to American allies such as Great Britain and France. This increased production of military supplies created many new jobs in industry.

African Americans were particularly in need of jobs at this time. The Great Depression had hit African Americans hard. By the end of the 1930s, the unemployment rate for white Americans was about 10 percent. The unemployment rate among African Americans was twice as high at 20 percent. Further, most African Americans were unable to find work outside of menial, unskilled positions. Industrial production jobs were skilled jobs that were highly desirable at this time. However, racial discrimination initially kept African Americans out of most of the new industrial jobs created by the beginning of World War II. For example, by 1940, more than one hundred thousand Americans were working in the aircraft industry. Only 240 of them (less than 0.2 percent) were African Americans.

This racial discrimination in industrial hiring prompted black leaders to take action. A. Philip Randolph was one of the most powerful African American leaders of the time. He was the president of the nation's only all-black union, the Brotherhood of Sleeping Car Porters. Randolph began planning a march in Washington, D.C., in early 1941. The purpose of the march would be to oppose industrial companies' refusal to hire African American workers. President Franklin D. Roosevelt wanted to convince Randolph to call off the march because Roosevelt thought it would undermine support for the war effort. Randolph and other black leaders agreed to call off the march in exchange for Roosevelt's support in ending racial discrimination in the defense industry.

Roosevelt made it possible for African Americans to secure high-paying industrial jobs when he signed Executive Order 8802 on June 25, 1941. An executive order is a document signed by the president that gives legally binding instructions on how to comply with the law. Executive Order 8802 prohibited government agencies and private companies that did business with the government (specifically, industrial businesses manufacturing military equipment) from refusing to hire African Americans. As a result, African Americans were able to share in the economic benefits of newly created industrial jobs.

African Americans Leave the South After Pearl Harbor

The United States became directly involved in World War II after Japan bombed the Pearl Harbor naval base in Hawaii at the end of 1941. The direct U.S. involvement generated an even greater need for industrial production. The armed forces needed tanks, ships, planes, guns, bullets, and numerous other supplies. The military's need for supplies created an enormous number of jobs in the industrial sector. However, most of the men who had traditionally worked in industrial jobs were on their way overseas as members of the military. They were no longer available to work at home. Almost all of these former industrial workers were white. By 1943, the United States was faced with shortages of workers in industries that were critical to the war effort.

These worker shortages created new job opportunities for African Americans. Most African Americans still lived in the South at this time, but new jobs were available at industrial plants and factories in cities in the North and the West. These available wartime industrial jobs helped begin what is known as the Second Great Migration. The Second Great Migration lasted from 1941 to 1970. It saw some five million African Americans leave the South and move to cities such as Oakland, California; Detroit, Michigan; Chicago, Illinois; and Los Angeles, California. This demographic shift contributed to major changes in the American economy.

Wartime industrial jobs helped bring the African American community out of the last stages of the Great Depression. Between April 1940 and April 1944, nine hundred thousand African Americans found new jobs. Of the 5.3 million African Americans who were employed in April 1944, 1.2 million worked in industrial jobs. What is more, these gains in employment lasted even after the war ended. African Americans' service in domestic industry during World War II permanently lowered racial barriers in American industry.

African American women were able to find work in factories during World War II because of the labor shortage caused by men going off to war. *The Library of Congress*

African American Women Play an Important Role

Women also helped fill the gap in the industrial workforce created by the beginning of World War II. Millions of women took jobs in industrial production that had previously been performed by men. Women's work in industry on the home front was an essential part of the American war effort. Six million American women took jobs outside the home for the first time. African American women played a big part in helping to sustain the war effort. Between 1940 and 1944, the percentage of African American women working in industrial jobs rose from about 7 percent to about 18 percent.

Industrial jobs created by World War II represented a unique opportunity for African American women. Most African American women had never before had the chance to work in a skilled, high-paying job. When the United States became involved in World War II in 1941, approximately 50 percent of all African American women who had jobs worked as domestic servants, mostly as maids or cooks. Industrial jobs offered a chance to develop job skills. They also paid much better wages. The average wage for a domestic servant was about two dollars and fifty cents a week. Many industrial jobs paid forty dollars a week.

Unfortunately, African American women encountered not only new opportunity but also old patterns of racial discrimination at many industrial jobs. Many African American women had to work night shifts and other odd hours while white women worked regular daytime hours. In addition, African American women were often forced to work the least desirable, most dangerous jobs. They often worked in hot temperatures surrounded by noxious (poisonous and smelly) chemicals or dangerous, explosive materials.

African American women earned good wages during World War II, but many of the gains they made in the workforce turned out to be temporary. Men who had been soldiers during World War II returned home and expected to be able to return to their jobs. African American women were often the first wartime employees to be fired to make room for returning soldiers. By 1948, the percentage of African American women in the workforce who worked as domestic servants had returned to pre–World War II levels.

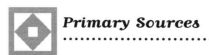

Primary Sources

◈ BOOKER T. WASHINGTON'S ATLANTA COMPROMISE SPEECH (1895)

Booker T. Washington (1856–1915) was the most famous African American leader of the late 1800s and early 1900s. Washington's philosophy and leadership focused on economic issues. He argued that African Americans needed to use hard work in fields such as agriculture and industry to overcome the discrimination they faced. Washington contended that political activism and lobbying for civil rights were not as important as attaining economic self-sufficiency.

Washington gave his most famous explanation of this philosophy in a speech at an exposition (business convention) in Atlanta, Georgia, in September 1895. The speech came to be known as the "Atlanta Compromise." Portions of the speech are reproduced below. In it, Washington explains to an almost all-white audience why he believes that African Americans should focus on developing their job skills instead of concentrating on politics. Washington argues that political equality will follow closely on the heels of economic productivity and accomplishment. He also suggests that it is in the best interests of whites in the South to offer jobs to African Americans.

• •

Mr. President and Gentlemen of the Board of Directors and Citizens:

Enterprise
Business venture or other undertaking

One-third of the population of the South is of the Negro race. No **enterprise** seeking the material, civil, or moral welfare of this section can disregard this element of our population and reach the highest success....

The opportunity here afforded will awaken among us a new era of industrial progress. Ignorant and inexperienced, it is not strange that in the first years of our new life we began at the top instead of at the bottom; that a seat in Congress or the State Legislature was more sought than real estate or industrial skill; that the political

Stump Speaking
A slang term for making political speeches

convention or **stump speaking** had more attractions than starting a dairy farm or truck garden.

A ship lost at sea for many days suddenly sighted a friendly vessel. From the mast of the unfortunate vessel was seen a signal: "Water, water; we die of thirst!" The answer from the friendly vessel at once came back: "Cast down your bucket where you are."

Heeding
Following or obeying

A second time the signal, "Water, water; send us water!" ran up from the distressed vessel, and was answered: "Cast down your bucket where you are." And a third and fourth signal for water was answered: "Cast down your bucket where you are." The

Injunction
Instruction or command

captain of the distressed vessel, at last **heeding** the **injunction,** cast down his bucket, and it came up full of fresh, sparkling water from the mouth of the Amazon River.

To those of my race who depend on bettering their condition in a foreign land, or who underestimate the importance of cultivating friendly relations with the Southern white man, who is their next door neighbor, I would say: "Cast down your bucket where you are"—cast it down in making friends in every manly way of the people of all races by whom we are surrounded.

Cast it down in agriculture, mechanics, in commerce, in domestic service, and in the professions. And in this connection it is well to bear in mind that whatever other sins the South may be called to bear, when it comes to business, pure and simple, it is in the South that the Negro is given a man's chance in the commercial world, and in nothing is this Exposition more eloquent than in emphasizing this chance. Our greatest danger is, that in the great leap from slavery to freedom we may overlook the fact that the masses of us are to live by the productions of our hands, and fail to keep in mind that we shall prosper in proportion as we learn to dignify and glorify common labor, and put brains and skill into the common occupations of life; shall prosper in proportion as we learn to draw the line between the superficial and the substantial, the ornamental **gewgaws** of life and the useful. No race can prosper till it learns that there is as much dignity in **tilling** a field as in writing a poem. It is at the bottom of life we must begin, and not at the top. Nor should we permit our grievances to overshadow our opportunities.

To those of the white race ... were I permitted, I would repeat what I say to my own race, "Cast down your bucket where you are." Cast it down among the 8,000,000 Negroes whose habits you know, whose **fidelity** and love you have tested in days when to have proved treacherous meant the ruin of your firesides. Cast down your bucket among those people who have, without strikes and labor wars, tilled your fields, cleared your forests, builded your railroads and cities, and brought forth treasures from the bowels of the earth, and helped make possible this magnificent representation of the progress of the South. Casting down your bucket among my people, helping and encouraging them as you are doing on these grounds, and, with education of head, hand and heart, you will find that they will buy your surplus land, make blossom the waste place in your fields, and run your factories. While doing this, you can be sure in the future, as in the past, that you and your families will be surrounded by the most patient, faithful, law-abiding, and unresentful people that the world has seen. As we have proved our loyalty to you in the past, in nursing your children, watching by the sick bed of your mothers and fathers, and often following them with tear-dimmed eyes to their graves, so in the future, in our humble way, we shall stand by you with a devotion that no foreigner can approach, ready to lay down our lives, if need be, in defense of yours, interlacing our industrial, commercial, civil, and religious life with yours in a way that shall make the interests of both races one. In all things that are purely social we can be as separate as the fingers, yet one as the hand in all things essential to mutual progress.

There is no defense or security for any of us except in the highest intelligence and development of all. If anywhere there are efforts tending to curtail the fullest growth

Gewgaws
Trinkets or decorative items that serve no function

Tilling
Planting, plowing, sowing, and raising crops

Fidelity
Faithfulness and loyalty

of the Negro, let these efforts be turned into stimulating, encouraging, and making him the most useful and intelligent citizen. Effort or means so invested will pay a thousand percent interest. These efforts will be twice blessed—"blessing him that gives and him that takes."

There is no escape through law of man or God from the inevitable:

"The laws of changeless justice bind
Oppressor with oppressed;
And close as sin and suffering joined
We march to fate abreast."

Constitute
Make up

Nearly sixteen millions of hands will aid you in pulling the load upwards, or they will pull against you the load downwards. We shall **constitute** one-third and more of the ignorance and crime of the South, or one-third its intelligence and progress; we shall contribute one-third to the business and industrial prosperity of the South, or we shall prove a **veritable** body of death, stagnating, depressing, **retarding** every effort to advance the body politic.

Veritable
Real and true, not imaginary and false

Retarding
Slowing down or making more difficult

Gentlemen of the Exposition, as we present to you humble effort at an exhibition of our progress, you must not expect over much. Starting thirty years ago with ownership here and there in a few quilts and pumpkins and chickens (gathered from miscellaneous sources), remember the path that has led from these to the invention and production of agricultural implements, buggies, steam engines, newspapers, books, statuary, carving, paintings, the management of drug stores and banks, has not been trodden without contact with thorns and thistles. While we take pride in what we exhibit as a result of our independent efforts, we do not for a moment forget that our part in this exhibition would fall far short of your expectations but for the constant help that has come to our educational life, not only from the Southern States, but especially from Northern **philanthropists,** who have made their gifts a constant stream of blessing and encouragement.

Philanthropists
People who regularly give money to charity

The wisest among my race understand that the agitation of questions of social equality is the extremist folly, and that progress in the enjoyment of all the privileges that will come to us must be the result of severe and constant struggle rather than of artificial forcing. No race that has anything to contribute to the markets of the world is long in any degree **ostracized.** It is important and right that all privileges of the law be ours, but it is vastly more important that we be prepared for the exercise of those privileges. The opportunity to earn a dollar in a factory just now is worth infinitely more than the opportunity to spend a dollar in an opera house....

Ostracized
Excluded from society or discriminated against

◈ FRANKLIN ROOSEVELT'S EXECUTIVE ORDER 8802 (1941)

Racial discrimination prevented most African Americans from being able to obtain industrial jobs in the years leading up to World War II (1939–45). Employment discrimination in the industrial sector was especially costly because industrial jobs required skilled labor and paid high wages. African American leaders threatened to organize a march on Washington in July 1941 to protest the lack of job opportunities in industry. President Franklin D. Roosevelt (1882–1945) wanted to prevent the march from taking place. He was worried that a protest march would decrease public support for the war effort. Roosevelt agreed to implement protections against racial discrimination in hiring in exchange for the cancellation of the march.

Roosevelt used Executive Order 8802 to provide those protections. An executive order is a document signed by the president that gives legally binding instructions on how to comply with the law. Roosevelt made history when he issued Executive Order 8802. It was the first time that the president had ever acted to prevent racial discrimination by private companies. It was also the first civil rights–related action by the federal government since the end of Reconstruction in 1877. The text of Executive Order 8802 is reproduced below. Executive Order 8802 prohibited government agencies and private companies that did business with the government (specifically, industrial businesses manufacturing military equipment) from refusing to hire African Americans. It also created a government agency to enforce the rules it created.

· ·

Reaffirming Policy Of Full Participation In The Defense Program By All Persons, Regardless Of Race, Creed, Color, Or National Origin, And Directing Certain Action In Furtherance Of Said Policy

June 25, 1941

WHEREAS it is the policy of the United States to encourage full participation in the national defense program by all citizens of the United States, regardless of race, creed, color, or national origin, in the firm belief that the democratic way of life within the Nation can be defended successfully only with the help and support of all groups within its borders; and

WHEREAS there is evidence that available and needed workers have been barred from employment in industries engaged in defense production solely because of considerations of race, **creed,** color, or national origin, to the **detriment** of workers' morale and of national unity:

NOW, THEREFORE, by virtue of the authority vested in me by the Constitution and the statutes, and as a **prerequisite** to the successful conduct of our national defense production effort, I do hereby reaffirm the policy of the United States that there shall be no discrimination in the employment of workers in defense industries or government because of race, creed, color, or national origin, and I do hereby declare that it is the duty of employers and of labor organizations, in furtherance of said policy and of this order, to provide for the full and **equitable** participation of all workers in

Creed
A person's fundamental beliefs, ideas, and values

Detriment
Injury or damage

Prerequisite
Something that is necessary

Equitable
Fair

Vocational

Relating to a job

defense industries, without discrimination because of race, creed, color, or national origin;

And it is hereby ordered as follows:

1. All departments and agencies of the Government of the United States concerned with **vocational** and training programs for defense production shall take special measures appropriate to assure that such programs are administered without discrimination because of race, creed, color, or national origin;

2. All contracting agencies of the Government of the United States shall include in all defense contracts hereafter negotiated by them a provision obligating the contractor not to discriminate against any worker because of race, creed, color, or national origin;

3. There is established in the Office of Production Management a Committee on Fair Employment Practice, which shall consist of a chairman and four other members to be appointed by the President. The Chairman and members of the Committee shall serve as such without compensation but shall be entitled to actual and necessary transportation, subsistence and other expenses incidental to performance of their duties. The Committee shall receive and investigate complaints of discrimination in violation of the provisions of this order and shall take appropriate steps to redress grievances which it finds to be valid. The Committee shall also recommend to the several departments and agencies of the Government of the United States and to the President all measures which may be deemed by it necessary or proper to effectuate the provisions of this order.

Franklin D. Roosevelt
The White House,
June 25, 1941

Research and Activity Ideas

1. Annie Turnbo Malone and Madame C. J. Walker were two of the first African American women to become very successful in business. Both Malone and Walker went into the cosmetics and hair-care business. Each made more than a million dollars selling products that were designed for and marketed to African American women. Prepare a speech to give in class in which you answer the following question: How were Malone and Walker able to build successful businesses in the field of cosmetics at a time when most job opportunities were not available to African American women? Is there something unique to the field of cosmetics that made their success possible? Why were white-owned businesses unable to take advantage of the opportunity that Malone and Walker found?

2. Sharecropping was the primary way that African Americans in the South made their living for many years after the end of the Civil War. Sharecropping was a very difficult life. Sharecroppers made very little money. It was also difficult for sharecroppers' children to move on to better careers because they frequently dropped out of school to help their parents on the farm. Write a research paper about sharecropping. How did the system of sharecropping emerge? What was day-to-day life like for sharecroppers and their families? Why did sharecroppers earn so little money? What are some ways that landowners used dishonesty or deception to prevent sharecroppers from earning a better living?

3. African Americans faced racial discrimination by labor unions in the late nineteenth and early twentieth centuries. After World War II, African Americans became a powerful force in organized labor, and many powerful unions actively aligned themselves with the goals of the civil rights movement. Prepare a timeline, starting in 1945 and ending in 1965, illustrating the many links between organized labor and the civil rights movement. Use the library and the Internet to conduct your research.

4. The South was home to many black-owned businesses during the era of segregation. Segregation, the process of using the law to force members of different races to live apart from each other, lasted from the late 1800s until the 1960s. Black-owned businesses often struggled to remain profitable after segregation ended. Many went out of business. Form a group with several of your classmates and discuss why the end of segregation might have caused so many black-owned businesses to close. If these businesses were losing African American customers to white-owned businesses, why were they not also gaining white customers from those businesses?

For More Information

BOOKS

Bundles, A'Lelia. *On Her Own Ground: The Life and Times of Madam C. J. Walker.* New York: Pocket Books, 2001.

Burrows, John H. *The Necessity of Myth: A History of the National Negro Business League.* Auburn, AL: Hickory Hill Press, 1988.

Clark Hine, Darlene. *A Shining Thread of Hope: The History of Black Women in America.* New York: Broadway Books, 1998.

Dudden, Faye E. *Serving Women: Household Service in Nineteenth-Century America.* Middletown, CT: Wesleyan University Press, 1983.

Harris, William. *Keeping the Faith: A. Philip Randolph, Milton P. Webster, and the Brotherhood of Sleeping Car Porters, 1927–1937.* Chicago: University of Illinois Press, 1991.

Honey, Maureen. *Bitter Fruit: African American Women in World War II.* Columbia: University of Missouri Press, 1999.

Hunter, Tera W. *To 'Joy My Freedom: Southern Black Women's Lives and Labors After the Civil War.* Cambridge, MA: Harvard University Press, 1997.

Lewis-Coleman, Daniel M. *Race Against Liberalism: Black Workers and the UAW in Detroit.* Champaign: University of Illinois Press, 2008.

Royce, Edward. *The Origins of Southern Sharecropping.* Philadelphia: Temple University Press, 1993.

PERIODICALS

Ammons, Lila. "The Evolution of Black-Owned Banks in the United States Between the 1880s and 1990s." *Journal of Black Studies,* vol. 26, no. 4 (March 1996): 467–489.

Barnes, Annie S. "White Mistresses and African-American Domestic Workers: Ideals for Change." *Anthropological Quarterly,* vol. 66, no. 1 (1993): 22–36.

Ingham, John N. "Building Businesses, Creating Communities: Residential Segregation and the Growth of African American Business in Southern Cities, 1880–1915." *Business History Review,* vol. 77, issue 4 (Winter 2002): 639–665.

WEB SITES

Brown, Sterling A. *A Photo Dossier on Sharecropping.* http://www.english.illinois .edu/maps/poets/a_f/brown/photos.htm (accessed on December 9, 2009).

Evans, Calvin. *Black Banks: Segregation's Gift to the Black Community.* http:// www.aframnews.com/html/interspire/articles/128/1/Black-Banks-Segregations- Gift-to-the-Black-Community/Page1.html (accessed on December 9, 2009).

Tuskegee University. *History of Tuskegee University.* http://www.tuskegee.edu/ Global/story.asp?S=1070392 (accessed on December 9, 2009).

Wormser, Richard. *Jim Crow Stories: Brotherhood of Sleeping Car Porters.* http://www .pbs.org/wnet/jimcrow/stories_org_brother.html (accessed on December 9, 2009).

Where Do I Learn More?

BOOKS

Barbeau, Arthur E., Florette Henri, and Bernard C. Nalty. *The Unknown Soldiers: African American Troops in World War I.* Cambridge, MA: Da Capo Press, 1996.

Bartleman, Frank. *Azusa Street.* New Kensington, PA: Whitaker House, 1982.

Bogle, Donald. *Bright Boulevards, Bold Dreams: The Story of Black Hollywood.* New York: One World/Ballantine, 2005.

Brophy, Alfred, and Randall Kennedy. *Reconstructing the Dreamland: The Tulsa Race Riot of 1921, Race Reparations, and Reconciliation.* London: Oxford University Press, 2002.

Cooper, Anna Julia. *A Voice from the South.* Xenia, OH: Aldine Printing House, 1892.

Du Bois, W. E. B. *The Souls of Black Folk.* Ed. Henry Louis Gates Jr. New York: W. W. Norton, 1999.

Hill, Laban Carrick. *Harlem Stomp! A Cultural History of the Harlem Renaissance.* New York: Little Brown, 2003.

Katz, William. *The Black West: A Documentary and Pictorial History of the African American Role in the Westward Expansion of the United States.* New York: Harlem Moon, 1971.

Large, David Clay. *The Nazi Games: The Olympics of 1936.* New York: W. W. Norton, 2007.

Lemann, Nicholas. *The Promised Land: The Great Black Migration and How It Changed America.* New York: Vintage, 1992.

Love, Spencie. *One Blood: The Death and Resurrection of Charles R. Drew.* Chapel Hill, NC: University of North Carolina Press, 1996.

Malcolm X, with Alex Haley. *The Autobiography of Malcolm X.* New York: Grove Press, 1965.

Robeson, Paul. *Here I Stand.* Boston: Beacon Press, 1958.

Robinson, Jackie, and Alfred Duckett. *I Never Had it Made: An Autobiography of Jackie Robinson.* New York: Putnam, 1972.

Thomas, Vivien T. *Partners of the Heart: Vivien Thomas and His Work with Alfred Blalock: An Autobiography.* Philadelphia: University of Pennsylvania Press, 1998.

Till-Mobley, Mamie. *Death of Innocence: The Story of the Hate Crime that Changed America.* New York: One World/Ballantine, 2003.

Ward, Geoffrey C. *Unforgivable Blackness: The Rise and Fall of Jack Johnson.* New York: Vintage, 2006.

Wells, Ida B. *Southern Horrors and Other Writings: The Anti-Lynching Campaign of Ida B. Wells, 1892–1900.* Ed. Jacqueline Jones Royster. New York: Bedford/ St. Martin's, 1996.

Wood, Sylvia. *Sylvia's Family Soul Food Cookbook: From Hemingway, South Carolina, To Harlem.* New York: William Morrow Cookbooks, 1999.

Woodward, C. Vann. *The Strange Career of Jim Crow.* New York: Oxford University Press, 1955.

WEB SITES

African American Odyssey: A Quest for Full Citizenship. Available at the Library of Congress Web site. http://memory.loc.gov/ammem/aaohtml/exhibit/aointro .html (accessed on March 1, 2010).

Chicago Defender. http://www.chicagodefender.com (accessed on March 1, 2010).

Documenting the American South. http://docsouth.unc.edu/index.html (accessed on March 1, 2010).

Duke Ellington: Celebrating 100 Years of the Man and His Music. http://www .dellington.org/ (accessed on March 1, 2010).

Jazz. Available on the PBS Web site at http://www.pbs.org/jazz/ (accessed on March 1, 2010).

Madame C. J. Walker Official Web site. http://www.madamcjwalker.com (accessed on March 1, 2010).

Mintz, S. "America's Reconstruction: People and Politics after the Civil War." *Digital History.* http://www.digitalhistory.uh.edu/reconstruction/index.html (accessed on March 1, 2010).

The Nation of Islam Official Web site. http://www.noi.org/ (accessed on March 1, 2010).

Rosa and Raymond Parks Institute for Self Development. http://www.rosaparks.org/ about.html (accessed on March 1, 2010).

Tuskegee University. http://www.tuskegee.edu/ (accessed on March 1, 2010).

Index

Boldface type indicates entries; *Italic* type indicates volume; (ill.) indicates illustrations.

X

X, Malcolm. *See* Malcolm X

Y

Yale University, *4:* 821, 857–58,
861
Yordan, Philip, *1:* 127–28

Young, Charles, *4:* 635, 649–52,
649 (ill.)
Young, Perry, *4:* 865

Z

Zeta Phi Beta sorority, *2:* 393
Zoot Suit Riots (1943), *4:* 732–33
zoot suits, *4:* 731–33, 732 (ill.)